Global Horror
Cinema Today

# Global Horror Cinema Today

*28 Representative Films
from 17 Countries*

Jon Towlson

McFarland & Company, Inc., Publishers
*Jefferson, North Carolina*

Library of Congress Cataloguing-in-Publication Data

Names: Towlson, Jon, 1967– author.
Title: Global horror cinema today : 28 representative films from 17 countries /
Jon Towlson.
Description: Jefferson, North Carolina : McFarland & Company, Inc., Publishers, 2021 |
Includes bibliographical references and index.
Identifiers: LCCN 2021027794 | ISBN 9781476671536 (paperback : acid free paper) ∞
ISBN 9781476643526 (ebook)
Subjects: LCSH: Horror films—History and criticism. | Motion pictures—History—
21st century. | BISAC: PERFORMING ARTS / Film / Genres / Horror
Classification: LCC PN1995.9.H6 T693 2021 | DDC 791.43/6164—dc23
LC record available at https://lccn.loc.gov/2021027794

British Library cataloguing data are available

ISBN (print) 978-1-4766-7153-6
ISBN (ebook) 978-1-4766-4352-6

Cover image: Virginia (Julieta Cardinali) has to chase the white coffin
to find her daughter in *Ataúd Blanco: El Juego Diabólico/White Coffin*
(2016, Del Toro Films/Energía Entusiasta).

Printed in the United States of America

*McFarland & Company, Inc., Publishers
Box 611, Jefferson, North Carolina 28640
www.mcfarlandpub.com*

# Table of Contents

# Table of Contents

# Preface

From Hollywood to Europe to Asia, the horror film is thriving. With international hits like *It Follows* (2014), *The Babadook* (2014), *Grave* (*Raw*, 2016), *Busanhaeng* (*Train to Busan*, 2016), *Get Out* (2016), *The Hounds of Love* (2016) and *The Girl with All the Gifts* (2016), filmmakers in countries as diverse as the U.S., Australia, Israel, Spain, France, Great Britain, Iran and South Korea are using the horror genre to address the emerging fears and anxieties of their cultures.

The present work investigates contemporary horror cinema around the globe with an emphasis on developments in the genre since 2012. Each chapter focuses on a different country; I look at what frightens the people of each of these nation states and ways in which horror crosses over to international audiences. It explores the genre's unique capacity to break cultural boundaries and speak to social, political and personal anxieties in a world cinema context. Above all, it provides an overview of current developments and emerging trends in contemporary global horror cinema.

This is *not* intended to be a complete A to Z survey of international horror films from 2012 onwards! Although I have tried to be as comprehensive as possible in terms of the films covered (some are discussed in more detail than others), this book is best thought of as a "snapshot": a *selection* of films that, in my view, represent the current state of play of contemporary horror cinema around the world. Each chapter provides a detailed analysis of two representative films from one country, with others mentioned in summary. It closely examines 28 international films in total, with approximately 75 or so discussed overall. The majority of these films were produced between 2014 and 2020. For ease of reference, the book is organized country by country; in the case of co-productions, the language of the film or nationality of the director/s has been taken into account. But it should be noted that one of the aims of this book is to explore the genre's unique capacity to break national boundaries, even as it speaks to cultural fears in its place of origin.

*Global Horror Cinema Today* has grown out of my journalism for various U.K. magazine and journals, including *Starburst, Scream* and *Digital Filmmaker Magazine*, for which I have covered a number of horror film festivals since 2012 and interviewed emerging international filmmakers. The introduction of digital technology (which has considerably lowered production and distribution costs) has produced an explosion of edgy low-budget horror from a new generation of directors. They include Ana Lily Amirpour and David Robert Mitchell in the States; Aharon Keshales and Navot Papushado in Israel, and Juan Carlos Medina in Spain. There's also been a boom in fanzines and blogs, and a proliferation of horror film festivals and conventions, so alternative voices are emerging; this can be seen in the increase in women and Black and indigenous filmmakers working in the genre: to name just a few, Jordan Peele (*Get Out*, 2016; *Us*, 2019) in the States, Jennifer Kent (*The Babadook*) in Australia, Julia Ducournau (*Raw*) in France and Alice Lowe (*Prevenge*, 2016) in Britain. All of these filmmakers and others besides are discussed in this book.

Interconnecting trends (briefly outlined below) are discussed in detail in each of the chapters that follow, and provide the context for analysis throughout the book.

## *Trends of Production and Consumption*

Not only in America but in many other countries, the horror film has become a staple genre of national cinemas, following a low point of production in the 1990s. The increased level of production worldwide is partly a response to wider issues of transnationalism in cinema, itself an effect of

Jay (Maika Monroe, with unidentified actor in background) is menaced by an unknown supernatural force after a sexual encounter in David Robert Mitchell's break-out hit *It Follows* (2014, RADiUS-TWC/Icon Film Distribution Ltd.).

the globalization of media industries. The global consumption of horror has encouraged productions that cross over boundaries of nation states, and created interconnections between audiences via social media and film festivals. In Europe especially, co-production between countries has been boosted by the involvement of industry funding bodies like Eurimages; while the recent boom of international festivals with a focus on horror cinema in Britain, the U.S., Canada, Australia and elsewhere has provided a marketplace for international product. The rise of VOD and specialist Blu-ray and DVD labels has opened new exhibition windows for horror films, creating ease of access and encouraging fandom across the world.

## Socio-Political Trends

Despite its international appeal, the horror film continues to explore specific national trauma in many countries, whether it be historical disturbance or present-day anxieties. In Spain, for example, the work of Mexican director Guillermo del Toro (*El espinazo del Diablo/The Devil's Backbone*, 2001) has inspired a new generation of filmmakers to engage with the political history of their country, often going against official discourses of modern democratic Spain. A film such as *Insensibles* (*Painless*, 2012) might be seen as an allegorical retrospective of Franco's Spain and the atrocities that took place during the Spanish Civil War. Filmmakers in Israel and South Korea, on the other hand, are using the horror film to address ongoing contemporary traumas relating to military violence in the occupied territories (Israel) or fears brought about by the threat of invasion by neighboring countries and/or the potential loss of democracy (South Korea). The South Korean films *Gamgi* (*Flu*, 2013) and *Train to Busan* draw heavily on American disaster movie tropes for their transnational appeal, while also addressing more provincial worries relating to the collapse of a liberal Korean society.

## Recessionary Narratives

Anxieties stemming from economic inequality and precarity can also be seen in the prevalence of urban vs. rural horror films around the globe and in the home invasion scenario of many contemporary horror films since the economic crash of 2008. The U.K. almost immediately saw a number of films concerned with the threat to middle-class society of a dispossessed underclass (so-called hoodie horror): *Eden Lake* (2008), *Cherry Tree Lane* (2010) and *Citadel* (2012). The trend (or subgenres) of urbanoia and suburbanioa horror in which fears of social exclusion or social abjection are exploited, has also become apparent in America, with films such as *Don't Breathe* (2016), and in Australia (*100 Bloody Acres*, 2012). Anxieties arising from the economic recession also play a part in other horror films outside of these subgenres, as a social backdrop in a number of recent American horror movies, including *Lovely Molly* (2012), *American Mary* (2012), *Starry Eyes* (2014) and *Pet* (2016). The U.K.'s recent "folk horror" revival can be seen as a result of growing economic insecurity among the middle class, with young people seeking alternatives to the cultural mainstream.

## Feminist and Black Developments

Internationally, there has been a move towards regaining control of sexual and ethnic identity by women actors and filmmakers, aided by digitalization widening access. There have also been attempts to deconstruct horror subgenres by feminist filmmakers, e.g., *The Love Witch* (2016) and *A Girl Walks Home Alone at Night* (2014). The rise of the female ghost and female serial killer-cannibal in recent horror films might be seen as a late "return of the repressed" redressing issues of gender (in)equality in America, Japan and Iran.

Similarly, in the U.S., the success of Jordan Peele's *Get Out* has led to new developments in Black horror filmmaking, with emerging directors like Peele and Nia DaCosta (*Candyman*, 2020) reclaiming race horror and (re)telling horror narratives from a Black perspective.

## Audience Reception and Trends

The Midnight Movie tradition of the '60s and '70s lives on in film festival late night slots, as can be seen in the weird esoterica of Belgium's *L'étrange couleur des larmes de ton corps* (*The Strange Color of Your Body's Tears*, 2013), Mexico's *Tenemos la carne* (*We Are the Flesh*, 2016) and the U.S.-U.K. indie hit *The Greasy Strangler* (2016). The Italian *giallo* has also seen a revival amongst cult film audiences; movies like *The Editor* (2014), *Francesca* (2015) and *Amer* (2009) are pastiches of the *giallo*, appropriating its tropes for the purposes of satire and deconstruction.

## Horror and Bodily Affect

Body horror has become a major trope in contemporary world horror cinema (and arguably has been since the 1980s): lending universality to the genre, connecting the themes, while personalizing fear. Linking together

**Feminist deconstruction: Samantha Robinson in** *The Love Witch* **(2016, Anna Biller Productions/Icon Film Distribution Ltd.).**

the socio-political, psychoanalytical and feminist, bodily abjection remains a common theme in contemporary international horror, to be found in most, if not all, of the titles mentioned above and many more besides.

## Acknowledgments

One of the great pleasures of being a film journalist is meeting wonderful people who work behind the scenes in film journalism and criticism, film production, distribution and exhibition. I would like to thank the following, each of whom has contributed in some way (often through discussion in the cinema bar!) to the writing of this book:

David Baldwin, Alan Berry, Allan Bryce, Mark Chambers, Tony Clarke, Martyn Conterio, Chris Cooke, Rich Cooper, Cat Dunn, Huw Eggington, Kat Ellinger, David Flint, James Gracey, Kier-La Janisse, Jess Love, Joseph Maddrey, Michael Mackenzie, David Maguire, Christian Martin, Shellie McMurdo, Bernice M. Murphy, Rob Nevitt, Shelley O'Brien, David Phillips, Steve Rawle, Naila Scargill, Simon Shaw, Steven Sheil, Andy Stanton, Lauren Stephenson, Donato Totaro, Martin Unsworth and Bethany White.

Special thanks, as always, to Joanne Rudling for her support and help with the preparation of the manuscript.

# Introduction

## States of Terror

Since the box office success of *The Blair Witch Project* (1999), horror cinema has entered its most sustained—and arguably most popular—cycle in history. To highlight how significant the current horror boom is, one need only compare it to previous cycles. Horror's first golden age in the 1930s lasted a mere six years in America—from 1931 to 1936—before it began a three-year hiatus and then a resumption in (slightly reduced) production that lasted from 1939 to 1945 or thereabouts. The horror boom of the 1970s—often thought of as the second golden age of horror cinema—began in 1968, picked up in pace around 1972 and lasted until about 1982 when increasing censorship at the dawn of the video age caused a dip in production. The current horror boom is still going strong 20 years in, with no sign of slowing.

Not only has the number of horror films increased since the new millennium, more countries are producing horror films now than at any time in the past. This book surveys 14 countries currently making horror movies, and the list is far from complete—Chile (*Cuesta Abajo/Downhill*, 2016), Georgia (*Nagmi/Landmine Goes Click*, 2015), Germany (*Freddy/Eddy*, [2016]), The Netherlands (*De Kuthoer/The Columnist*, 2019), Poland (*Córki dancing/The Lure*, 2015), Russia (*Marshrut postroen/Paranormal Drive* [2016], *Rassvet/Quiet Comes the Dawn* [2019], *Sputnik*, [2020]), South Africa (*From a House on Willow Street*, 2016; *Triggered*, 2020), and Switzerland (*Chimères*, 2013) have a nascent or small but consistent horror film production output. We might expect these countries to increase their output in the next few years, and others—like Laos—to follow suit. Still other countries, like India, Japan and the Philippines, have a thriving horror cinema (and really need books of their own to do justice to their contemporary output).

This raises the question: Why horror, and why horror *now*?

The increased level of horror production worldwide is, in part, a result of the globalization of the media industries that sees international distribution of cinema—including horror cinema—rapidly broadening through the growing number of exhibition windows available to consumers in many countries. While the access of Netflix in Brazil, for example, boosted an interest in American horror films in that country, indigenous Brazilian filmmakers have responded with films of their own, and these films have now found their way into international distribution. And the boom in Argentinian horror owes much to marketing platform Blood Window, which represents Argentina's product at such prominent genre marketplaces as Sitges, Montreal's Fantasia and Austin's Fantastic Fest. These—and other countries—are also joining the market in terms of co-productions.

Of course, horror cinema has, in a sense, been transnational for many years in terms of distribution and production. European horror co-production has a long history; Franju's early classic *Les Yeux Sans Visage/Eyes Without a Face* (1960), for example, was an Italian-French co-production. Recent European co-production has been boosted by industry bodies such as Eurimages; multilateral co-production agreements make individual works "national" in all countries involved in the co-production and therefore eligible for public funding in all those countries. It is not uncommon for a horror film now to be a co-production of several countries. This in itself encourages productions that increasingly cross over the cultural boundaries of individual nations. *The Strange Color of Your Body's Tears* is a good example of transnationalism in horror: A co-production between French, Belgian and Luxembourgian production companies, it combines retro elements of the Italian *giallo* with the experimental film tradition of Belgium.

Horror's global popularity has also been boosted by social media, blogs and online journals that have helped create interconnections between fans and filmmakers, critics and distributors—a flourishing international horror community. Added to this is the rapid growth of film festivals in Britain, the U.S., Canada, Australia and elsewhere that showcase horror. In countries like Portugal, horror film festivals provide an international venue for filmmakers and fans from Europe and beyond. They encourage production through the exhibition of short films and often promote experimentation within the genre. Festivals like Lisbon's MotelX provide access to new independently produced horror films for the local community as well as to international festival-goers. Many of the films shown in such festivals may not see release on disc or on streaming platforms; thus the festival circuit has become a vital exhibition window in itself for new horror productions.

Distribution has become increasingly difficult for independent filmmakers, no matter what genre they work in. Horror is easier than most, thanks to a number of specialist subscription streaming platforms and distributors. Shudder offers a mixed program of horror classics and newly produced movies, many of which are exclusive to that channel. In the U.K., the Horror Channel is a freeview television channel devoted to horror and science fiction. Amazon Prime, Netflix and Hulu also showcase new international horror films. Blu-ray and DVD distributors specializing in cult and genre films, such as Arrow in the U.K. and Shout! Factory in the U.S., are increasingly including new horror films on their release schedules. New distribution windows for horror continue to open, and thus encourage greater production and audience consumption.

As Brenda S. Gardenour Walter has observed, "[M]odern media and rapid communication technologies have made possible a language of transnational horror predicated neither on the Hollywood version of Gothic, nor on a single tradition from any given region."[1] It is striking that despite its transnational language, horror cinema continues to explore specific national trauma in many countries, whether it be previously repressed historical trauma or present-day anxieties. In Spain, Australia and Austria, to give three examples, filmmakers are engaging with the histories of their countries, questioning official discourses that have stressed political continuity at the expense of historical fact. Austria's *Ich Seh, Ich Seh* (*Goodnight Mommy*, 2014) opens with a clip from a *Heimat* film, showing a von Trapp–like family on a TV screen, a reference to Austria's abiding postwar self-image—a comment on the *Heimatfilme* as an avoidance of historical truth. Australia's *Killing Ground* (2017) forcefully evokes a sense of that country's violent present co-existing with its violent colonial past. The story's three time frames (the present, the recent past and the distant past) inevitably coincide; history is presented in terms of repeating cycles of violence. As *Killing Ground*'s director Damien Power has commented, "It happened 200 years ago, it happened last week, it's happening right now. And the chances are, it's going to happen again."[2] It's a comment that might relate equally well to a number of contemporary horror films from different countries.

While historical trauma preoccupies a number of filmmakers, particularly in countries with a colonial past, others use horror's transnational tropes to explore contemporary national anxieties, be it military violence and war (Israel), tensions with neighboring countries (South Korea), issues of immigration (Austria), political oppression (Iran) or ecological catastrophe (Brazil). Set in a Tehran apartment in the 1980s during the Iran-Iraq war, *Under the Shadow* (2016) is the story of a woman (a political activist) and her child tormented by a malevolent entity. It addresses the rapid internal, political and cultural transition following the 1979 Iranian Revolution, when decades of progress in women's rights were rolled back. Similarly, the 2008 Brazilian production *Mangue Negro* (*Mud Zombies*) weaves themes of poverty and environmental destruction into the tale of a poor fishing community whose livelihood is threatened by water pollution. It was the first part of a trilogy of eco-terror horror films by director Rodrigo Aragão that speak to fears of environmental pollution within the framework of the supernatural. Films like these draw on transnational horror tropes for their appeal, while addressing more provincial worries relating to their specific countries of origin.

Although socio-political trends may vary from country to country, relatively constant in contemporary horror produced after the global economic downturn of 2008 is the recessionary narrative which stresses economic inequality and precarity. This can take the form of the home invasion scenario, such as Miguel Ángel Vivas' *Secuestrados* (2010) in which masked thieves break into a young couple's home, or appear in less obvious ways as a backdrop to other subgenres. A number of "maternity" horrors, such as *Shelley* (2016) and even *The Babadook* (2014), take place against a social background of economic insecurity. Social inequality is often addressed obliquely in films which feature conflict between the urban and the rural, *Ataúd Blanco: El Juego Diabólico/ White Coffin* (2016), for example. The migrants of *Die Hölle/Cold Hell* (2017) and *Most Beautiful Island* (2017) struggle to survive in a hostile social and economic environment. Meanwhile, growing financial insecurity among the middle class underpins a number of contemporary horror films, including Juliana Rojas and Marco Dutra's *Trabalhar Cansa* (*Hard Labor*, 2011), Adrián Garcia Bogliano's *Penumbra* (2012) and Jorge Michel Grau's *Somos lo que hay* (*We Are What We Are*, 2010).

Contemporary horror has seen a corresponding "return of the repressed" in a number of countries, including in Southeast Asia, Iran, Mexico, Turkey and North America. According to Andrew Hock Soon Ng, women in Southeast Asian horror films, when transformed into or aligned with monsters, "discover a new and empowered sense of self otherwise denied them."[3] Likewise we can detect in the chador-veiled vampire at the heart of the Farsi-language *A Girl Walks Home Alone at Night* (2014), a female monster who is ultimately allowed to *be*. The woman protagonist of *La región salvaje* (*The Untamed,* 2016) similarly finds sexual fulfillment with a creature from the id, the one that lurks behind the rational façade of the everyday. Turkish director Can Evrenol has spoken explicitly of his desire to "embrace the return of the repressed,"[4] indicating how theories on horror, race, class and gender have been disseminated via academic film courses into filmmaking practice.

As independent production continues to grow, aided by digital technology, so alternative voices are emerging. More women filmmakers, and more ethnic and indigenous filmmakers, are going into the horror genre and bringing a new radicalism to it. The explosion of women horror directors since 2008 has been enormous. This goes against the traditional glass ceiling in the film industry. Feminist filmmakers such as Anna Biller have deconstructed the genre in terms of its gender representations; while women taking more active roles as central characters in horror film narratives have promoted a female-centric approach to horror. The Final Girl has been replaced by the *primary* girl: Women characters are at the heart of horror film narrative. This is true not just of North American horror films but of horror movies internationally. *The Babadook, Raw, White Coffin, Cold Hell, Através da Sombra/Through the Shadow* (2015), *Shelley, Prevenge, The Girl with All the Gifts, Under the Shadow, A Girl Walks Home Alone at Night, Vuelven* (*Tigers Are Not Afraid*, 2017), *The Untamed* and *Most Beautiful Island* supply examples of female-centric horror. The #MeToo movement, which exposed the sexual harassment systemic in the music and film industries, provides an undercurrent to other female-centric horror films such as *Starry Eyes* (2014) and *M.F.A.* (2017). France's *Revenge* (2017) reconfigured rape-revenge tropes in light of the movement.

As well as seeing more women filmmakers going into the horror genre, and the genre addressing feminist concerns, North America has started to produce more Black horror films than before, made by Black filmmakers, bringing new vision and a new radicalism. In the way it allegorized (and satirized) white liberal America's co-opting of Black identity, *Get Out* pushed Black horror into new areas. Peele's follow-up, *Us*, and Nia DeCosta's reimagining of *Candyman* further mark a reclamation of Black identity in horror, an attempt to seize the reins of Black representation from white Hollywood. Other indigenous filmmakers in North America have emerged, including Jeff Barnaby (*Blood Quantum*, 2019) and Nyla Innuksuk (*Slash/Back*, 2020), whose work uses horror to explore colonial trauma.

These voices might not have emerged without audiences that are receptive to, and supportive of, new approaches to horror. In many ways, specialist DVD distributors such as 88 Films and streaming services like Shudder function much like the "midnight movie" did in previous decades. In a similar fashion to contemporary horror fans, 1960s and 1970s audiences sought alternative cinema and this was provided not only by the drive-in, but also by the repertory theater, college cinemas and inner-city theaters showing exploitation double-bills and midnight movies. To these audiences, independent cinema, and particularly cult cinema, equated with countercultural alternatives. George A. Romero once commented on the emergence of cult movie audiences in the 1960s as evidence of "the clutching search of the public mass towards something new or as yet unexperienced."[5]

The appetite for the new, the as-yet-unexperienced and the esoteric is evident in the programming of film festivals and repertory cinemas internationally. The curation of festivals is often wildly imaginative, with films grouped into strands that serve to highlight current and emerging horror themes and tropes. The 2018's Hell de Janeiro, for example, features sidebars like "The Monstrous Female" ("which subverts the usual sexist horror trope of casting women as the victims, with a whole host of short films about female monsters"). Other films fall into more traditional categories such as "Cannibals, Murderers and Slayers" and "Ghosts, Science Fiction–Horror and Freaks." The public appetite for new, weird and esoteric work is reflected by the fact that public funding bodies (the British Film Institute, for one) now put money into midnight movies like *The Greasy Strangler* in recognition of the cult audience. The genre savvy of horror and cult movie fans is apparent in the popularity of the *giallo*—a subgenre that attracts fans and academics alike. The modern awareness of the *giallo* arguably stems from the increased availability of titles from distributors like Shameless, a "pulp-inspired, exploitation brand of discovery offering up carefully curated films that will delight horror and exploitation fans," as well as festival programmed retrospectives and a great deal of written analysis by genre scholars. U.K. critic Anton Bitel observed in 2016 that *giallo* "keeps returning from the grave in new, if backward-looking forms" as "reverent homages"—*I Know Who Killed Me* (2007), *Giallo* (2009), *Les nuits rouges du bourreau de jade* (*Red Nights*, 2009), *Los ojos de Julia* (*Julia's Eyes*, 2010), *Faces in the Crowd* (2001), *Tulpa* (2012), *The Editor*—and "artfully crafted distillations"[6]—*Berberian Sound Studio* (2012), *Amer* and *The Strange Color of Your Body's Tears*. It is precisely because the formula of the *giallo* is so marked that it becomes ripe for deconstruction by filmmakers in ways that are recognizable to genre fans.

That the intellectual aspect of horror is appreciated by contemporary filmmakers and genre fans has led a number of journalists to claim that we have entered a period of "post-horror" or "elevated horror" in which horror has transcended its traditional status as low-grade exploitation. For these commentators, horror is no longer lowbrow, but synonymous with art house cinema. This has prompted protest from a number of scholars: the implication of "post-horror" being that the genre before now was somewhat less than worthy. While horror has taken increasingly abstract forms in some recent films (e.g., *It Follows, It Comes at Night* [2017], *The Lighthouse* [2019]), it is debatable that we are moving beyond horror towards something new. Horror fiction, especially short fiction, has been taking this approach for a long time, and one might equally point to Val Lewton's RKO films of the 1940s as examples of "post-horror."

Perhaps critics are responding to the aesthetics of these horror productions: their heightened *mise en scène*, cinematography, editing and sound, and corresponding bodily affect; their ability to create horror without recourse to standard tropes and monsters. Certainly a film like *The Strange Color of Your Body's Tears* derives as much—if not more—meaning from its sensory effects on the viewer as it does from its genre deconstruction. It is as much a film to be *felt* as one to be understood. Likewise, *Baskin* (2015) represents a remarkable technical achievement in Turkish horror cinema: It affects the viewer in a profound and powerful manner though sound and image, and in its bold use of nightmare syntax. It is a horror film *experience.*

It follows that body horror remains a universal aspect of contemporary world horror cinema, embodying its themes, while personalizing fear. *Starry Eyes* is an example of this. Essentially it is an indictment of the Hollywood casting couch (presented in the film as a literal Faustian pact); its protagonist, a wannabe actress, has to endure a physical makeover in her bid for stardom. Her body undergoes a frightening transformation in the process: She suffers hair-loss, develops sores on her face and body, her teeth start to fall out. Linking the socio-political, psychoanalytical and feminist—such bodily decomposition, abjection, wounding and/or physical metamorphosis can be found in numerous works discussed in this book.

In the 2014 Canadian documentary *Why Horror?*, journalist and horror fan Tal Zimerman set out to explore the reasons why horror holds an abiding fascination for fans across the globe. His conclusion: that experiencing horror on screen enables us to deal with our real-life fears, be they societal fears or personal ones. If that is indeed the case, it would go some way to explain why we seem to need horror now more than ever. As global anxieties increase, so do private metaphysical ones. With the current COVID-19 pandemic, the world is entering a new period of uncertainty, to which world horror cinema will inevitably respond.

# 1

# Argentina

## *White Coffin* (2016) and *Francesca* (2015)

In 2008, *Visitante de invierno* (*Winter Visitor*), the first Argentine horror film made for the theatrical market in two decades, marked the resurgence of homegrown horror in that country. Where auteurist films had dominated the Argentinian industry in the '90s, genre became popular with national audiences at the turn of the millennium, prompting a number of Argentinian co-productions with U.S. studios, such as Daniel de la Vega's *Jennifer's Shadow* (2004, starring Faye Dunaway and Gina Philips) and a 2010 remake of the British thriller *And Soon the Darkness* (1970). Previously, young filmmakers had made ultra–low-budget horror films that went straight to DVD, providing a training ground for a movement of filmmakers—de la Vega, Sergio Esquenazi, Adrián and Ramiro Garcia Bogliano and Luciano Onetti among them—who came up from the Buenos Aires Rojo Sangre international horror film festival. However, recent international hits such as the Disney-backed *Ataúd Blanco—El Juego Diabólico* (*White Coffin*, 2016) have made horror a theatrical mainstay domestically as well as abroad. Since 2014, Argentina's government-funded INCAA Film Institute has put specific funding into horror films, prompting a boost in production; meanwhile, the Latin American genre film market has expanded rapidly with galas of Argentinian (and other Latin American) horror films programmed by marketers Blood Window, at Cannes, Sitges, Montreal's Fantasia and Austin's Fantastic Fest. As distributor Alejandro de Grazia stated simply in 2008, "People like horror in Argentina."[1]

This should come as no surprise, for Argentine horror has much to draw upon culturally and historically. Such films as *White Coffin* are infused with South American mythology and Catholic imagery, Catholicism being, in the words of Zebbie Watson, both "a staple of the culture and an integral part of the violent past of colonialism."[2] What's more, Argentine horror, as Watson observes, is informed by the country's indigenous myths, its rich tradition of fantastic literature, and—during the last century—dictatorship

13

and political violence in the name of social advance. *White Coffin*, for example, begins like a typical American "rural" horror—a car breaks down in the wilderness, a child is abducted—but it quickly moves into the realm of the fantastic, a world of magic and ritual. On the other hand, Onetti's *neo-giallo Francesca* shows that Argentine horror is equally capable of assimilating forms outside of its own cultural traditions. It is both homage to, and distillation of, the classic Italian *giallo*. Before I go on to discuss these films in detail, however, let's take a brief look at Argentina's horror movie history and its influence on contemporary Argentine horror production.

## Argentine Horror Film History

Argentine horror had admittedly inauspicious beginnings, mired in parody and sexploitation. One of the first horror films, *Una Mujer sin Cabeza* (*The Headless Woman*, 1947) was a ham-fisted comedy-horror starring the comic actress Niní Marshall as a gypsy circus performer on the lam. She takes refuge in an old dark house replete with secret passageways and ghostly goings-on. *El Vampire Negro* (*The Black Vampire*, 1953), directed by Román Viñoli Barreto, is somewhat misleading in title; it is a remake of Fritz Lang's *M* (1931) that compares favorably with both the original and Joseph Losey's 1951 version. Olga Zubarry plays a cabaret artiste attempting to protect her daughter from the child murderer who stalks the streets of Buenos Aires. Recently restored by the UCLA Film & Television Archive and screened at MoMA in 2016, *The Black Vampire* has been acclaimed for its *noir* atmosphere and its striking and dreamlike opening credit sequence. Nevertheless, the film remains more *noir* thriller than horror.

Argentina's first horror film director of note is arguably Emilio Vieyra. Born in Buenos Aires in 1920, he started out as an actor in 1940s comedies, before moving into exploitation movies as a director in the '60s. His first outing in the genre (and the first Argentinian vampire film), *Sangre de vírgenes* (*Blood of the Virgins*, 1967), is a queasy mix of the gothic and "swinging '60s" sexploitation: A group of tourists find themselves stranded in the Andes after their taxi breaks down, and they take refuge in an abandoned house which, it turns out, is haunted by aristocratic vampire Gustavo (Ricardo Bauleo) and his undead bride Ofelia (Susana Beltrán). Graphic for its time, *Blood of the Virgins* is memorable for its early scenes set in 19th century Argentina: Gustavo murders Ofelia's husband on her wedding night before claiming her for his own with his vampire's kiss; later, he goes to the cemetery (in broad daylight) to retrieve her from the grave. The ground splits apart, revealing Ofelia's coffin. The lid rises, and Ofelia's eyes open. Her hands leave the rosary that she clutches to her chest; she reaches out to Gustavo, who pulls her from the coffin, literally bringing her back from the dead. It might now be seen as an iconic image of Argentine horror: the woman reaching out from inside the coffin. (De la Vega borrowed the image for a key moment in *White Coffin* when his heroine, Virginia [Julieta Cardinali], is similarly raised from the dead.)

*La venganza del sexo* (1969), better known as *The Curious Doctor Humpp*, is now a genuine cult curio, largely thanks to Something Weird Video's DVD release in 2000 and, prior to that, Pete Tombs' work on Vieyra in his seminal book *Mondo Macabro*. Directed by Vieyra, *Doctor Humpp* mixes mad scientists, voyeurism and blood transfusion to delirious effect. Aldo Barbero plays the mysterious physician who seeks the elixir to eternal youth, obtained by sex, and at the cost of transforming the couples he kidnaps for this purpose into emotionless zombies. It turns out that a disembodied talking human brain is instructing him. The film's overall strangeness, which borders on the incoherent, is not helped by the fact that its original American distributor, Jerald Intrator, added 17 minutes of largely unrelated soft-core footage to the Argentinian production, slowing down the narrative pace. Only this bastardized North American version is currently available.

Vieyra's third foray into the horror film, *La bestia desnuda* (*The Naked Beast*, 1967), combines the *giallo* with vampirism. It is nevertheless the most even-handed of the three, if perhaps the least interesting. Barbero here plays a police inspector investigating a series of murders taking place behind the scenes of a musical TV show with a Grand Guignol backdrop; the killer hides his identity behind a Dracula mask. The best scenes take place in this studio, where performers are guillotined to the delight of a live audience. There is also an effective death sequence in which Beltrán finds herself in bed with the killer. Here Vieyra intercuts her undressing with shots of the murderer in his bathroom, injecting himself with some drug. As the killer advances on the naked and prone girl, we see his eyes in extreme closeup moving behind ghoulish contact lenses; then Beltrán's eyes react in terror before she is strangled. (Juxtaposing close shots of the killer's eyes with those of his victim is a Vieyra trademark; while the eye is a common trope of the *giallo* film—the *gli occhi*.)

Vieyra went on to a directing career of more than 30 features in a variety of genres, but his films would rarely rise above exploitation. Argentine horror, however, took a turn towards respectability in 1975 with the release of Leonardo Favio's fantasy *Nazareno Cruz y el lobo* (*Nazareno Cruz and the Wolf*). Favio's film draws on the indigenous South American myth of the Lobizón, a curse afflicting the seventh son of the family. Nazareno (Juan José Camero) is a young farmer in a Pampas village, rumored to have fallen victim to the werewolf curse. He falls in love with a beautiful peasant girl, Griselda (Marina Magali). The Devil appears to Nazareno and tries to get him to turn his back on Griselda; Nazareno refuses, and the Lobizón curse comes to pass, with tragic results. Favio is considered one of Argentina's greatest directors, and *Nazareno Cruz and the Wolf* bears comparison with such classics of world fantasy cinema as *Valerie a týden divu* (*Valerie and Her Week of Wonders*, 1970). Its depiction of the rural Pampas as home of the savage gaucho and a place of barbarism and exile would influence Argentinian horror films for many years to come.

## Contemporary Argentine Horror Films

Many recent Argentine horror films have combined the exploitation approach of Vieyra with the rural isolation of *Nazareno Cruz y el lobo*. Adrián Garcia Bogliano's early efforts, *Habitaciones para turistas* (*Room for Tourists*, 2004) and *36 Pasos* (*36 Steps*, 2006), employed female nudity, abandoned houses and masked killers, while displaying a distinctive shot-on-video, lo-fi aesthetic. *36 Steps*, in particular, owes a debt of gratitude to Tobe Hooper's *The Texas Chain Saw Massacre* (1974) in terms of imagery and plot mechanics. Five girls are abducted and forced to live together in a suburban house; they are dressed in skimpy clothes and made to plan a bizarre birthday party, all presumably for the voyeuristic pleasure of their unseen male captors. Only when the girls try to escape do these men ever appear—and administer swift, merciless punishment. Low-angle shots of the bikini-clad girls are bleached out by bright blue skies; characters suffer brutal, sometimes unexpected deaths; and a chain saw becomes the weapon of choice for the film's would-be Final Girl as she struggles against an allegorized male oppression that pits sister against sister. Bogliano may well have made the film as a satire of reality television and its sexualized role models—its fetishization of the female form—but *36 Steps* works best as an absurdist piece, a modern take on the Theatre of Cruelty.

Bogliano's wildly kinetic style is reflected in the speed with which he makes films. He has directed 13 features to date. In 2010, *Sudor Frío* (*Cold Sweat*) marked a breakthrough in terms of a higher budget and wider distribution. It showed to huge acclaim at the South by Southwest film festival in 2011 before MPI Media Group acquired it for DVD release in the U.S. *Cold Sweat* also saw a general shift in Bogliano's work from rural to urban horror, and a desire on his part to address through genre cinema the horrors of the military junta during the years of the Dirty War, when security forces employed systematic violence against left-wing activists, trade unionists, journalists, students and other alleged Peron sympathizers. In the film, two elderly men, former officers in the dictatorship, kidnap and torture young women in an old house filled with stolen explosives. Their murder weapon of choice is nitroglycerin, which they slather over the bodies of their victims, a twisted nod to Henri-Georges Clouzot's *The Wages of Fear* (1953). Not all of the women have been killed, however, as there exists in the basement a kind of containment camp of barely human survivors from experiments that the men have conducted over a 30-year period. Bogliano is careful to locate his political allegory within a historical framework: *Cold Sweat* opens with newsreel clips of public beatings and other human rights violations of the era. Here, Bogliano speaks from personal experience. His own family was victim to state terrorism; for posing an ideological threat to the junta, his uncle was one of the 22,000 who were killed (or "disappeared").

As Bogliano's career developed, his co-production ventures took him to Mexico for *Here Comes the Devil* (2012) and *Scherzo Diabolico* (2015) (co-produced with MPI Media Group), with a brief sojourn in the U.S. for the werewolf flick *Late Phases* (2014) (co-produced by Dark Sky Films and Glass Eye Pix). His latest Argentine film at the time of writing, *Penumbra* (2012), co-directed with his brother Ramiro, continued in the vein of urban horror and caustic social commentary. Cristina Brondo plays Marga, a money-grabbing lawyer who unwittingly rents her inherited Buenos Aires apartment to a death cult as the city experiences a rare solar eclipse. Over the course of a single morning, her life completely unravels: She loses her keys, gets into an altercation with a homeless man who approaches her for money, slips and hits her head, and begins to hear strange noises in the apartment she is trying to rent out. Much of the film is designed to illustrate the deep suspicion with which such wealthy foreigners are viewed in Argentina. Marga's misfortunes are brought on herself as a result of her being at odds with a country she clearly despises, but whose inhabitants she, as a Buenos Aires property owner, is willing to exploit for financial gain. Eventually, we do start to feel some sympathy for Marga, but only when the cult turns nasty. The pay-off is ironic: The suicide sect proves itself capable of self-sacrifice, a quality Marga is sadly lacking—and for which she gets her comeuppance.

Bogliano's first Swedish-language film, *Svart Cirkel* (*Black Circle*, 2017) is described as a supernatural horror story of "two sisters whose lives change dramatically after going through hypnosis using a mysterious vinyl album recorded in the 1970s."[3] Bogliano is clearly a filmmaker with much to say, although it remains to be seen if working away from his native land will bring out the best in him or dilute one of the most distinctive voices of modern Argentine horror.

With Bogliano currently away from home, other Argentine auteurs have risen to take to his place. Gabriel Grieco's debut as director, *Naturalesa muerta* (*Still Life*, 2014) uses the Argentinian cattle industry as a backdrop for a slasher murder mystery with an animal rights message. Ambitious young TV journalist Luz Cipriot goes behind the scenes to investigate the killings and uncovers some rather distasteful truths about the beef industry. Grieco drew on rural horror for *Still Life*, a film much influenced by '70s American revenge-of-nature flicks and Australian outback horrors such as *Long Weekend* (1978). Cipriot is strong, resourceful and sympathetic, and provides a welcome respite from the endless parade of bound-and-gagged women found in Argentine horror. But Grieco's follow-up, *Hipersomnia* (2016), featured chained women in abundance, and moved us back to Buenos Aires as the setting for a "thriller about human trafficking in Argentina."[4] Its fractured narrative seems more influenced by the surreal neo-noir of David Lynch's *Mulholland Drive* (2001) and Darren Aronofsky's *Black Swan* (2010), than by the desire to make a coherent statement on this social issue. Aspiring actress Milena (Yamila Saud) is cast in a play about human trafficking by a dubious producer (Gerardo Roman). She finds herself having dreams that she is one of a number of girls locked up by sex traffickers. In these dreams, Milena assumes a different identity and so she (and we) are uncertain as to whether these experiences are imagined or taking place in an alternate reality. Or are we in fact witnessing events out of chronological order? Is Milena's casting in the play merely a trap to lure her into prostitution and human trafficking? Grieco's blurring of the lines of fantasy and reality and/or temporality quickly becomes confusing; and then, disappointingly, *Hipersomnia* moves into the realm of torture porn, complete with a leather-masked killer menacing his chained-up female victim with a knife and bottled insects. The bland predictability of this final trope may be a deliberate ploy on Grieco's part, of course, but we are ultimately left unsure of what it is Grieco is trying to say in terms of the parallels that *Hipersomnia* appears to want to draw between human trafficking, prostitution and white slavery on the one hand and the acting profession on the other.

*Hipersomnia* and *Fase 7* (*Phase 7*, 2001)—a pandemic-apocalypse movie set in Buenos Aires—veer closely toward exploitation cinema, but other recent Argentine horror films have assumed the more respectable air of the costume film. *Los Innocentes* (*The Innocent*, 2015) is a plantation drama featuring revenge from beyond the grave. A rare Argentine contribution to Black horror, it utilizes the common tropes of slavery films—beatings, rapes, murders and lynchings.

In *Le Segunda muerta* (*The Second Death*, 2015), a policewoman investigating a murder in a small town in the Pampas encounters a clairvoyant boy who duly informs her that the killer she is hunting is the Virgin Mary.

*Resurrección* (*Resurrection*, 2015) emphasized a brooding atmosphere over conventional horror trappings, in a tale of a young 19th century priest struggling to keep his faith as yellow fever ravages his community. All three films owe an obvious debt to the "historical" horror of Guillermo del Toro, and their mix of ruralism, period drama and Catholic themes mark a clear attempt to find an international audience as well as a domestic one.

Argentine horror cinema, then, is as much concerned with the urbanization of modernity as it is with the ruralism of the past. As Philippa J. Page has noted, much Argentine theater, literature and film charts the progression from barbarism to civilization, the passage from nature to culture as deterioration, with the modern city portrayed as "an institutionalized urban style of barbarism." The Pampas, by contrast, often constitutes "a Utopian space of exile and freedom."[5] In Argentine horror cinema, however, the Pampas is also portrayed as barbaric, just like the city. There is, it seems, no escape from the barbarism of the past, and even religion is powerless in the face of such savagery. These themes are pronounced in *White Coffin*.

## White Coffin

De la Vega collaborated on *White Coffin*'s script with Ramiro and Adrián Garcia Bogliano; Luciano Onetti provided the music score. The film examines the possibility of a mother committing infanticide, "something that could be scarier than her own death."[6] The mother, Virginia, is on the run with her young daughter Rebecca (Fiorela Duranda) after a custody hearing has awarded the child's custody to her estranged husband. Virginia will resort to desperate measures to keep Rebecca, culminating in the savage act of which de la Vega speaks. In *The Hollywood News*' *White Coffin* review, Kat Hughes writes that it is about "the lengths a parent will go … to save their child from harm."[7] To this end, *White Coffin*'s plot itself functions as a kind of game designed to bring de la Vega's hypothesis to light (indeed, the film's subtitle translated is *The Diabolic Game*).

*White Coffin* opens on an isolated road. Virginia and Rebecca are fleeing from the husband. As they drive, they play a word association game (marking the beginning of the diabolical game of the title). They drive past the poster for a missing child, Natalia Coba, a sure sign of events to come. Later, de la Vega will explicitly reference John Carpenter's *Assault on Precinct 13* (1976); specifically, the *Assault* scene where a child is brutally gunned down as she buys ice cream. Child murder will become a link between the two films, as will the rigorous formalism of Carpenter. As Chris Banks remarks of *White Coffin*, it all begins in "relatively disciplined fashion."[8] De la Vega's deployment of classical Hollywood style *à la* Carpenter makes the film's subsequent departure into the Latin American tradition of the fantastic all the more startling.

As they stop near a cemetery, Rebecca becomes strangely fascinated by the graves. De la Vega frames her between headstones, seen from behind, her white crochet hair bun given prominence in the shot. From here on, images of Catholicism suffuse *White Coffin*: Old World religion pitted against the ritual sect behind the diabolical game that Virginia is forced to play. In many ways, we might read *White Coffin* as a comment on the failure of Catholicism in Argentina: a country where over 75 percent of the population is Roman Catholic but non-practicing; where religious beliefs have become largely deinstitutionalized. The imminent abduction of the child is already planted firmly in our minds. (Significantly, the town near which they have broken down, Moriah, owes its name to the Biblical mountain on which God tells Abraham to sacrifice his son, Isaac.) As Virginia changes a blown tire, she looks up and sees that Rebecca has vanished from the front seat. We share her panic until she spots her daughter on the roadside, Rebecca having stepped out of the car.

A mysterious stranger comes to Virginia's aid. Mason (Rafael Ferro) is a gaucho figure, a go-between who traverses the present and the past, Virginia's reality and the savagely fantastical world of the cult; it is he who will raise Virginia from the dead for a brief reprieve in order for her to save Rebecca (or at least make the attempt). And it is through Mason that the diabolical game is given shape. After Rebecca is abducted from a service station diner, Virginia chases the pick-up truck in which her daughter is held. The chase results in Virginia being killed in a crash. At this point, *White Coffin* moves into the realm of the fantastic, and in so doing, shifts from American horror movie traditions to Argentine ones. Carpenter is supplanted by Vieyra as, in a direct homage to the scene in *Blood of the Virgins,* Virginia is brought back to life in her casket by Mason, who literally pulls her by her hand from her grave.

The rules of the diabolical game gradually become known. Rebecca is one of three kidnapped children to be sacrificed by the cult. Virginia has to track down the titular white coffin and deliver it to the *cementerio de Moriah* where the children are held captive. She has only one day among the living to do this and save her child. What's more, she is in competition with Patricia (Verónica Intile) and Angela (Eleonora Wexler)—the mothers of the other children—for possession of the white coffin. Thus, we first assume that the game is diabolical because it pits mothers against each other for the lives of their children: Which of them is prepared to become the most savage in her attempt to save her child?

A good bit of the film's 70 minutes is devoted to the chase for the white coffin. The three women converge on a remote warehouse where the coffins are made. The game is diabolical, too, in the way that it involves the sacrilegious use of Christian symbols. The "carpenter" here is not Joseph or Jesus, but a maniac who cuts Patricia in half with his buzz saw. The dead woman's daughter is subsequently the first child to be sacrificed: burned to death while her screams are relayed to the two surviving mothers by mobile phone. A priest is shown to be complicit in the game; indeed, Catholicism becomes increasingly implicated by the film to the point where rituals of the Church become indistinct from those of the cult. In *White Coffin*, Catholicism has not only failed, but is inextricably tied to the barbarism of the past and the present.

Thus, the film reaches its crescendo in the *cementerio*. Here, de la Vega's hypothesis comes into its own. Virginia stabs Angela and, as the surviving mother, is given one final task: She must herself sacrifice the child who is not her own, by placing her in the white coffin on a funeral pyre. This she does, but the atrocity of the act results not in reward, but in punishment, so exquisitely cruel as to reveal the game's true diabolical nature. Rebecca is not to be freed; instead, she is to continue the cycle of sacrifice as a newly inaugurated cult member. She is to become an agent in the diabolical game. She is taking the place of the disgraced priest (whom Virginia has beheaded); her scalp, like that of the priest, is inked with a map designed to lead future victims of the game to Moriah.

*White Coffin* ends with Mason, the gaucho, leading Rebecca away from the *cementerio* as the distraught Virginia finally runs out of time. The mother brought back from the dead to save her child, and who would go to any lengths (even descend into barbarity) to do so, dies gripping the cross of a gravestone, her own "resurrection" failed.

## Francesca

If *White Coffin* followed specifically Argentine traditions, Luciano Onetti's *Francesca*, as a *neo-giallo*, sought transnational appeal by looking to European horror. Drawing on the works of Italian directors Dario Argento and Sergio Martino in particular, the multi-talented Onetti (who co-wrote, directed, photographed, edited and scored) treads a line between pastiche and homage, deconstruction and distillation, with enormous skill. Remarkably, *Francesca* is more than simply an homage to the tropes of the *giallo*; and unlike other (in the words of critic Anton Bitel) "artfully transcendent distillations"[9] such as *Amer* and *The Strange Color of Your Body's Tears*, it is a mystery thriller as concerned with the narrative conventions of *giallo* as it is with *giallo's* distinctive stylistic characteristics and iconography (even if its deconstruction of gender politics is not as pronounced). Onetti has stated that what attracted him and his brother Nicolás (who produced and co-wrote) to the genre was that its approach to style and narrative marked a departure: "The *giallo* narrative was so different, and even usually it had script errors. We think that the idea of the directors at that time was to shoot it with style, using gloves, traumas, zooms, the unfocused, great music, etc."[10] *Francesca* features the masked, leather-gloved psycho killers, set-piece murder scenes and garish *mise en scène* of the classic '70s *giallo*, but distills this iconography into a series of almost stand-alone symbols, emphasized by the insistent use of closeups. (Many sequences are made entirely of closeups.) Onetti's widescreen cinematography evokes the visual style of *giallo*, including zooms for dramatic impact, and the color grading has the look of a remastered '70s film. His progressive rock-inspired music score, heightened Foley sound effects and Italian dubbing deliberately mimic the sound of Italian '70s cinema. And "trauma" features prevalently, not only in the film's sensory effects, but also in its psychological themes of Freudian gender confusion and childhood-induced psychosis; Argento's *Profondo Rosso* (*Deep Red*, 1975) and *Tenebrae* (1982) being obvious influences.

    *Francesca* opens with a scene that might easily be mistaken for Argento. We see the wheels of an old-fashioned pram and a woman's legs. A shot of an antique rocking horse and the woman's plain black shoes, images which readily evoke childhood trauma. On the soundtrack plays a lullaby (as in *Deep Red*). Onetti cuts to a young girl with a doll. In the garden, she skewers the carcass of a dead bird. This is intercut with the mother, Nina (Silvina Grippaldi), rocking her baby in the pram. What is immediately apparent in the sequence, and continues throughout *Francesca*, is how, by utilizing just a few objects such as these antiques (and through sound), Onetti can evoke the *giallo* by the most minimal means.

    We see the girl enter the baby's room; we see her feet in child's shoes; the handle of the pram; and a mid-shot of the girl (whom we already assume to be the Francesca of the title), raising the skewer. A shock sound effect of a slicing blade is followed by a brief, almost subliminal shot of the skewer in a doll's face; the sound of the baby crying is mixed with Francesca's childish laughter, as she leans over the pram watching the baby's agony with sadistic glee. The camera then whip-pans from a closer shot of the skewer to the shocked face of Nina as she enters the room. Freeze-frame on her scream. The image bleeds to red and zooms in to a tight closeup of the distraught mother.

    This sequence is the "psychodramatic primal scene"[11] that Bitel identifies as a key trope of the *giallo*, and which informs the story to follow. Fifteen years later, a killer strikes the city, seemingly inspired by *The Divine*

*Giallo* imagery in the Argentinian poster of *Francesca* (2015, Guante Negro Films/Unearthed Films).

*Comedy.* The implication is that Francesca, whom we are told disappeared mysteriously shortly after the opening incident, has returned to redeem the world of sinners and damned souls. Her modus operandi includes leaving rare and valuable coins on the bodies of those she kills, in a reference to Dante. Francesca, we discover, was the daughter of a celebrated playwright and poet, Vittorio Visconti (Raul Gederlini), who himself becomes a suspect in the police investigation into the murders. Visconti is wheelchair-bound following an armed robbery of his house that left him crippled, and which resulted in Francesca's abduction. Naturally, nothing is what it seems and Onetti constantly plays with our expectations, especially in respect to the killer's identity. As befitting the *giallo*, a gender switch takes place as part of the film's final reveal. The lead investigator, Moretti (Luis Emilio Rodriquez), arrives at Visconti's home with the intention of arresting him. It is revealed in flashback that after Francesca mutilated her baby brother, Visconti strangled her and buried her in the garden. Moretti discovers that Francesca's mother Nina, who had been suffering from nervous breakdown ever since the incident 15 years ago, has committed suicide. As the pieces of the puzzle begin to fall into place, Onetti reprises the imagery of the opening. Moretti discovers the child's doll and rocking horse in a locked room, along with a tailor's mannequin dressed in the hat and coat of the killer. An empty wheelchair glides into the room behind Moretti, and he turns to see Visconti—able to walk after all—dressed in a woman's clothes. A fight ensues and Visconti is accidentally shot. As Moretti surveys the dying poet, a final twist sees the detective skewered from behind by a teenage boy with a facial disfigurement: Francesca's mutilated younger brother.

As Onetti has noted of classic *giallo* narrative, "Usually it had script errors,"[12] and so it is here, as these final reveals create new mysteries and ambiguities. However, the lack of resolution in *Francesca* is fully in keeping with the sense of postmodern abstraction characteristic of the *neo-giallo*. Nowhere is this more apparent than in *Francesca's* middle sequence, which, like the works of Cattet and Forzani, recasts the *giallo* on the levels of abstract experimental film, psychodrama or dream-film. The traumatized mother dreams of Francesca in a park playground. Onetti bleaches out the image and then applies a kaleidoscope effect. Soon after, we are presented with naked female mannequins bathed in magenta and cyan light. The killer's gloved hand caresses the broken head of one mannequin, emerging from the hole like a spider; the mannequin's breasts are similarly caressed. Onetti then cuts to the breasts of a real woman, fondled beneath her bra. We see the killer inspect photographic slides of flowers and vintage pornography. We see again the rocking horse from the opening scene; the baby holds a coin. The sequence serves little narrative function, nor does it present purely *giallo* symbolism. Instead, like Cattet and Forzani, and Peter Strickland's *Berberian Sound Studio* (2012), Onetti explores the intersection between the classic *giallo* and the European art cinema of the 1960s and '70s, invoking the influences on the '70s *gialli* of Antonioni, Alain Robbe-Grillet and other modernists of that era.

# 2

# Australia

## *The Babadook* (2014)
## and *Hounds of Love* (2016)

Australia has been enjoying a new golden age of horror cinema. Since the 2005 box office success of *Wolf Creek*, there have been more distributors specializing in horror and funding agencies such as Screen Australia aware of the specific needs of horror filmmakers and audiences. Horror festivals have grown too, with Sydney's Fantastic Planet and A Night of Horror, as well as Melbourne's Monster Fest and Underground Film Festival, all flourishing alongside Tasmania's Stranger with My Face.

Film critic Alexandra Heller-Nicholas reads the *Wolf Creek* franchise as "a scathing indictment on white Australia's rampant, increasing and unchecked xenophobia."[1] Indeed, the films (and TV series) present to the world a particular viewpoint of the Australian landscape and of masculinity that had been popularized by the Ozploitation films of the 1970s and 1980s: one of violence and repression of a society bred out of social isolation, segregation of the genders and abuse of the natural environment. These themes and images occur again and again in Australian horror films and arguably originated in *Wake in Fright* (1971), Ted Kotcheff's seminal Ozploitation movie that enjoyed much critical attention following its restoration in 2009, having previously languished in obscurity.

In the last couple of years, however, a new generation of filmmakers has sought to break with tradition in favor of a greater diversity of filmic representation. This chapter takes as its main case study Jennifer Kent's remarkable feature debut *The Babadook*, a film that relocates horror from the outback to create instead "a myth in a domestic setting." The film "doesn't feel particularly Australian," and eschews issues of masculinity normally associated with Australian horror to debunk cultural assumptions surrounding motherhood instead: Women, according to Kent, are "educated and conditioned to think that motherhood is an easy thing that just happens."[2] By grounding a bizarre supernatural premise in very real feelings of anxiety and depression, *The Babadook* goes some way toward redefining modern Australian horror, and links both visually and thematically to the work of earlier women directors in that country, such as Jane Campion and Ann Turner, who explored the gender socialization of children and adolescents in *Sweetie* (1989), *An Angel at My Table* (1990), *The Piano* (1993) and *Celia* (1988).

Ben Young's *Hounds of Love*, by contrast, dramatizes the conflict between the traditional masculine Ozploitation tropes and the emerging female perspective of new Australian horror in a scenario that, according to Luke Buckmaster, is "about the subjugation of women and male-inflicted abuse, from brutal violence involving strangers to psychological domination from long-term partners."[3]

## *Ozploitation from* Wake in Fright *to* Wolf Creek

> With *Ozploitation* and Australian Gothic, visions of wreckage-strewn tarmac and oppressively endless desert, killers on the road and spirits in the wilderness, post-colonial shame and fear of nature have been driven into our consciousness.—*Sci-Fi Now*[4]

The introduction of substantial government subsidies and tax incentives in the early '70s provided a huge boost to the Australian film industry; before that, the indigenous Australian film industry was hampered by competition from Hollywood and Britain. The result was a wave of films (now called Ozploitation) lasting from 1970 to the early 1990s. Ozploitation classics include *The Cars That Ate Paris* (1974), *Picnic at Hanging Rock* (1974), *Inn of the Damned* (1975), *The Last Wave* (1977), *Patrick* (1978), *Long Weekend* (1979), *Mad Max* (1979), *Dead Kids* (1981), *Roadgames* (1981), *Razorback* (1984) and *Dead-End Drive-In* (1986).

In a survey of Australian (and New Zealand) horror movies, author Robert Hood identifies the key tropes of Ozploitation:

> [A] dusty larger-than-life depiction of small-town industrial-rural life … exposes the violent and repressive nature of a society spawned out of isolation and the abuse of nature. Sexual segregation, antagonism toward the "outsider" … and an oppressive air of lethargy and frustration combine to present a grim picture of outback life. Man is brutalized and even social and sexual relations are predicated on violence. This is civilization in a state of moral collapse.[5]

According to Hood, these themes came to characterize Australian horror films from *Wake in Fright* onwards. Kotcheff's film opens with a 360-degree pan of Tiboonda, the outback town in which schoolteacher protagonist John Grant (Gary Bond) is destined to remain metaphorically and literally stuck. During the course of the narrative, Grant will find himself going similarly full circle, ending up back where he started. In the process, he is brutalized by the male "neanderthal" culture of New South Wales in which he finds himself mired. Attempts to reach Sydney by train (and beyond that, dreams of a life as a journalist in London) are thwarted by his own personal demons set loose in the Bundayabba, where he embarks on a lost weekend of booze, gambling and violence that culminates in a failed suicide attempt and Grant's subsequent return to Ground Zero: his final recognition that there is no progress to be made and "no escape." When *Wake in Fright* was released, it proved to be a hit at the Cannes Film Festival; less so at home in its native Australia. As Melbourne academic Lindsay Coleman has commented, *Wake in Fright* is the "tale of an outsider, made by outsiders,"[6] and as such its representations of Australian rural life as a living hell may have been almost unrecognizable to indigenous audiences. Certainly its re-release came at a time—following Ozploitation and *Wolf Creek*—when critics were divided over whether such representations were still considered valid by international audiences or merely quaint. This re-evaluation of Ozploitation by critics (and later by filmmakers) really started after the 2005 release of *Wolf Creek*.

Made for an estimated one million Australian dollars, with a total worldwide return of over 29 million U.S. dollars, *Wolf Creek*'s financial success at home and abroad prompted a resurgence of horror production in Australia, even as critics debated the value of the film itself. Loosely based on true events, *Wolf Creek* depicts the torture and murder of female backpackers by a bushman who takes them captive in an abandoned mining site in the outback. Its crazed serial killer, Mick Taylor (played by John Jarrett), has since become a horror film icon, reappearing in the 2013 sequel *Wolf Creek 2*, a TV serial running two six-episode seasons (2016 and 2017) and spin-off novels. The character, as a stereotype of Australian masculinity, is as closely related to Crocodile Dundee as he is to Ozploitation brethren. He is the shadow-side of Paul Hogan's chivalrous bushman: the merciless tourist-killer with a pathological hatred of "foreign vermin." In many ways, *Wolf Creek* might thus be seen as a postmodern pastiche of Ozploitation tropes. Taylor is without morality; his brutality knows no bounds; and his antagonism towards others is absolute. In its graphic presentation of violence and mutilation, *Wolf Creek* also draws on torture porn, on *Saw* (2004), and this, too, accounts for its popularity internationally as a horror film about sadism. For some critics, this mix is merely a cynical attempt at box office and *Wolf Creek* remains tasteless exploitation. Others have read allegorical meaning into the films: Heller-Nicholas sees the franchise as a scathing indictment of white Australia's increasing and unchecked xenophobia; citing the Australian government's mistreatment of asylum seekers

**Murderous outback: Crazed serial killer Mick Taylor (John Jarrett) menaces British tourist Paul Hammersmith (Ryan Corr) in *Wolf Creek 2* (2013, Image Entertainment).**

on Nauru and Manus Island as examples of issues Australian horror cinema "is perfectly situated to critique and explore." But regardless of *Wolf Creek*'s merits (or lack thereof, depending on your viewpoint) as a horror film, there is little doubt that it and other Australian horror films feed directly into what Heller-Nicholas describes as a "crucial aspect of disenfranchised white identity" linked to a "deep, defining shame of Australia's violent past and violent present."[7]

## Recent Australian Horror

The notion of Australia's violent present co-existing with its violent colonial past is forcefully evoked in Tasmanian filmmaker Damien Power's debut *Killing Ground* (2017). A young couple, Ian (Ian Meadows) and Sam (Harriet Dyer), embark on a camping trip to Gungilee Falls Creek, a remote spot that, we are told, was the site of the massacre of Koori tribe Aborigines many years before. It is also the location of a much more recent atrocity: The couple finds the campsite of a family who, it is revealed in a series of intricate flashbacks, was kidnapped and murdered just the previous day by ex-convicts "German" Shepherd (Aaron Pederson) and his young associate Chook Fowler (Aaron Glenane). When Ian and Sam are accosted by the two killers, a battle for survival ensues in a bushland "killing ground" whose very soil seems poisoned by the slaughter of two centuries previous.

Thematically and structurally, *Killing Ground* concerns the past impacting the present. The story's three time frames (the present, the recent past and the distant past) inevitably coincide; history is presented in terms of cycles of violence. As Power has commented, "It happened 200 years ago, it happened last week, it's happening right now. And the chances are, it's going to happen again."[8] Power consciously drew on Ozploitation tropes, particularly in terms of the "landscape and our fears about it." However, his influences extend to American survival horror films of the '70s such as *Deliverance* (1972). And in terms of its historical allegory, *Killing Ground* invites comparison with Wes Craven's *The Hills Have Eyes* (1977). "There wasn't much education about Aboriginal culture and the first Australians, no real acknowledgment of the more brutal or murderous aspects of settlement," Power has said of growing up in white middle-class Australia. "I've had to really take it upon myself to put myself in theaters and to read books that educate me." If *Killing Ground* speaks to "a nation that wishes it could somehow erase the horrors and predations of its colonialist past,"[9] as critic Anton Bitel suggests, it also offers no easy solution to the cycle of violence. The past cannot be erased, and rewriting the end of one's nightmares, as the murdered child attempts to do in the film, seems futile. The loss of their naiveté may be Ian and Sam's only consolation after such a horrific experience. It's a harsh lesson, and *Killing Ground* ends on a note of disillusionment.

Gympie, Queensland, provides the terrible place in *Charlie's Farm* (2014), a film which bears structural and thematic similarities to *Killing Ground*. Here, too, violent history is shown to impact the present. A group of backpackers make their way to the remote farm of the title, drawn by an urban legend: Years before, the farm was said to be inhabited by a family who killed and ate tourists. Hounded out by the local townsfolk, only the youngest child, Charlie, survives, and he continues the family tradition by murdering intruders. If *Killing Ground* relied heavily on survival horror for its plot, *Charlie's Farm* settles even more predictably into slasher mode, as the hulking grown-up Charlie slaughters the backpackers (including Tara Reid) one by one in a variety of gruesome ways. The inclusion of Kane Hodder, best known for his role as Jason in four of the *Friday the 13th* movies, perhaps signals the film's intention in this respect.

*100 Bloody Acres* (2012) offered more rural horror and tourist murder in South Australia, but with a heavy added dose of black comedy. Brothers Reg (Damon Herriman) and Lindsay (Angus Sampson) run an organic fertilizer business. One day they realize that the city-slicker backpackers who regularly hitchhike on the local highways are a cheap source of blood and bone for their meat grinder. But Reg develops feelings for one of the would-be victims he brings home to the farm to turn into bonemeal, and a rift develops between the two brothers that will ultimately see one of them join the queue for the grinder. Familial loyalty is the theme of *100 Bloody Acres*, but the treatment is off the wall: firmly in the tradition of Ozzie and Kiwi splatter-comedies like *Body Melt* (1993) and New Zealand's *Black Sheep* (2006).

The Australian wilderness provided a major source of inspiration for the micro-budget zombie road movie *Wyrmwood: Road of the Dead* (2015), directed with lo-fi aplomb by Kiah Roache-Turner. A mixture of *Dawn of the Dead*-style gore and *Mad Max* post-apocalypse production design (most of the film's weapons and vehicles were bought from eBay by the director and his producer brother Tristan), *Wyrmwood* was financed partly by an Indiegogo crowdfunding campaign, and filmed in the distinctive Blue Mountains just outside of Sydney. This "Ozpocalypse" is a bold late addition to Ozploitation; its influences extend to early Peter Jackson, George Miller and Sam Raimi.

These recent Australian horror movies draw on the Ozploitation tradition of using the outback as a key setting. Other new Australian horror films reject this trope in favor of urban or suburban locations. Along with this is a desire to move away from stories that deal with outback crime and transgression, towards domestic violence scenarios in a city or town setting. As producer Briony Kidd notes: "We're getting closer to depicting all facets of our identity, not just a few perspectives. Diversity, both in terms of the people who are getting a chance to make films and in terms of the styles and approaches adopted, can only be a good thing."[10] An increasing number of Australian horror films break the mold of Ozploitation in this way.

Heller-Nicholas claimed in 2016 that domestic violence in Australia is at "epidemic proportions and verging on a national emergency."[11] A number of recent horror films focus on this aspect of contemporary Australian society. Made on a budget of 11,000 Australian dollars, Joseph Sims-Dennett's second feature *Observance* (2015) is set almost entirely in a Sydney apartment. Critics have likened it to Roman Polanski's *Repulsion* (1965) and Christopher Nolan's micro-budget debut *Following* (1998) but its lineage possibly goes back to Hitchcock's *Rear Window* (1954) by way of Coppola's *The Conversation* (1974) and Krzysztof Kieślowski's *Krótki Film O Miłości* (*A Short Film About Love*, 1988). Private investigator Parker (Lindsay Farris) is hired to spy on a woman (Stephanie King) from an abandoned apartment. From this simple premise, the British-born Sims-Dennett weaves in dark psychological themes. Bizarre events begin to happen around the woman, making the investigator (who is already suffering psychological trauma following the recent death of his young son) question his sanity.

Is the apartment building harboring an evil presence that victimizes the woman? Or are the nightmarish visions of bodily decay that Parker appears to witness really hallucinations, signs of his imminent mental collapse? *Observance* is a slow-burning interior film, the themes of which extend beyond its country of origin. It could be set anywhere, and as if to underline this point, Sims-Dennett has his actors speak in American rather than Australian accents. This is also, of course, a commercial move on the part of the filmmakers: Despite its tiny budget, *Observance* would find theatrical distribution in Australia (by Umbrella Entertainment) and on demand/ VOD and DVD/Blu-ray (courtesy of Artsploitation Films).

Another micro-budget thriller revolving around interpersonal violence, the slightly outlandish *The Suicide Theory* (2014) was the directorial debut of Brisbane-based filmmaker Dru Brown. Steve Mouzakis is a hitman hired by a suicidal but seemingly indestructible client desperate to end his own life. (Aki Kaurismaki mined similar territory in his mordant murder-thriller *I Hired a Contract Killer*, 1990.) Brown spins the tale off into a foray of hallucination and fragmented reality that also owes much to Christopher Nolan's *Memento* (2000).

The Cairnes brothers (Cameron and Colin) followed *100 Bloody Acres* with another low-budget splatter-comedy, one that relocated the mayhem from the outback to the confines of an abandoned psychiatric hospital in Victoria. *Scare Campaign* (2016) involves a reality TV show designed to play scary pranks on people. Hit by dwindling ratings, the producers seize upon the idea of staging a prank in a mental asylum. But they prank the wrong person, and the crew faces the wrath of a seemingly insane serial killer.

As with all reality shows, the line between what is real and what is not is apt to become blurred. Coming after *Grave Encounters* (2011) and *SX_Tape* (2013), with which it shared the same basic scenario of reality TV in an asylum, *Scare Campaign* nevertheless manages to retain a sense of freshness achieved through its inventive twists, its mirrors-within-mirrors structure and energetic visuals.

Cate Shortland's third feature, *The Berlin Syndrome* (2017) represents the exact kind of departure from "the usual approach and style" that Briony Kidd talks about. It eschews an Australian setting in favor of a gray and miserable Berlin in winter (although interiors were filmed in Melbourne), and focuses unflinchingly on themes of domestic abuse and power and control in gender relationships. An adaptation of the novel by Melanie Joosten, it starts unpromisingly: While travelling alone in Berlin, Australian photographer Clare (Theresa Palmer) hooks up with schoolteacher Andi (Max Reimelt) and has a one-night stand with him. The next morning, Andi refuses to let her out of his Berlin apartment. What begins as a clichéd stranger-danger tale of kidnapping and captivity (with shades of John Fowles' 1963 novel *The Collector*) develops into a powerful study of the Stockholm Syndrome (as suggested by the film's title). Clare continues to have sexual feelings for her captor despite the threat he poses to her (it is revealed that he has murdered at least one of his previous victims). Living together in close proximity over time seems to normalize the situation for the couple, at least for a while. The film's point seems to be that Clare and Andi's relationship—an extreme one—is not that far removed from many relationships between men and women, based, as they often are, on power and control. In this sense, *The Berlin Syndrome* parallels Jennifer Lynch's *Chained* (2012), another story about a killer and his victim and their growing interdependence. Andi is, on the surface, a perfectly respectable— and respectful—English teacher, brought up in East Berlin by his university lecturer father before the collapse of the Wall. Underneath, of course, he is needy and possessive to the point of psychosis; this, it seems, is triggered partly by his mother defecting to the West when he was young, arousing within him feelings of abandonment. Andi's ordinariness (on one level) makes Clare's response to him—and thus the film itself—believable. In the end, though, this is resolutely Clare's story: the tale of a girl who, against her better judgment, becomes entangled in a toxic relationship that traps her spirit; but she manages to come out the end of it with a greater sense of self. It is that personal growth and newfound independence that ultimately frees her.

The years between Ozploitation and *Wolf Creek* saw a rise in the number of women directors emerging in the Australian film industry (partly thanks to film school scholarships earmarked especially for women). Gillian Armstrong, Jane Campion and Jocelyn Moorhouse attended the Australian Film, Television and Radio School (as did Cate Shortland) before making films that helped redefine cinema in terms of their gender perspectives. Shortland has acknowledged these filmmakers for "setting up situations to give young women access to film."[12] Indeed, there had been films with horror themes made by women directors in Australia prior to *The Babadook*. As Heller-Nicholas observes:

> In the excitement surrounding *The Babadook*, a lot of people forgot the earlier genre films made by women, particularly Tracey Moffatt's *beDevil* (which is, as far as I know, the only horror anthology made wholly by a single woman director) and Ann Turner's *Celia*, which was a direct influence on *The Babadook* in its story about a child becoming obsessed by a scary storybook that comes to life.[13]

Moffatt's approach to cinema was influenced by the works of Vincente Minnelli and Masaki Kobayashi (the latter's *Kwaidan* [1964] is much in evidence in terms of the narrative strategy of Moffatt's film) and by her own work as a visual artist and photographer. Like other Australian directors, especially and including the women above, Moffatt is very much concerned with finding new and personalized ways of seeing. As Stephen Curtis, her production designer on *beDevil* (1993), has said: "[Moffatt] is aware of the conventions, but in a wonderful, unselfconsciously brazen way, she is able to break them."[14] The same is true of Jennifer Kent, whose *The Babadook* bears the distilled imagery and idiosyncratic signature style of a committed visual artist exploring themes of death, loss, grief, abandonment and motherhood.

## The Babadook

Graduating in 1991 from the National Institute of Dramatic Art, Kent began her career as an actress, working primarily in TV, before becoming an assistant to Lars von Trier on his film *Dogville* (2003). In 2005, Kent directed her first film, a ten-minute short called *Monster*, which she would later develop into *The Babadook*. Aside from being an accomplished short film in itself, *Monster* acts as an intriguing preliminary "sketch" for *The Babadook*. In terms of filmic influences, Kent has cited a number of '60s, '70s and '80s horror films including *The Thing* (1982), *Halloween* (1978), *Les Yeux Sans Visage* (*Eyes Without a Face*, 1960), *The Texas Chain Saw Massacre* (1974), *Carnival of Souls* (1962) and *The Shining* (1980), as well as *Vampyr* (1932), *Nosferatu* (1922) and *Let the Right One In* (2008). These are all apparent in *Monster* as they are in *The Babadook*. Kent originally wanted to film *The Babadook* in black-and-white (as she had *Monster*), as she wanted to create a "heightened feel" that is still believable. She was also influenced by pre–1950 B-grade horror films, as the subject matter is "very theatrical," in addition to being "visually beautiful and terrifying."[15] As a rough draft of Kent's ideas, then, *Monster* is worth considering in more detail before moving on to *The Babadook*.

Like *The Babadook*, *Monster* shows the fraught relationship between a mother and her young son plagued by nightmares of a monster who lives in the closet. The mother is unable to cope with the disturbed behavior of her child until she herself is forced to concede that the monster is not imaginary.

*Monster* opens in situ. From under the bed we see the boy, who is dressed as a knight, attack one of his toys (a rag doll) with a plastic sword, an attempt to kill the monster that he fears so much. The studied use of camera angles, black and white photography, and closeups that emphasize the individual elements of the scene (the rag doll, the raised sword, the boy's face under the face shield of his knight helmet) are reminiscent of the heightened feel of Jane Campion's early short films (*Passionless Moments*, 1983; *A Girl's Own Story*, 1986; *Peel*, 1986); they present a quirky, skewed child's-eye view of the world. Kent then cuts to the mother, standing in the kitchen, her nerves already shredded by the boy's anxious hyperactivity. She is framed through the bars of the kitchen window to suggest domestic imprisonment. There are dishes unwashed in the sink; flies on left-over food. In a shot of a pan on the stove, we see stew bubbling (like the mother's temper).

After the mother sees that the boy has wet the bed (presumably not for the first time), she throws the rag doll into a closet. We begin to realize that this situation has been going on for some time and that it is building to a head. There follows an altercation with the boy: He kicks his mother and she responds with barely restrained physical violence. "It's just a doll," she screams. "No it isn't, it's real!" he insists. A sense of unreality grows as the woman later goes into the closet to get clothes, and glimpses the horrible face of the boy's supposedly imaginary monster.

There is an absence of music throughout; Kent relies instead on heightened sounds to create tension. At this point, we move into "horror," as the mother begins to share the boy's experiences of the monster. In the sequence that follows, Kent's images reflect iconic, classic horror films: There are moments and shots strongly reminiscent of *Vampyr, Nosferatu* and *The Haunting* (1963), among others.

From a pop-up book, Mother reads to her son the story of the Three Little Pigs and the Big Bad Wolf (the story book motif would, of course, play a major part in *The Babadook*). A floorboard creaks outside the bedroom door; the woman goes to investigate. Kent frames her through the bannisters of the stairs—a classic horror shot; then uses pixilation animation to create *Monster*'s finest jump scare. The monster speeds up the stairs towards us and into closeup. The surreal effect of combining live-action and pixilated stop-frame animation to show the monster's movement would be used to similar nightmarish effect in *The Babadook*. The sound drops out and Kent utilizes the iconography of silent horror for her confrontation between the mother and the monster. Prefiguring the babadook itself, the monster is shrouded in black, with long, pointy fingers; Kent fully reveals it in this sequence, as it appears to grow in size to physically dominate the mother and her child.

The film's major twist now takes place: Rather than back away from the monster, or succumb to it, the mother chastises it. "Get back to your room!" she commands. She stands firm against the monster, which shrinks away. In an epilogue, we see that the woman has regained control, and can now feel love toward her son (who is free of his nightmares). Recast as an unruly child, the monster is banished to its closet, from which it only briefly appears in order to take the glasses of milk left for it by the mother. Ultimately, then, *Monster* concerns the reclamation of the woman's natural matriarchal authority. This theme is also at the heart of *The Babadook*.

It is significant that Kent's *The Babadook* received praise from William Friedkin, director of the classic American horror film *The Exorcist* (1973). Kent's film uses *The Exorcist* as a major point of reference, while simultaneously recasting its tropes. In developing *The Babadook* to feature length, Kent has created a commentary on the "family horror" of *The Exorcist* (and other similar films); here, however, it is the mother (as opposed to the child as is the norm) who becomes "possessed." Thereby, *The Babadook* questions the usual representation in such films of the mother as martyr figure. Kent utilizes the conventions of demonic possession horror cinema established by *The Exorcist* in order to structure *The Babadook* and give it resonance as a horror film; however, it is the particular way that she reframes the film as social statement from a woman's perspective that gives it the sensibility of new Australian horror. Indeed, *The Babadook*'s first ten minutes arguably owe more to Australian women's cinema than to any horror film.

These first scenes establish the film's theme: The real horror of *The Babadook* is the horror of motherhood. Amelia (Essie Davis) is traumatized by the death of her husband Oskar (Benjamin Winspear), killed in a car crash while driving Amelia to hospital during her labor. It is suggested that Amelia subconsciously blames her son Sam (Noah Wiseman) for Oskar's death, and therefore for Amelia having to shoulder the burden of parenthood alone. Kent opens the film with a dream in which Amelia is in the passenger seat of the car before the accident. She is having contractions and doing her breathing exercises. In slow motion, the window beside her shatters and she is hurled about the car. Kent keeps the camera fixed to Amelia's face, evoking the subjectivity of the dream-state. The car crash is conflated with Amelia's experience of motherhood as a shattering, emotionally traumatic experience. We see Amelia fall downwards, into darkness, towards her bed; a striking visual device that blurs the boundaries of dream and reality.

She is awoken by Sam, who tells her, "I had the dream again." We are now back in *Monster* territory. Kent repeats the first shot of the short film: the camera under the bed, as Amelia and Sam check for monsters. Then the camera is in the closet, as Amelia tries to placate the boy. Another scene from the short is repeated as Amelia reads to him from a book on the Big Bad Wolf. Kent then cuts to Sam sleeping in Amelia's bed; we get the sense of her resentment at his intrusion on her space, of her feeling suffocated by his neediness. She moves away from him. An overhead shot emphasizes her desire to put space between them. Already the theme is established in this pre-credit sequence. Indeed, it is foregrounded in the emphatic use of

**Amelia (Essie Davis) and Samuel (Noah Wiseman) check under the bed for monsters in *The Babadook* (2014, IFC Films).**

camera angles to express Amelia's alienation from her child. This opening, then, is not unlike the sense of suburban domestic dislocation that Campion evokes in her early work: the aforementioned short films and her debut feature *Sweetie* (1989).

Like Campion, Kent situates her film in an ordinary, working-class milieu; Amelia's situation is exacerbated by her low-pay job as a care worker in an old people's home. Her role, it seems, is preordained on account of her gender and class. It is to care for others, and it is a thankless, menial task. Kent is careful, though, not to present Amelia as a victim. When Sam exhibits behavioral problems, the school notifies Amelia. She tells the authorities that Sam needs understanding and threatens to take him out of school. In the car on the way home, we see solidarity between Amelia and Sam, and it is clear that Sam is genuinely troubled.

However, Sam's increasingly bizarre behavior is causing Amelia to become socially isolated. Relations with her sister Claire (Hayley McElhinney) are strained. (Claire no longer wants to share her daughter's birthday party with Sam, as has been their tradition.) Neither Amelia nor Sam has friends of their own.

In the introductory scenes, then, Kent invokes generic tropes (the house might be haunted by a ghost or demon; Sam might be the archetypal devil child, like Damien in *The Omen*, 1976). But much more forcefully established is Amelia's sense of revulsion at her own child, which ultimately arises from her own social disempowerment. "We're all, as women, educated and conditioned to think that motherhood is an easy thing that just happens," Kent has stated. "But it's not always the case. I wanted to show a real woman who was drowning in that environment."[16] *The Babadook* debunks the cultural myths of motherhood, and does so by examining how those myths are generally perpetuated in representations of motherhood in the horror genre.

There is a sense of a shift towards classic horror tropes in the sequence that follows. The next door neighbor's dog goes to the closet, drawn by something only it can detect: a horror film cliché. The film then moves into its developmental scenes. One of the new elements that Kent added to the feature-length film is the book by which the babadook makes its entrance into Amelia's home. The book fulfills a similar narrative and thematic function to the Ouija board in *The Exorcist*; it is the charm or conduit that bridges the spirit realm and the real world through which malefic forces can enter. Kent also utilizes much of the filmic grammar of *The Exorcist* in the central sections of *The Babadook*: The camera emphasizes Amelia's isolation in the house, her growing sense of *das unheimliche*; it repeatedly tracks in towards her from behind, suggesting an unseen presence that haunts her. Kent sets up a sense of expectation; we are waiting for the jump scare.

Kent is in fact playing with our genre expectations here. We begin to think that Sam is becoming possessed as his complexion becomes pale and his behavior increasingly disturbed. When Amelia finds broken glass in her soup, she—and we—immediately suspect Sam, even when he says that the babadook did it. His behavior could be read as aggression towards his mother or he could in fact be trying to protect her. Intertextual references to *The Exorcist* abound. In a medical scene, Amelia tries to convince the doctor that something is seriously wrong with her child; the ensuing scene in which Amelia reassures Sam, "Take your pills and it will be fine," further echoes *The Exorcist*. However, Kent draws these parallels in order to sharply contrast the mother in *The Exorcist* with her counterpart in *The Babadook*. Amelia cannot cope with her child's affliction, whereas in Friedkin's film, Chris McNeil (Ellen Burstyn) becomes a martyr to it. Amelia wants to relieve her own burden by giving her son tranquilizers; Chris is acting in the interests of her daughter, selflessly following doctor's orders. Amelia, unlike Chris, is unable to tell her child that she loves him. In this way, the babadook is a test to see if Amelia is able to be a "mother" to her child. Thus the babadook book keeps reappearing after Amelia has seemingly destroyed it. ("The more you deny, the stronger I get.") At this point, the babadook's intentions are revealed, as is the inexorable direction of the film's narrative: to drive Amelia to kill her son, and herself. *The Shining* (1980) thus becomes the touchstone in *The Babadook*'s central section, as it becomes clear that Amelia, not Sam, is to become possessed by the baba-dook's evil spirit. It is worth emphasizing that Kent uses intertextuality to interrogate standard genre tropes, as well as to fashion a scary movie. We see this in Amelia's hallucination when, in her mind, she inserts the baba-dook figure into the early silent horror films that she watches on late night TV (most pointedly Georges Méliès' *Le Livre Magique* [*The Magic Book*], 1900). This suggests that Kent's intention with *The Babadook* is nothing less than to mark a complete revision of tropes that extend back to earliest film history. Amelia is to become the archetypal "demonic mother" (cf. *Psycho* [1960]; *Carrie* [1976]) but, again, this is merely a test, a form of abjection that ultimately leads Amelia to summon her maternal authority when she rejects the babadook's possession of her. Indeed, before this happens, *The Babadook* becomes a veritable compendium of possession movie clichés. Amelia chases her son up the stairs with a knife, and when he locks himself in the bedroom, she leers at the bedroom door like *The Shining*'s Jack Nicholson (even calling her son a "little pig") before kicking it off its hinges. A moment later, she floats across the room!

It is Sam's stark admission of the truth to Amelia that enables Kent to debunk the demonic mother convention. "I know you don't love me," he tells her. "The babadook won't let you. But I love you, mum." This statement leads Amelia to eject the babadook from within herself, and this returns us to *Monster* and the final confrontation between a mother and the social forces that have disempowered her. Thus we have the necessary replaying of Amelia's trauma as her dead husband Oskar returns from the darkness; Amelia's horror of seeing him die again (which simultaneously frees her from him). And—crucially—Amelia's separating herself from the social order that serves to subjugate her. By reclaiming her matriarchal author-ity, she is no longer victimized by the babadook. She simply rejects it (him): "You are nothing." This denial in turn disempowers the babadook, who, as in *Monster*, retreats to the cellar.

In a coda, Kent shows us Amelia's calm acceptance of her husband's death, and of Sam's maleness. She can cope now; she's in charge. As in *Monster*, the babadook is still to be part of her life, and a challenging one. (The final scene in the cellar makes it clear that the babadook is still a potentially destructive force.) However, Amelia can now feel love for her son, and *The Babadook* ends on that note, with Amelia content in the knowledge.

## Hounds of Love

[I]t involved psychopathic men and very vulnerable women. The man would find this vulnerable person and build her up and then tear her down to the point where she truly believed that she didn't have an identity outside of him. Then, he could manipulate her into doing anything that he wanted to keep them together.—Ben Young on *Hounds of Love*.[17]

Interestingly, Ben Young credits his mother, crime fiction writer Felicity Young, as the chief inspiration of his debut feature. Certainly, Young would take the raw material of true crime stories that he found in his mother's research archive and fashion them into a study of male-female power relationships, where sympathy clearly lies with the strength of women as mothers and independent agents. Young's film very much takes the female perspective of New Australian Horror; but at the same time, pits it against a backdrop of male psychopathology that is so familiar from Ozploitation (and numerous male serial killer movies of all nationalities) that it hardly needs exploring in further detail, even within the film itself. Instead, what Young offers in *Hounds of Love* is a story of women who struggle to forge lives outside of toxic male influence.

*Hounds of Love* opens in the suburbs of Perth in December 1987. Throughout the film, Young emphasizes the apparent normalcy of the setting, with its casual division of lower middle-class and working-class neighborhoods. The camera tracks across netball players in slow motion; it lingers on the lithe young limbs of the girls. We come to realize that we are seeing them from the psychological viewpoint of an unseen stalker parked near the netball courts. The voyeur turns out to be a couple, John White (Stephen Curry) and wife Evelyn (Emma Booth). They offer a lift home to one of the players, but instead take her to their house where they keep her bound and gagged in a room with boarded-up windows. The next morning, Evelyn clears bloody tissues from the girl's room while John shaves (admiring his own reaffirmed masculinity in the bathroom mirror). We see Evelyn in bed, listening as John assaults the girl in the next room. John later puts the girl's body in the trunk of the car, while Evelyn does the laundry. In this opening sequence, Young emphasizes the ritualistic actions of the couple; we realize that this cycle of abduction, rape and murder has become a routine for them. What is left ambiguous is how Evelyn feels about John's depravity. As his accomplice, how willing is she?

The film now introduces us to disaffected schoolgirl Vicki Maloney (Ashleigh Cummings) who, it quickly becomes clear, will become the couple's next victim. Vicki harbors resentment towards her mother Maggie (Susie Porter), who has recently separated from Vicki's father Trevor (Damien De Montemas). Vicki feels abandoned, and doesn't fully understand her mother's need for independence. Sneaking out of her mum's house, she is approached by John and Evelyn, who lure her back to theirs with the promise of "weed." She is chained to the bed and raped by John. However, Vicki and Evelyn are thrown together, as Evelyn is the one who

**A publicity still for *Hounds of Love* (2016, Gunpowder & Sky): Emma Booth and Stephen Curry play killer couple Evelyn and John White.**

has to tend to the captive girl. In order to survive, can Vicki somehow manage to drive a wedge between the couple?

*Hounds of Love* is based in part on the true-life serial killers David John Birnie and Catherine Margaret Birnie, who murdered four women in a Perth suburb in 1986. Young uses some details of the case in his film, including elements of Catherine's life. Like Evelyn in the film, Catherine entered into a relationship with the killer at an early age, and although she left David to have children with another man, returned to him shortly before the killing spree began. However, Catherine—unlike Evelyn—never gave up her devotion to David even after they were both convicted for the killings. Young is less interested in female psychopathology than he is in depicting the dynamics of abusive male-female relationships. Therefore, *Hounds of Love*'s central focus is Evelyn's growing realization that she is being manipulated by John; that he is playing on her emotional vulnerability to get what he wants. John solicits her compliance by lying to her, and by making promises that he has no intention of keeping (such as helping her regain custody of her children and being a father to them). We see how Evelyn has, over time, allowed herself to believe him. Vicki observes their relationship and delivers the truth that Evelyn cannot bring herself to accept: "He just uses you," Vicki tells her. "He doesn't love you." To end the cycle of abuse, Evelyn must break free from her dependence on John. Vicki, as an outsider, helps her to see this.

John's psychopathology, as previously mentioned, can be seen as a distillation of Ozploitation's toxic masculinity: His sexual relations are entirely predicated on violence. Young makes it clear that John's sexual depravity arises from the need to affirm his masculinity through the domination of women. Young thus counterpoints the sexual abuse that John inflicts on Vicki with his psychological domination of Evelyn. Both are his attempts to subjugate women. His need is made more urgent because he himself is dominated by another male: Gary (Fletcher Humphrys) extorts money from John and humiliates him by stealing his cigarettes. Significantly, when Evelyn stabs John at the end, to be free of him, it is presented as a necessary act of emasculation.

Young ultimately departs from the Birnie case to explore wider cultural themes but Vicki, an intelligent and resourceful survivor, certainly shares those same characteristics with her real-life counterpart, Kate Moir, who also managed to escape by climbing through a window. *Hounds of Love* ends as Vicki is reunited with her mother, who has not given up searching for her daughter. Vicky is finally able to appreciate her mother's strength, and to fully understand the need for a woman to have independence.

# 3

# Austria

## *Goodnight Mommy* (2014)
## and *Cold Hell* (2017)

Largely because of its box office success in the States (grossing $1,168,902 on its 2015 release there), *Ich Seh, Ich Seh* (*Goodnight Mommy*) has been called "the rebirth of the Austrian horror film."[1] In a country that produces on average only 20 films per year, of which one or two at most might be described as horror, this claim may seem a little precipitous. However, given the international prestige of directors Michael Haneke and Ulrich Seidl, who, since the '90s, have come to characterize an Austrian art house cinema that is dark and disturbing, it is perhaps not surprising that the horror film has started to take root in that country, even if its growth has remained slow.

"In Austria, there isn't much of a horror film tradition," admits *Goodnight Mommy*'s co-writer-co-director, Veronika Franz.[2] In fact, in the 1980s and '90s there was no horror production of which to speak. One of the reasons for this may be that the Austrian film industry operates on state funding and that, during those decades (in Franz's words), "Austria wanted to represent itself as an art film country. It was thought that horror films had no stories and were filled with clichés."

The first tentative horror productions of the new millennium, *In 3 Tagen bist du tot* (*Dead in Three Days*, 2006), its sequel *In 3 Tagen bist du tot 2* (*Dead in Three Days 2*, 2008) and *Silent, Blood Night* (2006), based as they are on the post–*Scream* (1996) American slasher, did little to dispel that viewpoint (despite *Dead in Three Days* being Austria's highest grossing film of 2006). Austrian filmmakers looking for a tradition in horror prior to that had only *The Hands of Orlac* (1924), *Parapsycho—Spektrum der Angst* (*Parapsycho—Spectrum of Fear*, 1975) and the controversial *Angst* (*Fear*, 1983) as reference points. It is not surprising, then, that *Goodnight Mommy* should find itself as easily slotted into the Austrian art house category as into the genre of horror cinema, sharing as it does the kind of

43

clinical violence often associated with Haneke's work, even if its themes of family, identity and physical disfigurement are more readily identifiable as horror film concerns.

Indeed, *Goodnight Mommy*'s art house–horror crossover has inspired other Austrian filmmakers to move into the genre—or to attempt to straddle the two. Such a director is Stefan Ruzowitsky, whose films (which include *Die Hölle/Cold Hell*, 2017) can be seen as further signs of horror's rebirth in Austria.

## Austrian Horror History

Following the worldwide distribution of Germany's *Das Cabinet des Dr. Caligari* (*The Cabinet of Dr. Caligari*, 1920), silent cinema in Austria produced a number of notable early horror entries, including one genuine classic. *Der Graf von Cagliostro* (*The Count of Cagliostro*, 1920) starred *Caligari*'s Conrad Veidt and was one of the first attempts to dramatize the life of 18th century occultist Guiseppe Balsamo Cagliostro. *Das grinsende Gesicht* (*The Grinning Face*, 1921) marked an early adaptation of Victor Hugo's novel *The Man Who Laughs*, with Franz Höbling as Gwynplaine (a role that Veidt played in the superior 1928 version). In 1921, Michael Curtiz directed the lackluster *Labyrinth des Grauens* (*Labyrinth of Horror*), one of many movies he churned out for Sascha Films in Austria in the '20s before moving on to Hollywood. The undisputed masterpiece of this era is 1924's *Orlacs Hände* (*The Hands of Orlac*). *Caligari*'s Veidt and director Robert Wiene reunited to produce an adaptation of Maurice Renard's 1920 novel *Les Mains D'Orlac* that remains one of the most financially and critically successful Austrian films ever made.

From this early highpoint in cinema history, Austrian horror production underwent a long hiatus that—with just a few stand-alones—would last for the best part of the next 80 years. Hyperinflation and growing competition from the U.S. sent the Austrian film industry into decline in the late 1920s; Austria's annexation by Germany in the late 1930s, and subsequent confiscation of its film companies by the Nazis, limited production to non-propaganda light comedies. The end of World War II saw the rural and sentimental *Heimatfilme* celebrating a romanticized Austrian identity and idealizing the country's past. By the 1970s, Austria's film industry had bottomed out, with production hitting an all-time low of five to ten films per year, many of them sex comedies co-produced by West Germany. Even in the 1980s, when Austrian cinema rediscovered other genres beside comedy, horror did not flourish.

Only two Austrian horror films of note were made in the 1970s and

1980s. The Austrian–West German *Parapsycho—Spectrum of Fear* has the look and attitude of New German Cinema—a sense of social criticism informs the film—but at heart it is just as indebted to Amicus as it is to the work of Fassbinder, Kluge or Wenders. This tale of Viennese residents afflicted by unexplained phenomena—reincarnation, extrasensory perception and telekinesis—is told as a trio of stories, evoking the classic horror anthology movie. But it does so with a level of cold brutality (graphic gore, nudity and actual autopsy footage) that marks it as a precursor of later Austrian horror films.

*Fear*, the sole feature of director Gerald Kargl, takes this brutality to the extreme in a deliberately de-romanticized account of a sociopath's murder of a family after he randomly invades their home. Based loosely on the real-life case of Werner Kniesek, who butchered a widow and her two children (one of whom was disabled), Kargl portrays his killer as a pathetic figure, a deluded, disorganized individual who is neither charismatic nor particularly intelligent—a debunking of Hollywood's mythologized serial killer and a harking back instead to Peter Lorre's disturbed child killer in Fritz Lang's *M* (1931). Much of the film takes place in real time, and is shot in elaborate POV style to evoke the killer's schizophrenia. In terms of its approach to screen violence, *Fear* is unrelentingly realistic, which led to the film going unreleased in the States, Britain and Germany. Thereby unable to recoup his production costs, Kargl was left without the means to continue making films. *Fear* has since received positive critical attention and a belated (2015) DVD release by Cult Epics. It can now be seen as a crucial stepping stone in the development of Austrian horror cinema.

## Recent Austrian Horror Films

Co-funded by the Austrian Film Institute and the Vienna Film Fund, *Dead in Three Days* was an attempt to cash in on the success of teen slashers in the States, and managed to secure worldwide distribution (including a DVD release in America by Dimension Extreme). Writer-director Andreas Prochaska borrows liberally from films like *I Know What You Did Last Summer* (1997): On the day of their high school graduation, five friends each receive a text message telling them, "In three days you will be dead," and find themselves trying to outwit a serial killer determined to make good his threat. It's an over-familiar premise, but Prochaska puts a distinctly Austrian spin on standard slasher tropes. Much harsher in tone and visual style than its American counterparts, *Dead in Three Days* benefits hugely from its locations in the Traunviertel region of Upper Austria, with its mountains and lakes, and cold, hard light bringing stark realism to the proceedings. The Ebensee setting adds a resonance rarely found in American slashers, the town having been close by to a Nazi concentration camp in which 20,000 inmates perished. If recent Austrian horror cinema (indeed, recent Austrian cinema generally) has "national guilt at its heart," as critic Ryan Gilbey has suggested,[3] then *Dead in Three Days* might be seen as a tacit acknowledgment of this.

Prochaska's 2008 sequel *Dead in Three Days 2* did not do as well financially, failing to secure a release in the States. Even so, it is another attempt to broaden Austrian horror by drawing on typically American subgenres, in this case the backwoods survival horror: The first film's Final Girl, Nina (played by actor-director Sabrina Reiter), here finds herself trapped in a snowbound hotel run by a family of deviants, one of whom has distinctly homicidal tendencies. Again, Prochaska makes powerful use of the Austrian landscape and the film includes starkly realistic violence; but the emphasis on abduction and false imprisonment in the sequel speaks to contemporary true-crime stories such as the kidnapping of Natascha Kampusch (who was held captive in a cellar by her abductor for eight years) and the Josef Fritzl case in which an Austrian man kept his daughter, and the children he fathered with her, prisoner in the basement of his house for 24 years. (Prochaska actually names his killer Josef in the film.)

*Dead in Three Days'* success led to other Austrian companies producing slashers, with generally mediocre results. In a Swiss-Austrian co-production, *One Way Trip* (2011), a group of youngsters head for the Swiss mountains to get high on magic mushrooms. In a remote farmhouse, they fall victim to a deranged farmer and his equally psychotic daughter. Shot in 3D, *One Way Trip* drew inevitable comparisons with the Irish horror film *Shrooms* (2007), and is generally considered the inferior of the two.

*Blutgletscher* (*Blood Glacier*, 2013), produced by Allegro Films who made *Dead in Three Days*, borrowed liberally from John Carpenter's *The Thing* (1982) in its story of a team of scientists, studying climate change in the Austrian alps, discovering hybrid creatures created by the mysterious "blood glacier" of the title. An enjoyable but generic B movie, it uses the alpine scenery to good effect but has little to say about climate change, or anything else. However, writer-director Dominik Hartl managed to put together a genuine crowd-pleaser in the delirious *Angriff der Lederhosenzombies* (*Attack of the Lederhosen Zombies*, 2016), which uses many of the same elements: South Tyrol setting, widescreen cinematography and a clear appreciation of cult comedy-horror splatter films, from Peter Jackson's *Braindead* (aka *Dead Alive*, 1992) to Tommy Wirkola's low-budget Norwegian zomcom *Død snø* (*Dead Snow*, 2009). As the title suggests, there is much satirizing of Austria's reputation as a popular skiing destination, and of the country's traditional cinematic image abroad *à la The Sound of Music*

(1965). In its own way, *Attack of the Lederhosen Zombies* stands alongside *Goodnight Mommy* as one of the most distinctively "Austrian" horror films made in recent years. The plot, such as it is, sees a snowboarder and his girl-friend trapped in an alpine hotel infested with zombies. Like many zom-coms, its *raison d'etre* is to showcase the inventive special effects; in this case, zombies are dispatched by ski pole, snowblower and snow board by characters wearing traditional alpine garb. (The women wear Dirndl dresses, the men Tyrolean trilby hats.) It's very silly, but at the same time also very knowing. Beneath the gruesome fun, there is the concern with questioning national identity that more serious Austrian films share.

A further sign of Austria's horror re-emergence is the recent Austrian–North American co-production *The Dark* (2018), co-directed by Columbia University alumni Justin P. Lange and Austrian cinematographer Klemens Hufnagl. The story of a flesh-eating undead girl who haunts the forest where she was murdered, and the blind boy whom she befriends, it was made with the support of the Austrian Film Institute and shot in Canada. It's a somber, depressive piece of work, concerned with child abuse and a lingering unease about the past. As such, it seems to fit in well with Austrian horror cinema's main preoccupations.

Despite the lack of a firm horror tradition, the dark and disturbing nature of modern Austrian art house cinema has had a clear influence on art house–horror hybrids like *Goodnight Mommy*. The Natascha Kampusch case, for example, provided the inspiration for Markus Schleinzer's *Michael* (2011), the frank story of a pedophile who keeps a ten-year-old boy locked in his basement. Schleinzer's detached fly-on-the-wall style and controversial subject matter evokes the bleakness of Haneke's work while also keying in modern horror cinema's obsession with physical confinement and abuse. (Jennifer Lynch's *Chained* is just one of many recent films in the horror genre to explore these tropes; while the art house drama *Room* [2015] shared largely the same theme.) Little known outside of Austria, *Michael* deserves a mention for drawing together art house and horror and paving the way for *Goodnight Mommy*.

## Goodnight Mommy

*Goodnight Mommy*, according to Franz's co-writer-co-director Severin Fiala, is about a "clash of perspectives and people not communicating clearly or talking to each other."[4] This, in Fiala's words, is what connects the film to Austrian cinema "where crises arise because the people aren't talking to each other." In *Goodnight Mommy*, there's alienation between a mother (Susanne Wuest) and her children after the mother returns from hospital with her face bandaged. Her twin sons, Lukas (Lukas Schwarz) and Elias (Elias Schwarz), come to suspect that the woman is not their mother but a stranger who has stolen their mother's face and identity. The film plays on the psychological condition known as the Capgras Syndrome, the delusion that a loved one has been replaced by an imposter. But the film's underlying theme is the loss of trust within the family—conflict between the generations—and this is what aligns it with horror cinema, Franju's *Les Yeux Sans Visage* (*Eyes Without a Face*) being an obvious touchstone. Indeed, the war guilt that Ryan Gilbey speaks of in relation to *Goodnight Mommy* is something that both films share. Franju's horror of Vichy France's collaboration with the Nazis is transcribed by Franz and Fiala into a more generalized unease over the unwillingness of postwar Austria to confront the Anschluss, as Franz told *Film Comment* in 2015:

> They didn't talk about Hitler.... It was only 25 years ago when the Austrian Chancellor [Franz Vranitzky] first publicly said in parliament that Austria was not a victim—Austria was guilty. I mean, that was 25 years ago! Until then, Austria would always say: "Oh, we were the first victims of Hitler's Germany" even knowing that Hitler was Austrian. [*Laughs*] And I think that's very typically Austrian—kind of avoiding the truth.[5]

*Goodnight Mommy* opens with a clip from a *Heimat* film, showing a von Trapp–like family on a TV screen, a reference to Austria's abiding postwar self-image—a comment on *Heimatfilme* as an avoidance of historical truth. In contrast, Franz and Fiala present their family home as modernistic and isolated; and the beauty of the Austrian countryside rendered with a cold precision that works against the schmaltzy golden hues of *Heimatfilme*.

The isolated homestead also works to the horror genre, of course. The twins are forbidden by their mother from opening the blinds during the day; they are allowed only to play outside, and when in the house they must maintain strict silence, as the mother tells them she needs to rest after her surgery. Right from the start, this serves only to create a sense of alienation between mother and children. More alarming is the cruel behavior she begins to exhibit toward her sons. She pointedly ignores Lukas and physically abuses Elias. Reasoning that their real mother would never act in such a way toward them, the boys determine to expose the woman as an imposter.

The film's use of alternating points of view between the boys and their mother serves to make the other monstrous. The first two-thirds of the film are taken from the perspective of Lukas and Elias; they view their mother as increasingly cold, distant and callous. The boys gain our sympathy as we share their growing suspicion of the woman and their antipathy towards her. In a striking early scene, they test their mother with a game of "Who

**Lukas Schwarz and Elias Schwarz as murderous twins Lukas and Elias in *Ich seh, Ich seh/Goodnight Mommy* (2014, RADiUS-TWC).**

am I?" sticking a Post-It with "Mama" written on it to her bandaged forehead. Her inability to give the correct answer indicates to the boys that being their mother is not how she identifies herself, and their misgivings develop from there. But if this woman is not who she says she is, who is she really?

This is only one enigma with which we are presented during the film's developmental sequences: in addition, we don't know why the woman is bandaged and why the boys might think she is an imposter. Is she simply a vain, uncaring, selfish woman who places her appearance before her relationship with her sons? Has her hospitalization served to increase the distance that was already there between her and the boys? These uncertainties help to imbue *Goodnight Mommy* with a rich ambiguity that serves it well. We feel the lack of communication within this family keenly. Franz and Fiala went on to explore this theme in their next film, the family gaslighting horror *The Lodge* (2019), filmed in Quebec.

The film then switches perspectives to that of the mother and this serves to make the clash of perspectives between them seemingly irreconcilable. Here, from the mother's point of view, the boys take on a cruel guise as they determine to make the woman reveal her true identity by torturing a confession out of her. They tie her to the bed, bind her mouth with tape (and later Super Glue) and try to exact the truth from her.

These later scenes are difficult to watch, and key into Austrian cinema's preoccupation with confronting the viewer. As one reviewer put it, "Torture porn filtered through a traditional family dynamic, the movie seems engineered to exploit phobias."[6] The family's dysfunction becomes truly monstrous, the physical torment increasingly graphic, but underneath is always this question of personal and national identity—an issue that Austrian art house horror films seem determined to force. Hence, the film's final twist that explains the mother's behavior, and Elias's alienation from her, satisfies the viewer looking for a rationale to the story, while making its message overt. The ending openly satirizes the von Trapp film shown at the start, as Elias, Lukas and their mother are reunited in a glowing cornfield, now re-cast as an idealized *Heimatfilme* version of family and national identity. The filmmakers seem to be saying that the lack of communication between generations, their clash of perspectives, remains a problem.

This mirroring of opposing perspectives "not talking to each other" is reflected in the film's very structure, in the symmetry of the opening and closing scenes, and extends to the twinning theme and the doubling imagery throughout. Intriguingly, *Goodnight Mommy*'s Austrian title is *Ich Seh, Ich Seh*, which loosely translates as "I See, I See" (the German children's game of "I Spy"); perhaps also a reference to the conjunction of "visual" and "self"—perspectives governed by subjectivity.

## Cold Hell

Subjective perspectives also inform *Cold Hell*, Ruzowitsky's extraordinary melding of immigrant drama and serial killer thriller set in a modern Vienna made to look like a neon-soaked nightmare. Violetta Schurawlow plays Özge, a young Turkish woman who has left her homeland to make a new life in Austria. She works as a taxi driver for the husband of her cousin Ranya (Verena Altenberger). After hours, her hobby is kickboxing, a tough sport that serves as an outlet after the hostility that she faces from her customers and the police. One night she witnesses the murder of a prostitute by a serial killer who targets Muslim women. Because Özge saw his face, he turns his attentions to her, and she is forced to go into hiding. When the killer murders Ranya, Özge decides to take the law into her own hands and confronts the killer herself.

*Cold Hell* is very much a film of two halves. The first half documents Özge's struggle to survive in a brutal and brutalizing environment. We see her face misogyny and Islamophobia as part of her daily life as a Turkish Muslim woman in Vienna; we see the precarity of her existence as an economic migrant, forced to drive a taxi to survive. Her support network is meager: She has split up with her boyfriend; her relationship with her parents is fraught; her only friend is Ranya. The threat from the serial killer, which renders her homeless, with no one to turn to, leaves her to the mercies of the police investigator (Tobias Moretti). The second half of the film

**Violetta Schuralawlow plays Özge, the Turkish immigrant menaced by a serial killer, in** *Die Hölle/Cold Hell* **(2017, Shudder).**

presents a rebirth of Özge—from victim to heroine—as she takes control, defeats the killer and, in the process, regains the ability to feel tenderness and love for another person.

The subjectivity of the film—which presents the immigrant experience from Özge's perspective—is convincing and brings to mind works like Fassbinder's *Angst essen Seele auf* (*Fear Eats the Soul*, 1974) and Fatih Akin's *Gegen die Wand/Head-On* (2004). *Cold Hell* certainly shares the harshness of these films in their frank depiction of the xenophobia experienced by Muslim immigrants in Austria-Germany. (The title *Cold Hell* has a double meaning in this respect.)

However, *Cold Hell* also compares to William Friedkin's work (specifically *The French Connection*, 1971, and *Cruising*, 1980) in the unflinching way that the dark underbelly of a city is exposed. It shares with Friedkin in both its strengths (its documentary realism) and its weaknesses (its contrivances of plot). The weaknesses become apparent in the second half, which contrives to give Özge an overly defined "journey" or character arc. We learn that she has been sexually abused by her father—this explains her hardness, her inability to express her feelings in ways other than through violence. When she later sleeps with Moretti's detective, it is another contrivance, this time to show the softening of her character, as she rediscovers human tenderness. Neither contrivance is necessary to the film, as the structure of events—and the film's subjectivity—suggest that trajectory without the need to make it pointed. Crucially, these rather conventional

feature film, *O Segredo da Múmia* (*The Secret of the Mummy*), in 1982. Clearly inspired by Marins, Cardoso adds liberal amounts of sex to his tale of an Egyptian mummy brought to life by a discredited professor; but while Marins generally plays his horror straight, Cardoso's tongue is firmly in cheek. A patchwork of Super 8, found documentary footage and homage to Universal's classic horror films of the 1930s and 1940s, *The Secret of the Mummy* has a cult underground vibe reminiscent of the more camp efforts of American filmmakers like Mike and George Kuchar and Joe Sarno.

Cardoso continued in the same vein with *As Sete Vampiras* (*Seven Vampires*, 1986), which parodied both the Brazilian *chanchada* (musical-comedy) and Hollywood vampire movies of the past. The slender plot is an obvious nod to *The Little Shop of Horrors* (1960, remade in 1986): A carnivorous exotic plant (housed in a nightclub) turns people into blood suckers. Randal Johnson and Robert Stam describe it as a "Brazilianized synthesis of Roger Corman and Mel Brooks,"[5] in the way that Cardoso attempts to give new life to generic clichés, "vampirizing, as it were, preexisting films and genres, absorbing and transforming the 'blood' of other texts."

Cardoso's latest horror-satire to date is *Um Lobisomem na Amazônia* (*A Werewolf in the Amazon*, 2005). Paul Naschy stars as Dr. Moreau, a mad scientist (based on the H.G. Wells character). He has created a werewolf that runs amok in the rain forest (actually Rio de Janeiro) killing a group of friends who came to the Amazon in search of hallucinogenic tea. Cardoso mixes his trademark comedy with nudity and lesbian sex, and introduces the use of hand-held video sequences in order to keep up with the found-footage horror of *The Blair Witch Project*. It's an eccentric mix even for Cardoso. In the U.S., *A Werewolf in the Amazon* sat on the shelf until 2016, when the aptly named Camp Motion Pictures picked it up for digital streaming and a DVD release as part of a Cardoso box set that helped him find a new generation of fans and admirers. He is certainly one of Brazil's underrated film talents.

Walter Hugo Khouri is celebrated for erotic psychological dramas that explore the sexual mores of the middle classes in Brazil's conservative 1960s and 1970s. He has moved into horror territory on at least two occasions. *O Anjo da Noite* (*The Angel of the Night*, 1974) riffed on the terrorized babysitter theme of films like *Fright* (1972) as well as on the Gothic literature of Henry James. Selma Egri plays Ana, a young student who flees Rio's hustle and bustle to the mountain retreat of Petrópolis where she takes the post of nanny in a gloomy mansion. She starts to receive threatening phone calls that she eventually discovers are being made from inside the house. Who is the anonymous male caller? Is it one of the other servants? Is it Augusto, the Black night watchman (Eliezer Gomes) who befriends

Ana? Or could it be Ana's young charge, Marcelo (Pedro Coelho)? Khouri explores the social and sexual tensions of the time, drawing on the Gothic feminism of *The Turn of the Screw* and its influences over the years, particularly in terms of the paranoid, persecuted woman trope that underlies Khouri's scenario. The black and white cinematography evokes that of *The Innocents* (Jack Clayton's 1961 adaptation of James' classic novel) but also has a Bergman-esque quality in keeping with the psycho-sexual elements of the story.

Khouri trod similar territory in 1978 with *As Filhas do Fogo* (*The Daughters of Fire*), in which two young women, staying in a colonial mansion in the Rio Grande do Sul countryside, find themselves embroiled in paranormal events. They meet an elderly lady who claims to be able to communicate with the dead, and several mysterious deaths occur. Khouri uses this scenario to explore issues of gender and homosexuality that lie at the heart of many Gothic tropes and conventions (the two protagonists have a lesbian relationship). In his later films, Khouri moved further into areas of sexuality; but his two films in the horror genre remain distinctive works, and have been subject to recent rediscovery by a new generation of critics who recognize them as important entries in the Brazilian horror canon.

Brazil's erotic movie industry, originating in the Boca do Lixo district of São Paulo, gave rise to a number of films that combined the *pornochanchada* (sex melodrama) with supernatural horror. Although the *Cinema de Boca* is more readily identifiable with crime films, kung fu movies, action and comedy (B movie exploitation genres then more popular than horror), Marins' influence via the success of the Coffin Joe series can be seen in the works of Garret, Doo and Castillini in the late 1970s and early 1980s.

Garret's *Excitação* opens memorably with a man committing suicide in a secluded beach house. A noose dangles from the ceiling; Garret frames the man's face in the background. Then we have a shot of the chair on which the man will climb in order to hang himself. Garret shows us the knot of the rope, and then a graphic match to the knot in the man's tie, which he takes off in preparation. He places the noose around his neck and we see his legs go limp after he kicks over the chair. Finally, Garret cuts to an extreme closeup of the man's eye. It's a striking juxtaposition of images and Garret continues in this style throughout the sequences that follow. A couple from the city moves into the house; she has a history of psychotic disturbance and soon begins to experience strange phenomena in the house: Objects appear to move by themselves and attack the woman, and she has visions of the hanged man. Are these visions hallucinations, or is the couple being haunted by the man's ghost? The premise is a familiar one (very similar to José Ramón Larraz's 1974 film *Symptoms*, among others) but Garret has an impressive command of the genre, and brings a sure touch to the ghostly set pieces.

Director John Doo's *Nifas Diabólicas* (*Diabolical Nymphs*) comes across as a surreal road movie of sex, death and magic. Hitchhikers Circe and Ursula (Patrícia Scalvi and Aldine Müller), who seem to share a telepathic link, are picked up by family man Rodrigo (Sergio Hingst). He drives them to a deserted beach, where the women take turns seducing him. Jealousy inexplicably flares up between Ursula and Circe, each of whom appears to want Rodrigo for her own. A fight develops in which Circe, with the help of Rodrigo, seemingly murders Ursula with a rock. As Circe and Rodrigo flee in the car, the bloody figure of Ursula materializes in the back seat, causing a crash which the viewer assumes is fatal to all. But shortly afterwards, in an enigmatic twist, both women appear again, completely unhurt (although Rodrigo is presumably dead). They swap clothes and personas, and in what now seems to be some kind of never-ending diabolical game, resume their hitchhiking to find a new male victim. Filmed on location, *vérité*-style, *Nifas Diabólicas* is an odd, unsettling movie, all the more so because nothing is explained. It takes the oft-used pornographic male fantasy of women hitchhikers picked up by lone men, and turns it on its head.

Patrícia Scalvi also appeared in husband Luiz Castillini's *A Reencarnação do Sexo* (*The Reincarnation of Sex*), a melancholy ghost story about a pair of young lovers (Scalvi and Artur Roveder) whose relationship is forbidden by the girl's parents. When the boy is murdered, the girl dies of a broken heart. Their vengeful ghosts remain in the parents' house where they exert a malefic influence on couples who move in, driving them to violence and murder during the act of sex. If, as Roberto Pinheiro Machado has claimed, the *pornochanchada* is often concerned with "a strange form of eroticism full of mixed feelings of love, hate, jealousy and anger,"[6] then Castillini's film is a case in point. At times, the combining of these elements with horror motifs makes for a queasy mix.

## Recent Brazilian Horror

As Bahiana observes, "films with fantastical themes have historically been rare in Brazilian cinema,"[7] and the tradition of Marins has not carried forward into all of the most recent Brazilian horror movies. Instead, as previously noted, it is the increased availability in Brazil of mainly American horror films (thanks largely to Netflix, which made Brazil its first Latin American territory in 2011) that has generated interest in the genre among audiences and filmmakers alike. A number of recent horror film festivals, such as the Morce-GO Goiás Horror Film Festival in Goiânia, Fantaspoa International Fantastic Film Festival in Porto Alegre, the Rock Horror in Rio Film Festival in São Paulo and Hell de Janeiro—Festival Internacional de Terror do Rio, offer programs of international releases as well as home-grown features and shorts, many of which debut at these festivals. The programming is often imaginative, with films grouped into strands that serve to highlight current and emerging horror themes and tropes. Thus, the 2018 Hell de Janeiro, as previously noted, featured strands like "The Monstrous Female" ("which subverts the usual sexist horror trope of casting women as the victims, with a whole host of short films about female monsters"), as well as films that fall into more traditional categories such as "Cannibals, Murderers and Slayers" and "Ghosts, Science Fiction–Horror and Freaks."[8]

Opening 2018's Fantaspoa was *Mata Negri* (*The Black Forest*, 2018), directed by Rodrigo Aragão, one of the leading lights of Brazilian horror. His career has been sustained until now by low-budget production and the film festival circuit. Born in 1977, he was raised on *Star Wars* and early Peter Jackson and Sam Raimi movies, some of which he saw in his father's cinema in the tourist resort of Guarapari in the eastern Brazilian state of Espírito Santo where he grew up. An interest in special effects makeup and prosthetics drew him into moviemaking as a teenager. His debut feature, *Mud Zombies*, was shot on a $15,000 budget with minimal crew on a plot of empty land behind his house. Aragão handled all the special effects and the film took him three years to complete. Set in Espírito Santo, it weaves themes of poverty and environmental destruction into the tale of a poor fishing community whose livelihood is threatened by water pollution. One night, zombies rise from the contaminated swamp to attack the locals. Luis (Walderrama Dos Santos), a dorky young crab-picker, has to save the day and his love Raquel (Kika de Oliveira). *Mud Zombies* has been compared to Jackson's *Braindead* (*Dead Alive*, 1992) but perhaps does not have the same impact as that splatstick classic. Despite the originality of its premise and admittedly impressive effects, Aragão's script stretches thin over a 105-minute running time; it would have been better as a short film. Having said that, there is no doubt that *Mud Zombies* remains a milestone in Brazilian horror, not least because, even by 2013 and his third film, Aragão was still described as the only Brazilian filmmaker making horror movies at that time. After *Mud Zombies*, he made *A Doite do Chupacabras* (*The Night of the Chupacabras*, 2011), the story of two feuding families whose war is interrupted when they are attacked by a blood-sucking monster (the Chupacabra of South American legend). *Mar Negro* (*Black Sea*, 2013) followed, completing his "eco-terror" trilogy in which a fisherman suffers the bite from a sea creature that turns him into a zombie. The infection quickly spreads through the Espírito Santo village, as locals take refuge in a brothel.

A fitting showcase for Aragão's remarkable gore effects, *Black Sea* boasted a larger budget than his previous outings and it had a DVD release in Germany (under the title *Bloodbath*). *The Black Forest* sees Aragão changing gears somewhat, moving away from zombies and monsters into fantasy and black magic: An ancient book grants wealth and power to those who possess it, but also unleashes terrible evil. It falls into the hands of an albino girl who lives in a forest. She must fight bandits, witches and supernatural forces to protect the book from a powerful demon who wants it for his own.

Aragão attempts to combine 1980s horror homage with a Brazilian seasoning, featuring themes of poverty, discrimination and environmental pollution within the framework of the supernatural, while other filmmakers choose a more psychological approach. Tomas Portella's *Isolados* takes the familiar plot of a couple trapped in a remote house with a serial killer and imbues it with claustrophobia and a fair degree of suspense. Portella and cinematographer Gustavo Hadba make the most of the rain forest setting (filmed in Rio de Janeiro) and Rembrandt-inspired visuals but *Isolados* was little seen outside of Brazil, and even there it received limited release.

*The Trace We Leave Behind* is an equally ambitious horror-thriller that starts with the rational and gradually leads us into ghostly ambiguity in a manner reminiscent of Polanski and Brad Anderson. (J.C. Feyer's film shares striking similarities to Anderson's *Session 9* [2001].) At a Rio mental hospital about to close due to budget cuts, a young doctor called João (Rafael Cardoso) has the task of transferring patients. What seems like a straightforward job becomes anything but when one patient, a young girl, goes missing. He sets out to find her, a quest that quickly becomes an obsession, and as he searches the labyrinth of corridors and dormitories, he discovers its terrible history, and the empty, decaying hospital starts to take on a life of its own. Is the hospital haunted, or is João cracking under the pressure and slowly losing his mind? Feyer leaves these ambiguities intact and focuses instead on the nightmarish, oppressive hospital location, making it a character in its own right, one that overwhelms João.

Underlying the story is a seam of social critique. The hospital is closing due to government corruption; while money is pumped into the 2014 World Cup, essential services are denied the necessary funding. As the main administrator, João shoulders the guilt for the hospital closure; and thus *The Trace We Leave Behind* becomes a topical political commentary on Brazil's neglect of its most vulnerable citizens.

As previously mentioned, the recessionary narrative has played a large part in the modern Brazilian horror film from 2008 onwards. Juliana Rojas and Marco Dutra's *Hard Labor* has been described as "*The Shining* meets a Vittorio de Sica film"[9] for the way it locates horror in the capriciousness of the Brazilian labor market. Helena (Helena Albergaria), a middle-aged, middle-class housewife, opens a modest grocer's shop in São Paulo after her husband Octávio (Marat Descartes) loses his white collar office job as a result of the economic downturn. Helena's determination to keep her new business afloat becomes eroded by the strain of dealing with a sullen house-keeper, thieving employees and a souring of her personal relationships. Then the shop itself seems to turn against her: The plumbing fails and the building is plagued by a foul smell that seems to come from inside the walls. Rojas and Dutra build an unsettling atmosphere even if the film stumbles in its reveal of the mysterious forces at play. The difficult nature of labor relations is the film's true subject, the hierarchy of employer-employee and its extension into Brazil's class system. But *Hard Labor* ultimately holds back from drawing political conclusions. By the final reel, it has shifted instead into vaguely supernatural realms.

After working on solo projects, Rojas and Dutra reunited for *Good Manners*, the story of two women raising a strange wolf child in an isolated São Paulo condo. Like *Hard Labor*, it is a conscious attempt to use the horror genre to explore issues of social identity. The filmmakers said that their aim was to delve into the two main female characters and "their conflicts of class, race and desire."[10] The wolf child is also finding out about his own nature. There is a process of self-understanding that all three must go through. The coming-of-age elements of werewolf folklore provide the film's mystical backdrop, to the extent that *Good Manners* becomes a fairy tale in itself, while the São Paulo setting helps to give it grounding in reality.

## Through the Shadow

Like *The Angel of the Night*, *Through the Shadow* uses Henry James' *Turn of the Screw* as its primary influence. However, in transposing the story from 19th century England to Brazil in the 1930s, writer-director Walter Lima, Jr., weaves a colonial theme into James' classic story of sexual repression and class tension. As Lima remarks, "That was my challenge—to keep the rich nuances of James' narrative from being lost in such a radical 'transcreation,' geographically and historically speaking."[11] As such, *Through the Shadow* also evokes the colonial horror of *I Walked with a Zombie* (1943) whose ur-text is, of course, Charlotte Bronte's *Jane Eyre*—the archetypal "governess" story.

Virginia Cavendish plays Laura, a nun tasked with looking after two orphans, a boy and a girl living on their uncle's coffee plantation. The previous governess, we later learn, died following a sexual affair with another plantation employee. Laura comes to believe that their ghostly spirits exert

**Governess Laura (Virginia Cavendish) is blindfolded by her orphan charges in** *Através da Sombra/Through the Shadow* **(2015, Europa Filmes).**

a malefic influence on the children, especially Antonio (Xande Valois), who makes inappropriate advances towards the governess.

What attracted Lima to the James story was, in his words, "its ambiguous approach to the theme of sexual repression through the Eros and Thanatos conflict in a Victorian cultural milieu."[12] As in the James story, sexual repression underlies *Through the Shadow* and drives the plot: Laura is secretly in love with the master of the house, Mr. Aphonso (Domingos Montagner), but she represses her desire. Meanwhile, she begins to see apparitions of her drowned predecessor and the lover: Ghostly figures appear at windows and on the roof of the house. Laura begins to doubt her own sanity and is almost driven out of the house by these experiences. But her sense of duty and concern for her charges make her stay.

In contrast to the ghostly atmosphere of *The Innocents*, Lima films *Through the Shadow* in a classical style that favors realism and follows the tradition of Marins. Thus, the intervention of seemingly supernatural forces is given greater ambiguity. The fantastic is downplayed in favor of Laura's psychological state: her sexual repression returning in uncanny form and projected onto the children whom she believes "belong to him and her," the previous governess and her lover. Laura's hallucinations become more extreme as she begins to imagine the dead lovers during the act of sexual intercourse. Her terror turns into hysteria as she attempts to expel the spirits of the lovers from the house before they can take possession of the children. As in *The Innocents*, the notion of sexual repression and spirit possession become fused together in Laura's mind when she is kissed in an adult way by Antonio. But in *Through the Shadow*, themes of class and colonialism are also raised by the figures of the dead lovers (named Bento and Isabel), as well as by the two Black employees on the estate who are shown to be involved in a sexual relationship. As reviewer Jennie Kermode has remarked, "Class divisions remain potent, often marked out by skin colour. Antonio spying on amorous servants hints at the taboos that have shaped the lives of those on the estate."[13]

*Through the Shadow* links the theme of sexual repression to social commentary on racial, gender and class oppression. Here the context of the coffee plantation as the film's setting becomes significant. Indeed, the film reaches its conclusion in the coffee fields. Only Laura and Antonio are left in the house, as the little girl has been sent away with the housekeeper to save her from the ghosts' evil influence. Laura tries similarly to drive Bento's spirit from Antonio (an act that we might read as the governess's attempt to suppress the boy's awakening sexuality). Fleeing, Antonio sees Bento's apparition, and, as in James' original novel, dies in Laura's arms. "I came to take you," she tells him, before kissing him one last time.

*Through the Shadow* ends on a shot of the house on the coffee plantation, emphasizing its colonial context as the film's cultural milieu: Themes of sexual repression and gender, race and class oppression are thereby triangulated with the Gothic and colonialism.

## Our Evil

While *Through the Shadow* places an emphasis on social-political allegory, the ambiguity of Henry James' tale finds its correlation in the gradual giving way from psychological horror to supernatural intervention. Likewise, *Our Evil*, Samuel Galli's feature debut as writer-director, starts out as one subgenre—serial killer thriller—and gradually morphs into something else entirely, a supernatural horror film. (This shift from one type of film to another resembles Ben Wheatley's *Kill List* [2011].) *Sci-Fi Now* describes *Our Evil* as "a brutal hitman/serial killer thriller that evokes both *The Sixth Sense* and *The Exorcist*."[14] The comparison is apt. Galli's stripped-down, minimalist style disguises a clever plot that slowly reveals its themes and takes on meaning.

The film opens in a Brazilian suburb, behind the proverbial white picket fence. Arthur (Ademir Esteves), a middle-aged man who lives alone, is awoken by voices in his head. He goes onto the Dark Web where he trawls through atrocity videos marked "assassins." He watches a snuff movie of a teenage girl who is scalped and then shot in the head by an unseen

"EVOKES *THE SIXTH SENSE* AND *THE EXORCIST*"
PROJECTED FIGURES

★★★★
"A DARK MORAL HEART"
BRITFLICKS

★★★★
"IMAGINATIVE, AMBITIOUS"
HORROR TALK

"SHOCKING, GRIPPING"
FRIGHTFEST

"BREATHTAKINGLY BRUTAL"
HORROR CHANNEL

A FILM BY
SAMUEL GALLI

# OUR EVIL

The British poster for Samuel Galli's *Mal Nosso/Our Evil* (2017, Dark Star Pictures/Matchbox Films).

executioner. He contacts the website and sets up a meeting with the assassin, Charles (Ricardo Casella). His instructions to the hitman are given on a USB key, including an encrypted file that can only be accessed after the job is done. The narrative focus then shifts briefly from Arthur to the hitman who, following their meeting, picks up a pair of prostitutes and, seemingly for his own enjoyment, brutally murders them. This extended sequence—coming as it does so early in the film—seems gratuitous, but later makes sense as Galli's full intentions become clear.

The action returns to Arthur as he makes preparations for his daughter Michele's twentieth birthday. He bakes a cake for her and we soon realize that Michele (Luara Pepita) is the intended victim of Arthur's hitman. Both Michele and Arthur are shot dead. Returning home after the job, Charles opens a beer and orders pizza, and then plays the encrypted file on the USB key. In an address to camera, Arthur begins to explain the voices in his head and the reason why he had Michele (and himself) murdered.

As reviewer Benedict Seal comments, *Our Evil* "shape shifts and transforms before the viewer from French extremism to South American spirituality."[15] Thus, the film starts with graphic realism and gradually introduces the fantastic. In flashback, we learn that the young Arthur is able to communicate with the dead. He uses the gift of mediumship to help those who have died and their loved ones. In this, he is aided by a mentor, a clown who appears to him in the afterworld. "Special people are born to help and sacrifice," he is told. We then discover how Arthur met Michele. Her mother, whom Arthur had tried to help, was killed by a demon entity. Michele is similarly marked. Arthur learns that the entity will take possession of her on her twentieth birthday, unless Arthur takes the necessary steps. However, he is told that he cannot end Michele's life by his own hand; instead he must "choose someone who deserves to suffer, pass sentence and send him to Hell."

At this point, *Our Evil*'s narrative comes full circle, as we are brought to where the film began and Galli's clever pay-off. As Arthur and Michelle reunite in the afterworld, the demon comes for Charles. Like Coffin Joe, he is an evil man punished by supernatural intervention. *Our Evil* shows us that the spirit of José Mojica Marins, the cornerstone of Brazil's horror film tradition, lives on in contemporary cinema.

# 5

# Britain

*Prevenge* (2016)
and *The Girl with All the Gifts* (2016)

Since the success of Hammer's *The Woman in Black* (2012), in the U.K. there has been a move away from hoodie horror—prevalent between 2008 and 2012—towards the traditional ghost story and a folk horror revival. This has not been without controversy, as the British Board of Film Classification has taken a firmer stance on the tone of a work in relation to horror films where it was felt that a "sense of threat" may be equal to, if not more significant than, the level of violence on screen in terms of its potential harm to the viewer.[1]

This chapter will start by discussing the transition in British horror films from the social-political concerns of the early noughties to a renewed interest in the supernatural in more recent years. The British folk horror revival coincides with a surge of interest in psychogeography, hauntology, folklore, costumes and cultural rituals, carnivalia, paganism and eco-activism, and a return to the pastoral. Among the films significant in this respect are *A Field in England* (2013) and *Wake Wood* (2009), which revive the tropes of the folk horror classics *The Wicker Man* (1973) and *The Blood on Satan's Claw* (1971).

However, as the main focus films of the chapter, I have chosen examples of two less-analyzed but arguably equally British horror subgenres: comedy-horror social satire and British post-apocalyptic horror. Both genres have rich traditions in British horror (stemming from literature and theater, respectively). Both have links to folk horror and elements of the gothic, but draw on other traditions as well, such as British science fiction literature (in the case of *The Girl with All the Gifts*) and satirical theater (*Prevenge*). It is perhaps impossible to disconnect these subgenres from one another completely: It could be argued that these traditions are interlinked and that tropes of two or more subgenres can be found in a number of recent British horror films, *Eden Lake* (2008), for example. Therefore the discussion that follows will necessarily reflect the fluidity of these subgenres.

## From Hoodie Horror to Folk Horror to Ghosts

As I stated in this book's preface, anxieties stemming from economic inequality and precarity resulting from 2008's economic crash can be seen in the prevalence of urban vs. rural horror films around the globe and in the home invasion scenario of many contemporary horror films internationally. (*Green Room* [USA, 2015] springs to mind, telling of the threat of white power skinheads to a group of punk musicians trapped inside a secluded music venue.) In the U.K., there have been a number of films concerned with the threat to middle-class society of a dispossessed underclass (so-called hoodie horror) such as *Eden Lake, Cherry Tree Lane* (2010) and *Citadel* (2012). This cycle of urbanoia and suburbanoia, in which fears of social exclusion or social abjection are exploited, has extended to films outside of the horror genre (such as the thriller *Harry Brown* [2009], starring Michael Caine as an aging vigilante wiping out drug dealers on a council housing estate).

Anxieties arising from the economic recession have grown during the years of government-administered austerity measures which, up until 2020 and the COVID-19 pandemic, saw huge cuts to public spending. Like the hoodie horror cycle, the more recent folk horror revival can be seen as a result of growing economic insecurity among the middle class, with young people seeking alternatives to the cultural mainstream. In this way, the two subgenres are more closely linked than they would first appear to be.

Shellie McMurdo describes how moral panic over "chav culture" in the early noughties gave rise to fears about the threat of an unruly working class youth subculture, which found expression in films like *Eden Lake*. Such cultural manifestations of class conflict in the British horror film, according to McMurdo, draw on the tropes of American hillbilly horror (e.g., the *Wrong Turn* franchise, 2003–2014) to embody in their underclass antagonists the idea of "a polluted poor white identity, with poisoned blood that will infect future generations."[2] McMurdo argues that British eugenics beliefs from the early 1900s have carried through into the cultural figure of the "chav," whose characterization (in hoodie horror) is of a polluted body "that needs to be kept separate from the populace by way of exclusion from executive homes in gated communities, for fear of contamination by monstrous poverty." In other words, hoodie horror draws on historical fears of (in McMurdo's words) the rise of the "monstrous poor": At the heart of the British eugenics movement was "a belief that the poor and feeble-minded bred at an alarmingly high rate when compared to the higher classes." This translates as "a clear Us vs. Them mentality that has filtered into both American and British rural horror cinema." Such beliefs are ingrained in British and American culture(s) to the extent that they are liable to resurface under certain social conditions.

The folk horror subgenre is somewhat nebulous, and its influence on contemporary British horror production has been limited to a small number of releases. Interestingly, American films such as Robert Eggers' *The Witch* (2015) and Ari Aster's *Midsommer* (2019) have received wider publicity than their English counterparts, which have tended to be marketed as programmers or art house product. In Britain, releases include the "new" Hammer's *Wake Wood* (2009) and Ben Wheatley's *A Field in England* (2013). Wheatley's film (and also his *Kill List* [2011] which appropriated a number of folk horror tropes within its hybrid formula) certainly has its share of admirers, but didn't have the box office success of the studio-backed American movies.

An almost unknown British film that consciously drew on 1970s folk horror is *The Fallow Field* (2009), directed by Leigh Dovey. After struggling to find distribution (like so many indie horror films) for over three years, Dovey's debut feature was picked up by the Australian company Monster Pictures in 2013. With other releases like Scott Leberecht's excellent *Midnight Son* (2011) and Eric Falardeau's hard-hitting body horror *Thanatamorphose* (2012), Monster Pictures has in recent years established itself as a leading distributor of quality independent horror.

When amnesiac Matt (Steve Garry) wakes up in the wilderness with no recollection of the past seven days, he retraces his steps to a remote farm owned by Calham (Michael Dacre), a sadist who abducts his victims and subjects them to torture in a shed. Matt finds himself a victim to Calham's twisted games, but things are not quite what they seem and there is more to Matt's *déjà vu* than anyone could have known—except Calham. Meanwhile, the fallow field where Calham buries bodies yields a strange and terrible secret.

Billed as a cross between *Wolf Creek* and *Memento* (2000), *The Fallow Field* also owes more than a little to British rural horror films of the 1970s, such as *The Wicker Man* and *The Blood on Satan's Claw*. In this case, the countryside that provides the setting of *The Fallow Field* becomes more than just a backdrop, but a character in itself. It is this twist that makes *The Fallow Field* all the more memorable, taking it beyond what at first appears to be a *Haute Tension* (*High Tension*, 2003) type of story into something more mystical and M.R. James–inspired. This genre-bending could have been unconvincing in lesser hands but *The Fallow Field* benefits from strong direction by Dovey and impressive performances by Dacre and Garry (in what is essentially a two-hander) that root it in reality. Despite the rural setting, *The Fallow Field* is a claustrophobic piece of work and well-served by cinematographer Nick Kindon, who lends the surrounding countryside (and the farm itself) a real air of menace.

*The Fallow Field* was shot on a meager budget but Dovey confines his story to the farm and the surrounding countryside, and this helps keep the tension high throughout. The early scenes, before Matt arrives on the farm, have the feel of domestic TV drama, and it is only when we get out into the countryside, with its sense of isolation, that *The Fallow Field*'s cinematic qualities take hold. Capturing some of the bleak tone and threat of 1970s horror, and with a slowly building sense of dread as well as some sudden shocks and visceral scenes, it is an effective pastiche of '70s folk horror.

Himself a fan of the genre, Dovey grew up watching late night BBC horror double-bills and manages to invoke them in his first feature. Having said that, one of *The Fallow Field*'s strengths is its unpredictability. Just when you think you have a handle on the story, Dovey wrong-foots the viewer and makes his film all the more effective for its clever genre-bending.

Writing in the popular British horror publication *Scream*, Kat Ellinger provides a basic definition of folk horror. Although she admits that the term is somewhat vague, and ever-expanding in light of the renewed interest surrounding the genre, she is nevertheless able to pinpoint some fundamentals: "In order to qualify, a film must have some aspect of folk magic or ritual, and a rural setting (so superstition can breed amongst local residents, thus making them a threat to outsiders)."[3] In terms of this description, *The Fallow Field* would certainly qualify as folk horror. Broader definitions potentially open up the classification to many more films.

Adam Scovell further defines folk horror by the three foundational works that together make up what he describes as the "folk horror chain": *Witchfinder General* (1968), *The Blood on Satan's Claw* and *The Wicker Man*. Scovell claims that this trinity is linked together by a number of shared elements. The first is topography: The landscape in folk horror has an "adverse effect on the social and moral identity of its inhabitants."[4] In *The Wicker Man*, the residents of the Scottish island make human sacrifices to the land, so that it will be fertile for their crops. In *The Blood on Satan's Claw*, an 18th-century village is possessed by a demon that literally appears from within the plowed furrows.

Scovell's second definition is the isolation of the environment in which the horror takes place: "The landscape must in some way isolate a key body of characters … [I]t is an inhospitable place because it is in some way different from society as a whole [and] people are cut off from [the] established social progress of the wider world."[5] This is most apparent in *The Wicker Man*, which tells the story of a policeman (Edward Woodward) from the mainland who travels to the island in response to a missing person report. He finds that the people are trapped in time, still practicing Celtic paganism. This halting of social progress leads to, in Scovell's words, skewed belief systems and morality: "From a post–Enlightenment perspective … folklore, superstition, and even to some extent religion, form through this very physical but also psychical isolation. This is also skewed within the context of the general social status quo of the era in which the films are made."[6]

In terms of plot events, folk horror often revolves around a happening event or summoning: some action that results from this skewed social consciousness with all of its horrific fallout. In *Witchfinder General*, the summoning might be seen as the arrival of the witchfinder, Matthew Hopkins (Vincent Price) into a Norfolk village to root out sorcery and witchcraft, with ghastly consequences for all concerned. The summoning in *The Blood on Satan's Claw* is the black mass that the villagers perform that conjures up the demon, Behemoth; while the happening in *The Wicker Man* is the ritual sacrifice of the missing girl, which is later reprised when Woodward's policeman is burned alive inside the Wicker Man.

These elements of the folk horror chain allow the crossover of folk horror into other horror subgenres, including hoodie horror. Dawn Keetley argues that *Eden Lake* exemplifies the principal elements of folk horror as defined by Scovell: "It is set in a lush natural landscape; Jenny and Steve become isolated, removed from their familiar urban environment; and they soon realize with horror that they are beset by characters whose moral beliefs are at best bewilderingly skewed, at worst entirely absent."[7] Although lacking supernatural elements, *Eden Lake* evokes the idea of rural ritual in its scene of the "hoodies" around the campfire in the woods, and when the gang members attempt to burn the protagonists. The landscape seems to act upon the characters, in particular Jenny (Kelly Reilly), inciting in her "a strength, a violence, that she (and we) had no idea she possessed…." *Eden Lake* ends with the imminent sacrifice of Jenny by the gang, although, as Keetley points out, "[T]he scaffold, the gestures, of sacrifice are present, but there's no substance, no belief, no meaning, no purpose, no sense of renewal." In the end, *Eden Lake* works as both hoodie horror and folk horror because it literalizes the media image of the teenage "hoodie" as modern folk devil.

The widening—by Scovell *et al.*—of folk horror definitions beyond the principal components to include the philosophical concepts of hauntology, psychogeography and the urban wyrd, allows us to see a number of recent British "ghost" films as hybrid forms of folk horror. *The Canal* (2014) managed to combine all three concepts, to varying degrees, in a tale of supernatural dread. A film archivist (Rupert Evans) becomes obsessed with a reel of footage which appears to show a murder taking place in his house many decades before. When he discovers his wife is having an affair with her work colleague, the archivist resists the urge to murder her with a hammer, and instead tosses it into the nearby canal. Gradually his life becomes unspooled, after his wife's body is later discovered in the canal. Her death is ruled as accidental. The archivist starts to investigate a century-spanning series of murders that took place in and around his house and canal, and becomes convinced that an evil influence from the past is exerting control on the present. He begins to see ghostly visions of himself as the murderer, acting out the will of an unseen presence.

The notion of a protagonist caught in a kind of ghostly time-loop of the past and present recurred in Gareth Tunley's low-budget mystery thriller *The Ghoul* (2016). Set in a *noir*-ish London, the plot involves a detective (Tom Meeten) who goes undercover as a patient to investigate a psychotherapist suspected of murder. In the process, he starts to question his own identity and—when his leads bring him back to where he started—his own sanity. Critics compared *The Ghoul* to David Lynch's *Lost Highway* (1997) in terms of a story that seems to both twist in and double back on itself. Tunley actually constructed the events of the film to act as a kind of Möbius Strip: By the end, the detective finds himself returning to the start but has become someone else in the process. The effect makes for what *Empire* describes as "powerful, disturbing and intense viewing."[8]

Written and directed by Elliot Goldner, *The Borderlands* (2013) follows the investigation of paranormal events at a church in sleepy Devon. Gray (Robin Hill), a mouthy technician is recruited to film the progress of veteran priest-cum-paranormal investigator Deacon (Gordon Kennedy) as he looks into an apparent miracle that occurred in the church. *The Borderlands* was filmed as a found-footage horror; humorous banter between the likable pair turns to sheer terror as events prove to be inexplicable.

One of *The Borderlands'* most appealing aspects is its focus on the developing relationship between Deacon and Gray as they comes to grips with the paranormal activity. The humor grows naturally from characters who try to make the most of a strange, frightening situation. But the film also has a genuine air of folk horror, helped by the antiquity of the locations. The church featured in the film was built in 1100. The cottage where Deacon and Gray stay is north of Newton Abbot in Devon, another historical English site which dates back to the Neolithic period. The film crew also shot in Chislehurst caves in Kent, man-made chalkstone caves built around the same time as the church. Ancient history seems to seep into the film through the very pores of these places, much like in Nigel Kneale's classic of British television folk horror, *The Stone Tape* (1972).

## Prevenge

Alice Lowe's *Prevenge* falls very much into the category of the type of British comedy-horror that could also be described as a spoofy social satire. This approach was popularized by the success of *Shaun of the Dead* (2004) but it also has roots in television comedy, and in the camp horror of Antony Balch's *Horror Hospital* (1973) and the movies produced by Amicus in the 1970s.

Lowe made her name as an actor in the cult TV series *Black Mirror* (2011–2014) and *Garth Marenghi's Darkplace* (2004); both evoked a kind of genre pastiche that mixed sci-fi–horror tropes with a knowing humor and sly social satire. Her background in fringe comedy theater informs her work, much in the same way that spoofing '70s British horror has inspired a number of her contemporaries. She is a regular collaborator of filmmakers Edgar Wright and Ben Wheatley. Wheatley directed her in 2012's *Sightseers* (which she co-wrote with Steve Oram).

*Sightseers* is an interesting forerunner of *Prevenge* in terms of its dark comedic tone and its wry approach to genre mixing and matching. It tells the story of a seemingly average English couple, Chris and Tina (Lowe and Oram) who go on a caravanning holiday and end up murdering many of the people they encounter along the way. It satirized the very British

Ruth (Alice Lowe) makes herself up for Halloween and another revenge killing in *Prevenge* (2016, Shudder).

obsession with touring caravan holidays and fused it with the American killer couple road movie (for example, 1973's *Badlands*). Critics described it as a mix of Mike Leigh and "outright grue."[9] It is true that *Sightseers* plays very much on the kind of comedy of embarrassment for which Leigh is known, but the grotesque nature of the characters and their situation perhaps owes more to the iconic comedy TV series *The League of Gentlemen* (1999–2002). Co-written and starring Mark Gatiss, Steve Pemberton and Reece Sheersmith, the show draws on many of the tropes of British horror cinema, including folk horror. Set in the fictional northern town of Royston Vasey, it is populated by grotesque, often disturbing characters, and the humor is darkly comic. Although only a modest success when first broadcast, the series has since attracted a cult following and generated a number of revivals and spin-off shows.

Many of the characters were based on people the actors had encountered in real life; a large source of inspiration for the series came from the British horror films that Sheersmith, Pemberton and Gatiss grow up watching. For example, there is more than a little of the camp of *The Abominable Dr. Phibes* (1971) and *Dr. Phibes Rises Again* (1972), and the aforementioned *Horror Hospital*. But the comic-grotesque characters are contrasted by genuinely macabre elements, much like those found in the Amicus movies *Tales from the Crypt* (1972) and *From Beyond the Grave* (1974). It might be said that the tradition of *The League of Gentleman* goes back to Sweeney Todd, the Demon Barber of Fleet Street, whose origins are in the *Penny Dreadful* serials published in a weekly magazine during the Victorian age. As Ian Cooper remarks, the Sweeney Todd character has proved remarkably enduring: "It would become a staple in the repertoire of Tod Slaughter, must surely be the only story to inspire both an Andy Milligan film (*Bloodthirsty Butchers*, 1970) and a Stephen Sondheim musical."[10] In many ways, Ruth (Lowe) in *Prevenge* is a modern-day Sweeney Todd, hacking and slicing her way through a number of unsuspecting victims in a series of comedy-horror vignettes.

*Prevenge* opens in a pet shop as Ruth goes in, ostensibly to buy a pet for her child. The owner (Marc Bessant) is as slimy as the reptiles he tries to get Ruth to touch. Ruth cuts his throat and leaves him to die alongside the snakes and tarantulas. We learn that Ruth is seven months pregnant (Lowe actually made the film during her own pregnancy), and has lost her husband, the father of her unborn child. In a series of seemingly random episodes, she goes on a killing spree that seems to be at the behest of her child, who speaks to her from inside her womb. She is apparently committing these murders for the sake of the baby.

Lowe deliberately creates a sense of enigma throughout; we begin to piece together her motives only gradually. Interspersed with the killings are scenes between Ruth and her midwife (Jo Hartley), which convey the sort of social realism for which Leigh is noted. The characters are recognizable types, perhaps even caricatures. The most grotesque of them is Ruth's second victim, DJ Dan (Tom Davies), an egocentric pub disc jockey, whom Ruth attempts to pick up for sex. Returning to his place, Ruth castrates him with a knife. This killing is observed by Dan's dementia-suffering mother, who happily plays along: Ruth puts the old woman to bed and kisses her good night before cleaning up Dan's blood.

Eventually we begin to piece together the backstory and the reason for Ruth's "prevenge" killings: Her husband, a rock climber, died in a fall while under the supervision of his trainer, Tom (Kayvan Novak). Ruth's victims are the members of the climbing expedition who survived (Tom cut the rope joining them all together on the cliff, sacrificing Ruth's husband so that the others could live). This plot, although cleverly revealed in a way that keeps the viewer guessing, functions as a clothesline upon which to hang the individual vignettes; this makes *Prevenge* essentially a series of two-handers between Ruth and her victims. In each vignette, an awkward social encounter leads to murder. This structure does become repetitive at times. Only when Ruth suddenly goes into labor during the penultimate killing does *Prevenge* move toward some kind of resolution. Hospitalized after giving birth to a daughter, Ruth realizes her child is a normal baby, not a psychopathic killer. This raises a number of questions for the viewer. Is Ruth herself experiencing some kind of pre-partum psychosis? Or is she unhinged by the death of her husband? Are the killings a figment of her imagination? Just as it seems that *Prevenge* might move toward a conventional conclusion, Lowe performs a *volte-face* and has Ruth commit one final killing in order to complete her "prevenge."

Thus *Prevenge* fits into a number of contemporary horror subgenres quite intriguingly. As an expression of the fears of pregnancy and childbirth, it is a maternity horror movie alongside films like *Delivery* (2013), *Still/Born* (2017) and *Shelley*. Critic Peter Bradshaw noted in his *Guardian* review of the film that Lowe is not afraid to make Ruth unsympathetic as a comment on the way that pregnancy is often romanticized. As Bradshaw remarks: Lowe plays Ruth as a pregnant woman with "an intense and rational awareness that, despite the sentimental propaganda, pregnancy is a grueling, painful and violent business, made even more traumatic by the condescending way women in her situation are habitually treated."[11] Alongside this is the serial killer thriller element that Lowe as actor-writer had already explored with Oram in *Sightseers*. In *Prevenge*, the format is similar: Killing becomes a way for the character to gain the upper hand during her encounters with others. As such, Ruth is a sociopathic character, much like the one she played in *Sightseers*. Her inability to connect with others is partly what makes the film so compelling. In *Prevenge*, there is a deep sense of disenchantment with interpersonal relationships, a mourning of the lack of love or inability to love. Self-righteous anger or resentment is a stronger motivation for the protagonists. Just as her *Sightseers* character is unable to go the full mile with her partner at the conclusion of the film (where they make a suicide pact that only one is ultimately willing to fulfill), the conclusion of *Prevenge* sees Ruth abandoning her baby in the hospital in order to hunt down her final victim.

## The Girl with All the Gifts

Based on the novel by M.R. Carey, *The Girl with All the Gifts* tells the story of a near-future catastrophe that leaves the human race on the verge of extinction. Humanity has been infected with a disease caused by a parasitic fungus that turns people into flesh-eating zombies. A team of scientists, aided by the British military, experiment on a group of children who are second generation hybrids. Although they are human in the sense that they can think and learn, they are also flesh-eaters. One girl, Melanie (Sennia Nannua), becomes central to the scientists' bid to find a cure. However, when the facility is attacked by a horde of flesh-eaters, Melanie and a small group of human survivors are forced to flee to the city, where they discover that the fungus has spread to buildings and developed seed pods which, if released, will wipe out the whole of mankind.

As an example of post-apocalyptic science fiction–horror, the film (directed by Colm McCarthy from a screenplay by M.R. Carey) owes a clear debt to the success of *28 Days Later* (2002) but, like that film, it has roots that go back further into early British science fiction. In his book *English Gothic*, Jonathan Rigby described Danny Boyle's groundbreaking film as owing "multiple debts to, among others, the novels *I Am Legend* and *The Death of Grass*, the 1975 TV series *Survivors* and, above all, George Romero's seminal zombie trilogy."[12] With respect to Rigby, we might trace the lineage of both *28 Days Later* and *The Girl with All the Gifts* further back still to the origins of British post-apocalyptic literature and M.P. Shiel's *The Purple Cloud*.

Written in 1901, *The Purple Cloud* has been described as the first post-apocalyptic "Last Man on Earth" science fiction novel. Jefferson, a polar explorer, discovers a cloud of purple gas that spreads from the North Pole to wipe out the whole of humanity. Returning to his native London, he searches vainly for other survivors. Eventually he meets a woman with whom he falls in love. Together they flee the cloud as it continues its devastation across Europe.

Shiel's story was adapted into the 1959 film *The World, the Flesh and the Devil*, which is generally considered to be one of the first doomsday science fiction films (alongside Arch Oboler's *Five*, 1951), but its influence can be clearly felt in Richard Matheson's aforementioned *I Am Legend*, written in 1954. Itself spawning a number of cinema adaptations including *The Last Man on Earth* (1964), *The Omega Man* (1971) and *I Am Legend* (2007), Matheson's seminal novel also inspired an unofficial adaptation in Romero's *Night of the Living Dead* (1968), thus creating an interesting loop of influences back to *The Girl with All the Gifts*.

While *The Purple Cloud* has undoubtedly led to many American post-apocalyptic "last man" films and novels, it has had a strong influence on the genre in Britain as well. Rigby mentions the 1970s TV series *Survivors* as part of the genealogy of *28 Days Later*. In *Survivors*, humankind is wiped out by a man-made biological plague. Only a handful of people are left: city dwellers who come together on an abandoned farm and have to learn the skills of agriculture and animal husbandry to survive. *Survivors* showcased one of the key themes of British science fiction in the 1970s: the collapse of modern society forcing people back onto the land, back into the fields, and a return to the old, pre–industrial revolution days. In showing the fallibility of modern society, and a sense of rural renewal, *Survivors* also taps into folk horror; as do other influential British sci-fi TV programs like *Doomwatch* (1972) and the Quatermass series of TV and radio plays (1953–1996). Keetley describes *Doomwatch* as a hybrid of folk horror and ecological horror: It offers "a powerful critique of the ways in which governments and corporations are poisoning both the ecosystem and rural populations."[13]

Perhaps the most famous British post-apocalyptic science fiction–horror novel is John Wyndham's *The Day of the Triffids*, which spawned a 1962 film adaptation as well as two British TV versions (1981 and 2009). Written in 1951, *Triffids* carries the influence of *The Purple Cloud* (by way of H.G. Wells' *The War of the Worlds*, 1898) in its storyline of a small group of survivors battling the carnivorous plants known as Triffids, after a meteor shower has rendered most of the population blind. Cited as an inspiration for *28 Days Later*, its influence can also be seen in *The Girl with All the Gifts*. Much British post-apocalyptic science fiction deals with ecological disaster and this is brought to the fore in Wyndham's novel. Although Wyndham leaves the exact origins of the Triffids a mystery, the novel speculates on the possibility of "the outcome of a series of ingenious biological meddlings"[14] that may have accidentally led to the breeding of the carnivorous plants. *The Girl with All the Gifts* nods to *Triffids* in making its ultimate threat a voracious fungus which eventually turns the city into a verdant growth of roots and deadly spores.

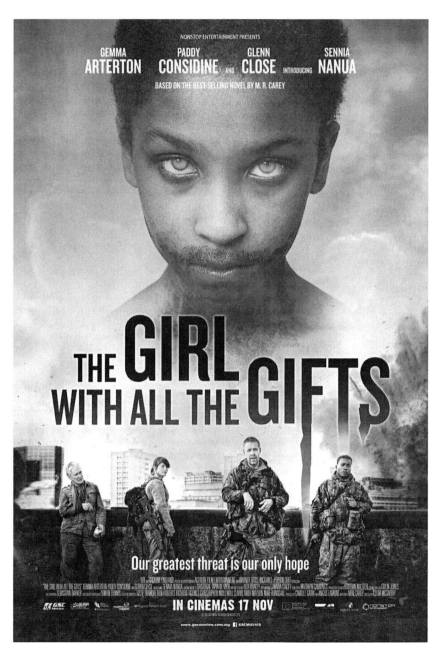

The British poster for *The Girl with All the Gifts* (2016, Saban Films/Warner Home Video).

Socio-political readings of post-apocalyptic science fiction have varied throughout the years, as meanings have been linked to changing historical concerns, even as the overarching premise of these stories is, of course, the imminent collapse (and subsequently renewal) of modern society. Much has been made of the fact that the producers cast a Black child as the hero of the film adaptation of *The Girl with All the Gifts*. Equally significant is that the story's hero is, in fact, its monster. The conclusion of *The Girl with All the Gifts* sees Melanie release the deadly pods, in effect wiping out the whole of humanity. Only the hybrids will survive, creating a new race: "Why should it be us who die for you?" Melanie asks the scientists. The human race (as we know it) is eradicated, and with it, the status quo. It is an audacious ending to a horror film, but whether future horror films will follow its lead in making the monster their true hero, and leaving social authority discredited, remains to be seen.

# 6

# Denmark

## Shelley (2016)
## and What We Become (2015)

The success of Tomas Alfredson's *Låt den rätte komma in* (*Let the Right One In*, 2008) heralded a new wave of Scandinavian-Nordic horror that saw Denmark, Sweden, Norway and Finland become major exporters of horror films. With many of these as co-productions, it is perhaps not surprising that Scandinavian horror films, in the words of Josh Millican, "carry a shared aesthetic and mood, no doubt influenced by the region's geography and climate."[1]

*Død snø* (*Dead Snow*, 2009) put Norway on the map for horror fans, due to its splatstick mix of Nazisploitation and zombie movie tropes. The success of Tommy Wirkola's comedy-horror spawned a 2014 sequel, *Død snø 2* (*Dead Snow: Red vs. Dead*). Prior to *Dead Snow*, *Fritt vilt* (*Cold Prey*, 2006) had transposed the American post–*Scream* teen slasher to the Norwegian mountains (*Fritt vilt II/Cold Prey 2* and *Fritt vilt III/Cold Prey 3* followed in 2008 and 2010, respectively); while Pål Øie's psychological thriller *Skjult* (*Hidden*, 2009), made at the same time as *Dead Snow,* showed that Norway was capable of producing horror films that did not rely on satire or on slasher conventions. Other notable Norwegian entries include Pål Sletaune's twisty "Babycall" thriller *The Monitor* (2011), Aleksander L. Nordaas' supernatural horror *Thale* (2010) and perhaps best known of all, André Øvredal's found-footage fantasy, *Trolljegeren* (*Trollhunter*, 2010).

While not as prolific a producer as Norway, Finland's film industry enjoyed a revival in the 2000s that led to a small number of noteworthy horror movies. *Bodom* (*Lake Bodom*, 2017) took an infamous unsolved 1960 crime case, the Bodominjärvi Murders (which involved the killings of three teenagers in the Espoo lake district), and made it the basis of an accomplished meta-slasher. Prior to that, the Christmas horror film *Rare Exports* (2010) had received international exposure and reviews praising it for its dark revisionist approach to Northern European folklore; and *Sauna*

(2008) looked to 16th-century history and the Russo-Swedish war as the setting for a story of two brothers who stumble across a mysterious village on the Finland-Russia border where they encounter ghosts and a spa with seemingly magical properties.

Reykjavik hosted the first-ever Icelandic horror film festival, Frosterbiter, in 2016, partly as a platform for that country's emerging horror filmmakers. Two distinguished Icelandic horror-thrillers were released the following year. Erlingur Thoroddsen's enigmatic and moody ghost story *Rökkur* (*Rift*, 2017) saw Björn Stefánsson traveling to a secluded cabin in the Icelandic countryside to come to the aid of his ex-lover who seems to be suffering a breakdown. As they attempt to repair their relationship, mysterious goings-on outside the cabin alert them to the possibility that they may not be alone in the wilderness. Thoroddsen directed with a strong sense of atmosphere and breathtaking visual detail. Not a lot happens, but *Rift* hypnotizes the viewer all the same.

Thematically, Óskar Thór Axelsson's *Ég man þig* (*I Remember You*, 2017) is very much in the Scandinavian thriller tradition, dealing with the afterlife from the perspective of those still living but deeply grieving. After an elderly woman is found hanged in a remote church, Freyr (Jóhannes Haukur Jóhannesson), a police psychiatrist still mourning the disappearance of his son several years earlier, discovers that this is but one of a series of strange deaths involving senior citizens in the area. When Freyr finds strange cross marks burned into her body, he realizes that the link between the deaths is that all of the victims attended the same church school as children. Meanwhile, three city dwellers restoring an old cabin across the bay begin to experience supernatural happenings. As the past returns to haunt each of the characters, the stories begin to intertwine in often disturbing ways. Axelsson's first foray into supernatural horror saw him building on the moody crime thriller tropes of his Icelandic TV series *Trapped* (2016–2019). *I Remember You* shares much of the same atmosphere, sense of isolation and labyrinthine plotting. Intriguing too is the time frame of the story, and it is here that Axelsson delivers one of the film's twists: The two plotlines come together in a way that surprises the viewer even while snapping the film into focus. Like many Scandi-thrillers, *I Remember You* is a slow burn, but a satisfying one; fans of Nordic Noir found much to enjoy in this dark tale of loss, memory and ghostly goings-on in Iceland's chilly Westfjords.

Sweden has hosted a number of recent high profile co-productions with the U.S. and the U.K., including *Stitches* (2012) and Ari Aster's *Midsommar* (2019). However, the country has a strong tradition of homegrown horror films that dates back to 1921 and Victor Sjöström's *Körkarlen* (*The Phantom Carriage*). Sweden's burgeoning exploitation cinema gave rise to

Elena (Cosmina Stratan) attempts to phone home in *Shelley* (2016, IFC Midnight).

a number of notable mystery thrillers in the late 1950s, such as *Mannekäng i rött* (*Mannequin in Red*, 1958) and *Vita frun* (*Lady in White*, 1962); while the 1970s Swedish *Sensationsfilms* brought sex and horror in the form of Torgny Wickman's *Skräcken har 1000 ögon* (*Sensuous Sorceress*, 1970) and Joseph W. Sarno's *Vampire Ecstasy/The Devil's Plaything* (1974). More "legitimate" Gothic works also appeared, such as Calvin Floyd's *Terror of Frankenstein* (1977) and *The Sleep of Death* (1980). With the rise of home video in the 1980s came a boom in production and such straight-to-video titles as *Mask of Murder* (1985), *The Visitors* (1988) and *Scorched Heat* (1987).

Following the international success of *Let the Right One In*, there was a glut of Swedish horror films that followed a similar supernatural theme: *Marianne* (2011), *Mara* (2014), *Alena* (2015), *Thelma* (2017). These have attempted to capture the bleak realism of Alfredson's groundbreaking vampire film, as well as its existential tone, but none have the same impact, or the complexity.

The atmosphere of modern Nordic horror can instead be best found in two recent Danish films: *Shelley* and *Sorgenfri* (*What We Become*). These films will be discussed in detail later in the chapter.

## Danish Horror

Early Danish horror films were usually realist in nature, often with a fixation on witchcraft and demonology. Perhaps the most celebrated are, of course, the works of Benjamin Christensen and Carl Theodor Dreyer.

Christensen's *Haxan* (1922) still has the power to transfix with its hypnotic and highly sexualized imagery. More influential on contemporary Nordic horror, though, are Dreyer's austere depictions of medievalism and religion in *Prästänkan* (*The Parson's Widow*, 1919), *Blade af Satan's bog* (*Leaves from Satan's Book*, 1920) and *Vredens dag* (*Day of Wrath*, 1955). Arguably, these non-supernatural titles have exerted as great an influence on current Nordic horror as Dreyer's fantasy-horror classic *Vampyr* (1932) in terms of their brooding atmosphere and realistic approach.

A key theme in the works of both Christensen and Dreyer is the woman as object of persecution, and we can see this influence very strongly in the films of Lars von Trier; a number of his movies—such as *Antichrist* (2009) and *The House That Jack Built* (2018), as well as the TV series *The Kingdom* (1994–1997)—fit firmly into the horror genre. Trier's international success has indisputably helped establish Nordic art-house horror as a recognizable brand.

The most financially successful Danish horror film to date is Ole Bornedal's *Nattevagten* (*Nightwatch*, 1994), in which Martin (Nikolaj Coster-Waldau), a law student, takes a job as night watchman in a Copenhagen morgue, only to find himself pitted against a serial killer. *Nightwatch* grossed more than *Jurassic Park* (1993) in its native Denmark. Coinciding with the rise of the Nordic Noir mystery-thriller novel following the success of Peter Høeg's *Miss Smilla's Feeling for Snow* in 1992, *Nightwatch* shares much in common with Nordic Noir literature. Copenhagen is made to look deliberately bleak, and the film is imbued with a sense of moral complexity as Martin finds himself a suspect in the killings after having tampered with bodies in the mortuary. As has been written of Nordic Noir, the genre "depicts a tension between the apparently still and bland social surface in the Nordic countries, and the murder, misogyny, rape and racism it depicts as lying underneath."[2] *Nightwatch* certainly shares this in common with Nordic Noir literature, to the extent that the failure of Bornedal's 1997 American remake can be attributed to the relocation of the story from Copenhagen to Los Angeles, thereby removing the Nordic context.

Bornedal followed the *Nightwatch* films with 2007's *Vikaren* (*The Substitute*), a science fiction-teen horror that played on the tropes of *Invasion of the Body Snatchers* (1956). The substitute of the title is played by Paprika Steen, an extraterrestrial who takes the form of a sixth grade class teacher in a Danish school. The theme was done better by Robert Rodriguez in *The Faculty* (1998), made ten years earlier. Bornedal's connection with Hollywood saw him return to the U.S. to shoot *The Possession* (2012), based on the Hebrew legend of the Dybbuk Box.

Denmark's oldest film studio, Nordisk, financed and distributed two noteworthy horror films in *Kollegiet* (*Room 205*, 2007) and *Når dyrene*

*drømmer* (*When Animals Dream*, 2014). Martin Barnewitz directed the former, an interesting take on the urban myth–inspired horror movie popularized by *Candyman* (1992; 2020) and the *Urban Legends* franchise. Katy,
a Copenhagen student (Neel Rønholt), moves into a dormitory room only
to find it haunted by the ghost of a former murdered resident. When Katy
inadvertently releases the spirit, it goes on a killing spree through the cam-
pus, and Katy finds herself accused of the murders. Despite the deriva-
tive plot, the theme of social isolation translates well, and Barnewitz films
with a bleak realism that contrasts the story's overly familiar supernatural elements. Co-produced with Sam Raimi's Ghost House Pictures and
distributed in the U.S. by Lionsgate, *Room 205* is deliberately designed for
transnational appeal. The film was remade in Germany as *205—Zimmer der
Angst* (*205—Room of Fear,* 2011); an American remake produced by Raimi
and Robert Tapert was mooted in 2009 but has yet to appear.

    *When Animals Dream*, the feature debut of director Jonas Alexander
Arnby, also took social ostracism as its theme, in a mix of werewolf film
and coming-of-age movie that prompted critics to describe it as *Let the
Right One In* meets *Ginger Snaps* (2000). However, with its desolate Danish fishing village setting giving home to a dour religious community, Arnby's film is equally reminiscent of Trier's *Breaking the Waves* (1996) and is a
much more indigenously "Danish" horror movie than *Room 205*. On leaving school, shy teenager Marie (Sonia Suhl) goes to work in the village's fish
processing plant where she is ostracized by her co-workers. At the same
time, she undergoes strange physical changes that mark her as a threat to
those around her. Arnby carefully details Marie's bleak environment—
church, home, factory—as places of spiritual entrapment that her physical transformation (which naturally coincides with her sexual awakening)
might allow her to escape from. However, unleashing her inner beast pro-
vokes a predictable response from her religious oppressors. In its examina-
tion of persecuted women branded as witches, *When Animals Dream* harks
back to Christensen and Dreyer, bringing Danish horror cinema full circle.

# Shelley

    While the persecution of women by the patriarchy has lent Dan-
ish horror a key theme from Christensen and Dreyer onwards, *Shelley*,
the feature film debut of Iranian-Danish director Ali Abbasi, riffs on the
anti-bourgeois dramas of Thomas Vinterberg (*Festen/The Celebration,*
1998) and Trier (*Idioterne/The Idiots,* 1998) in its depiction of a wealthy
Danish family torn apart from within. As a "maternity" horror film, it also
draws heavily on *Rosemary's Baby* (1968)—deliberately so in the advertising

of the film, with a marketing campaign that closely resembled that of Polanski's classic.

The story concerns a childless couple, Kasper (Peter Christoffersen) and Louise (Ellen Dorrit Petersen), who engage the services of Romanian maid Elena (Cosima Stratan) to help them around their lakeside home while Louise recovers from surgery. A close friendship develops between the two women. Elena confides in her employer that she is saving money so that she can provide a home for her son back in Romania; Louise reveals to Elena that she is unable to conceive a baby herself. The couple make Elena a proposition: They will give her a large sum of money if she will be their surrogate. Elena agrees to this for the sake of her son's future, but as she goes through pregnancy she becomes increasingly convinced that the baby inside her (which she calls Shelley) is malignant and is trying to kill her from within. Eventually Louise and Kasper have to care for the stricken girl. In an act of desperation, Elena tries to abort the pregnancy with a knitting needle, and dies of an internal hemorrhage. The baby is delivered safely to her adopted parents, but seems to exert a malefic influence on them, resulting in attempted suicide and, finally, murder.

Although the story invokes the "devil child" tropes of horror films like *Rosemary's Baby*, it becomes clear that Abbasi is more interested in exploring the nature of the relationship between the surrogate and her benefactors—one that hinges on Elena's poverty and the couple's wealth. For Abassi, evil is born of exploitative social interaction. The Romanian immigrant finds her body being used for the benefit of those who possess the economic power that she lacks. It is possible to interpret Elena's conviction that the baby inside her is "evil" as stemming from her unconscious rejection of her situation.

During the first part of the film, Abassi concentrates on the developing bond between the two women. It later becomes clear that their friendship is not one of equals. Louise and Kasper apparently reject bourgeois norms (as expressed by their desire to live in the wilderness, without electricity, and self-sufficient in growing their own food), but like the commune members in the films of Vinterberg and Trier, they are unable to overcome ideology that governs their social interactions. (Several critics have picked up on this theme in the film, likening Elena's situation to the general exploitation of the East European migrant worker by the wealthy West.)

A number of reviewers have also linked the baby's name Shelley to Mary Shelley, author of *Frankenstein; Or, the Modern Prometheus* (1818). We might see "Shelley" as a symbol of the social evil that arises from Elena's exploitation by her employers, which results in Elena's loss of agency. "Shelley" therefore continues to exert an evil influence after Elena's death. She becomes a kind of Frankenstein's Monster, a "hideous progeny," born

**A pregnant Elena (Cosmina Stratan) faces her wealthy benefactor Louise (Ellen Dorrit Peterson) in a chilly, atmospheric shot from *Shelley* (2016, IFC Midnight).**

of Elena's mistreatment at the hands of Kasper and Louise. Kasper, at least, seems to understand this and, overcome with fear and shame, attempts to kill both "Shelley" and himself by carbon monoxide poisoning. But Louise's need to keep the child is such that she murders Kasper and takes the baby.

*Shelley* ends enigmatically. Louise, who has finally lost her mind, rocks the baby that is now unequivocally hers, as a mysterious man in black stands in the room with them. The figure might be Satan or Death, or a witness to the evil that has torn the family apart from within.

## What We Become

The notion of the family being torn apart by forces arising from the family dynamic is also explored in Bo Mikkelsen's debut feature *What We Become*, which depicts the outbreak of a zombie virus in the Copenhagen suburbs from the perspective of a Danish family. The film begins at the end, with the mother, Pernille (Mille Dinesen) cradling her dead child as intruders break into her bedroom. The rest of the film serves as a flashback leading up to that point, essentially a revelation of "what we become" as a society alienated by modernity. As a zombie movie, it draws heavily on *Night of the Living Dead* (1968) as well as on variations such as *28 Weeks Later* (2007). (The opening scene of *28 Weeks Later*, showing a family trapped in the darkness of their own home, was a major influence on Mikkelson.) The tropes of *Night of the Living Dead* combine with the Nordic Noir tradition of realism and a concern with the tension between an apparently bland social surface and the violence underlying it. Like Romero, Mikkelsen approaches the zombie metaphor from a socially critical angle.

The film's original title, *Sorgenfri*, refers to the real-life suburb in Greater Copenhagen enclosed by lake and forest that serves as the film's setting (and is also home to Mikkelsen). Gustav (Benjamin Engell), the family's teenage son, dreams of breaking free from the suburbs that entrap him and his family. We first see him at Lake Furesøen on the outskirts of Sorgenfri, where he and his family spend their holidays. (In the film's book-end conclusion, Gustav will flee into the forest.) Suburbia has created in the family a sense of insularity; disconnection from wider society and from each other. His mother Pernille and father Dino (Troels Lyby) can no longer communicate with each other or with Gustav, and instead dote on their youngest child, Maj (Ella Solgaard). When a new family moves in across the street, Gustav is immediately attracted to the teenage daughter, Sonja (Marie Boda), who awakens in him a sense of rebellion and a desire to reach out from the confines of his family's situation.

The zombie virus metaphorically arises from within suburbia, and, as in Romero's movies, the authorities are shown as ruthless in their attempts to contain it and hold onto power. The residents are forced to remain in their own homes, in lockdown, and their houses are tented by thick black polythene. They are quite literally kept in the dark, isolated from others, with their understanding of what is happening is limited to local TV news reports that hide the truth. In an interview, Mikkelsen has spoken in terms of "how well-functioning societies have plenty of money while some are kept outside."[3] So it is in *What We Become*. It depicts suburbia itself, even before the zombie outbreak, as a form of social quarantine. Residents, uninformed about the outside world, become blinkered and docile as a result. Dino unquestioningly follows orders given by the military who keep him and his family prisoners in their own homes. When Gustav attempts to bring Sonja and her injured mother into the house, Dino objects, repeating what he has been told by the authorities: "It's best for each family to stay in their own home."

However, when it becomes clear that the military are shooting the "patients" in a nearby school-cum-field hospital, rebellion begins to grow among the residents. Significantly, the compartmentalized living space of the nuclear family—the bedrock of suburbia—breaks down as more survivors seek shelter in the house and the residents start to band together as a community. Suburban ennui gives way to the survival instinct and Gustav's family starts to take control. They are forced to communicate.

Also like the Romero movies, in *What We Become* those characters unable to break away from ideology are destined to perish. Mikkelsen's key

**Therese Damsgaard is one of the walking dead neighbors in *Sorgenfri/What We Become* (2016, IFC Midnight).**

theme was, in his words, "Can one keep love for his neighbor when everything is taken from one? Or when you yourself become a bestial predator?"[4] The film explores this primarily through Dino's character, who is ultimately unable to overcome selfish individualism when he encounters a woman outside the house in possession of food. He seizes her meager supplies for himself and his family and leaves the woman to die in a zombie attack. This seals Dino's own fate, and that of his wife and daughter, and it is at this point in the narrative that we are returned to the opening scene, with Pernille cradling Maj during the final zombie siege of the house. The motif of a family destroyed from within becomes literal when the zombie-infected Maj kills her mother and then turns on Dino.

Like *Night of the Living Dead*, *What We Become* ends inconclusively. The final shot shows that Gustav and Sonja, the only survivors of the Sorgenfri zombie outbreak, have managed to escape the enclosure, and the confines of the suburbs, and are fleeing into the forest. Behind them, the zombie virus has spread beyond Sorgenfri and into the wider suburbs of Copenhagen, marking the beginning of an apocalypse that military air strikes are failing to contain. Gustav may have broken free but his future survival—alongside that of the entire human race—is far from certain.

# 7

# France-Belgium-Luxembourg

*The Strange Color of Your Body's Tears* (2013)
and *Raw* (2016)

This chapter examines two contemporary European horror co-productions, taking as its focus (a) the work of husband-and-wife filmmakers Bruno Forzani and Hélèn Cattet, and (b) Julia Ducournau's debut feature, *Grave* (*Raw*), a French-Belgium thriller that won a FIPRESCI prize for Best First Film at the 2016 Cannes Film Festival.

The current revival of the *giallo*, a form of exotic murder thriller popularized in '70s Italian cinema, can itself be seen as an example of transnationalism; the recognition given to past directors of *gialli* like Sergio Martino (*All the Colors of the Dark; Your Vice Is a Locked Room and Only I Have the Key*, both 1972) has been made possible by festival revivals and DVD sales internationally. The films of Cattet and Forzani are co-productions that combine retro elements of the *giallo* within the experimental film tradition of their native Belgium. Their first feature, *Amer*, has been described as a *neo-giallo*, and an exploration of female sexual awakening as "glimpsed through a prism of traditional *giallo* convention."[1] In their follow-up *The Strange Color of Your Body's Tears*, Cattet and Forzani rupture classical narrative in favor of style. The film both celebrates and critiques *giallo* iconography, and can perhaps be best understood as an art house pastiche mash-up of thriller, '60s art film and avant-garde psychodrama. Literary pulp fiction also inspired Cattet and Forzani's third film, *Let the Corpses Tan* (2017), based on Jean Patrick Manchette's 1971 crime novel. Although taking a more straightforward narrative approach, the formal aesthetics of the genre are heightened to an abstract level.

The hype and hysteria surrounding Julia Ducournau's *Raw* on its festival release in 2016 threatened to overshadow what is a highly accomplished film. Despite reports of people fainting or vomiting (ambulance intervention was reportedly required during its screening at the Toronto Film Festival), it is apparent that this is a visceral debut by an adroit new voice in cinema. Although there are graphic moments in *Raw*, the real horror is the social coercion, *vis-à-vis* university and family, of young veterinarian Justine (Garance Marillier), a vegetarian who resorts to cannibalism in order to conform and gain social acceptance. Peer pressure, hazing and sibling rivalry fuel her growing psychosis, and there are strong Freudian undertones throughout, but the ultimate message of *Raw* is a feminist one, manifest when the real cause of Justine's sickness becomes clear in the film's final moments. A late entry in the New French Extremity (there are clear comparisons to be made with Claire Denis' *Trouble Every Day*, 2001), *Raw* also crosses over into the art house arena as a French social realist fable in the vein of Jean-Pierre and Luc Dardenne's work depicting young people on the fringes of society.

## Exploitation vs. Art House Traditions in French Horror Cinema

As Jordan Hageman has observed, "France never was prominent in Horror until the French New Wave of Extremity."[2] It has never had an exploitation film industry the likes of, say, Brazil's *Cinema de Boca*. In terms of genre moviemaking, the crime film has been much more prominent as French product than has horror. French horror cinema, where it does feature in that country's history, has tended toward an art house approach rather than an exploitation one. Of course, France can lay claim to the first-ever "horror" film in George Méliès' *Le manoir du diable* (*The Haunted Castle*, 1896), but the tradition of the *fantastique* that carried into Louis Feuillade's silent films (*Fantômas*, 1913; *Les Vampires*, 1915–1916) arguably diverted into the *bande dessineé* (comic books and cartoon strips) in the '60s and '70s and French television in the '80s. Horror films tended to arise from within the *oeuvres* of directors not generally associated with the genre, and thus were anomalies, albeit, in several cases, important ones.

Jean Epstein's *La chute de la maison Usher* (*The Fall of the House of Usher*, 1928), with its mist and lightning effects, shadow photography and ghostly atmospherics, helped define the genre cinematically. Epstein belonged to the Impressionist school at the time of filming. Henri Langlois praised *The Fall of the House of Usher* as "the cinematic equivalent of Debussy's works."[3] Epstein's co-scenarist and assistant during production was Luis Buñuel; if the horror genre is indeed the meeting of surrealism and expressionism, as has often been claimed, then *The Fall of the House of Usher* is a key progenitor.

Another, often overlooked early entry in French horror is *Le Main du Diable* (*The Devil's Hand*), produced and directed by Maurice Tourneur in

1943. The story of a struggling artist who acquires a severed hand as a lucky talisman, this variation on the W.W. Jacobs classic "The Monkey's Paw" has inspired a number of films since, including the "Disembodied Hand" segment of the Amicus anthology *Dr. Terror's House of Horrors* (1965). Tourneur's poetic realism situates *The Devil's Hand* firmly within French national cinema of the '40s; however, the film's themes are common to the horror genre. The passing of the cursed talisman motif was used memorably by Jacques Tourneur in *Curse of the Demon* (1957); that film also shares the Jungian psychology of *The Devil's Hand*, knowledge of psychoanalysis having been passed onto Jacques by his father Maurice. Some scholars have, in fact, read *The Devil's Hand* as an allegory of the German Occupation: Its horror elements, in the words of Frank Lafond, "may well express an anxiety experienced by every Frenchman opposed to the German invasion, in their souls if not through action."[4]

One of the most commercially successfully horror films made in France, *Les Diaboliques* (*Diabolique*, 1955) had an undeniable impact on the development of the genre overseas, if not necessarily at home. Hammer and, of course, Alfred Hitchcock picked up on the film's popularity and built on its success with significant contributions to the psychological thriller in the '60s. Clouzot himself followed *Diabolique* with the spy thriller *Les Espions* (*The Spies*, 1957), and would not return to horror cinema. Neither did *Diabolique* lead to a glut of French horror productions or co-productions. The *Nouvelle Vague* filmmakers disparaged Clouzot's films and genre cinema in general, and it would be five years before the next French horror films of note.

Roger Vadim's *Et mourir de Plaisir* (*Blood and Roses*, 1960) and Georges Franju's French-Italian co-production *Les Yeux Sans Visage* (*Eyes Without a Face*, 1960) followed in the art horror tradition, eschewing the popular suspense thriller approach of Clouzot. Franju's film in particular has greatly influenced contemporary horror cinema, while Vadim's adaptation of Sheridan Le Fanu's 1872 vampire novel *Carmilla* might be seen as a major influence on Jean Rollin's art horror films of the '60s and '70s.

*Eyes Without a Face* continues to exert a strange fascination on horror film fans and lovers of world cinema. Reviled on its first release, it met with international disgust and was slammed by critics, but has subsequently grown in acclaim and is now considered a classic. It started as an attempt to cash in on the success of Hammer horror films in France in the late 1950s. Franju, who up to that point had only directed a handful of shorts, documentaries and one feature, was engaged as director on the strict proviso that he avoid three things (gore, animal cruelty and mad scientists), so as not to upset European censors. Of course, he ended up including all three. Franju's use of body horror—especially in the cosmetic surgery sequences—is matter-of-factly shocking and finds echoes in the work of a number of contemporary filmmakers in the New French Extremity.

Franju himself was an enigmatic figure. He came from a relatively lowly background; after leaving school, he worked in insurance and he packed crates in a noodle factory before his military service in Algeria. Then in 1936 he started the *Cinémathèque Française* with Langlois and, after the war, made *Hotel Des Invalides* (1952) and *Le Sang Des Betes* (*Blood of the Beasts*, 1949), two films in which horror and modernity intersect in much the same way as they do in *Eyes Without a Face*. Franju was influenced by the surrealism of Cocteau. His films address, albeit in allegorical fashion, the atrocities of the Nazis, and a postwar Europe stained by the horrors of the Second World War. Franju turned government-sponsored documentaries about war veterans, factories and meat processing plants into virtual snuff movies, showing the industrialized slaughter of the modern world. In *Blood of the Beasts*, Franju contrasts the dispassionate butchery of animals with the seemingly oblivious bourgeois normalcy of the surrounding Parisian suburbs. Gasper Noé would achieve much the same effect in the shocking butchery of a horse at the start of his short film *Carné* (1991).

Franju is a poet rather than a storyteller and if *Eyes Without a Face* seems slow by today's standards (perhaps by any standards), it's a film that builds atmosphere, what Franju described as "horror in homeopathic doses." Horror and art cinema have always been closely connected, but *Eyes Without a Face* is arguably the quintessential art house horror movie. Its influence has been acknowledged by numerous European directors including Dario Argento, Lucio Fulci and Harry Kumel. The medical horrors of Jess Franco—*Gritos en la noche* (*The Awful Dr. Orloff*, 1962) and his late-in-the-day slasher *Faceless* (1987)—also owe a huge debt to Franju's film. *Eyes Without a Face* has its own precedents in Feuillade's silent fantasy films, of which Franju was a big fan, and in the early works of F.W. Murnau; and there is also the influence of Tod Browning, James Whale and the numerous mad scientists and disfigured monsters of the Universal movies of the 1930s.

A female vampire emerges from a grandfather clock at the stroke of midnight: This iconic moment from *Le Frisson des Vampires* (*Sex and the Vampire*, 1970) may be the "master image" of Jean Rollin, and compares with the equally striking imagery of *Blood and Roses* (such as the violent tableau of a female vampire impaled by a wooden stake and fallen on a barbed wire fence). Often derided as a Eurotrash director, or confused with Jess Franco, Rollin has not received serious critical attention until relatively recently. Partly this is because his career has fallen into two very distinct categories.

On the one hand, there are the personal works, those that are imbued with Rollin's sensibilities; strange, often visually beautiful films that can only be described as art-horror. Rollin's first work, *Le Viol du Vampire* (*The Rape of the Vampire*, 1968), is said to have caused a riot in the Paris cinema where it was first shown because it broke the conventions of the Hammer vampire film, replacing them with Rollin's own idiosyncratic thematic preoccupations and striking visual sense. Other films in this category include *Requiem pour un Vampire* (*Requiem for a Vampire*, 1971) and his later *Fascination* (1979) and *La Morte Vivante* (*The Living Dead Girl*, 1982). David Hinds aptly describes Rollin's personal films as "gentle, romantic and playful. They often embody an innocent fairy tale ambience. They do not aim to directly shock the viewer, but immerse them in another world."[5]

On the other hand, there are those films on which Rollin worked only as a director-for-hire; impersonal projects that Rollin made under pseudonyms, including hardcore pornographic titles. Rollin did them for the money and put very little of himself into them; they are often shoddy affairs. These exploitative films have tended to overshadow his personal work. Amongst these jobbing titles is perhaps his best-known film, *Le Lac des Morts Vivants* (*Zombie Lake*, 1981), upon which much of his reputation has unfortunately been based.

However, recent scholarship by Hinds and others has done much to restore Rollin's stock as one the most original European horror directors. Indeed, it is possible to argue that, until recently, Jean Rollin was France's only horror auteur.

## New French Extremity

"New French Extremity" is the term coined by journalist James Quandt for the series of transgressive films produced in France and Belgium in the last two decades, including works by Noé, Claire Denis, Catherine Breillat and François Ozon, as well as individual titles such as *Baise-Moi* (2000), *Le pornographe* (*The Pornographer*, 2001), *Intimité* (*Intimacy*, 2001) and *Dans ma peau* (*In My Skin*, 2002). These films, which have received considerable international attention, are characterized by a desire to shock, although critics are divided as to whether the deliberate breaking of taboos in these films is linked to a genuine desire on the behalf of the filmmakers to shock audiences into political consciousness.

A number of distinguished horror films have been linked to the movement: *Haute Tension* (*High Tension*, 2003), *Calvaire* (2004), *Sheitan* (*Satan*, 2006), *Ils* (*Them*, 2006), *Frontiere(s)* (*Frontier[s]*, 2007), *À l'intérieur* (*Inside*, 2007) and *Martyrs* (2008).

Despite the emergence of the French and Belgian horror film in recent years, *Martyrs'* director Pascal Laugier is quick to disabuse us of any notion that the horror genre has become part of French mainstream cinema: "My country produces almost 200 films a year but there are only two or three horror films. It's still a hell to find the money, a hell to convince people that we are legitimate to make this kind of film in France."[6]

This suggests that New French Extremity (and the horror films within it) provides an alternative to French national cinema, a challenge to national identities. But to what extent can these films in themselves be considered progressive? Certainly their tradition seems to be that of French "shock" art and literature originated by De Sade, Artaud, Bataille—a tradition anchored in the philosophy of nihilism, an extreme skepticism that denies all human values, all human forms of communication, and therefore the possibility of progressive change. Critics have detected a disturbing undercurrent of fascism in many of these films (Noé's work is often seen as particularly problematic, especially in his treatment of homosexuality). This is not peculiar to French cinema; the torture porn subgenre of horror, starting with *Saw* in 2004, is redolent of it.

New French Extremity can perhaps be seen most significantly as a response to the rise of right-wing extremism in France during the last two decades, a response that filmmakers are still in the process of working through. In her book *Films of the New French Extremity: Visceral Horror and National Identity*, Alexandra West writes: "At the turn of the millennium, France was at a crossroads. The turmoil brewing within the country was becoming untenable. Police brutality, xenophobia and riots were an everyday occurrence but few voices ever spoke out about the injustices outside of news reports."[7]

Of the horror films attached to the movement, *Frontier(s)* is perhaps the most politically minded: A family of degenerate murderers, led by a former Nazi, imprisons and tortures a group of young people who stumble into the family's inn on the Belgian border. Set against a backdrop of Paris riots following the fictional election of an extremist right-wing candidate into the French presidency, *Frontier(s)* functions as a political allegory about a degenerate "old guard" set on annihilating the young. The fact that the young people are a mix of races and sympathetically portrayed emphasizes the Nazi undercurrents of the torture that they undergo at the hands of the elders. Director Xavier Gens explains that the story "came from events in 2002 when we had presidential elections in France. There was an extreme right party in the second round. That was the most horrible day of my life."[8]

The capture-torture motif of *Frontier(s)* is also central to *Martyrs*, but in this film the political intentions are less overt, more ambiguous. The film begins with a young girl, Lucie (Mylène Jampanoï), escaping from a disused abattoir where she has been imprisoned and physically abused by mysterious captors. From there, the film develops into a tale of friendship: Lucie, tormented by "survivor guilt," is taken in by an orphanage where she meets Anna (Morjana Alaoui), who attempts to help her. Up to this point, *Martyrs* appears to be about the phenomenon of parents imprisoning their children in order to abuse them—cf. Josef Fritzl—and its psychological effects on the victims. But then it makes a sudden *volte-face* as the mysterious captors are revealed to be a society of aged super-rich inflicting torture on young women in a bid to discover the secrets of the afterlife. This shift in story direction comes across as muddled and confused (and somewhat unconvincing), and while there is no doubt that *Martyrs* is a visceral piece of work, this confusion about what it is trying to say, together with its unremitting bleakness, ultimately detracts from the film. The overall impression is one of nihilism. *Martyrs* was remade by Blumhouse Productions in 2015, reworked to give it "a glimmer of hope."

Whereas *Martyrs* fell somewhere between a progressive and nihilistic vision exploring the notion of a degenerate older generation abusing its young, *Inside* might be labeled as reactionary horror because of its dread of the woman's body. A young pregnant woman is the victim of a home invasion by a stranger (Beatrice Dalle) who seeks to take her unborn baby. The film presents pregnancy and motherhood in a generally negative light. Firstly, in Beatrice Dalle's character is the personification of the psychologically disturbed mother who would seek to harm another in her obsessive need for a child to replace the one she lost. Then there is the depiction of childbirth itself as something to be loathed (shown in the film as an impromptu Caesarian performed with a pair of scissors). *Inside* might be considered a study in what Barbara Creed called the Monstrous-Feminine, and a reminder that transgressive horror often invokes revulsion of the body.

A number of directors associated with horror films of the New French Extremity—Laugier, Gens, Alexandre Bustillo and Alexandre Aja—have gone on to make films for the Hollywood studios. Their subsequent work has often invoked the hardcore horror of New French Extremity, but has lacked its socio-political context. New French Extremity has, however, inspired new voices within the French film industry, in particular a number of women directors who have brought a feminist perspective to the horror film.

*Revenge* (2017), the feature debut of writer-director Coralie Fargeat, takes the rape-revenge exploitation movie paradigm and mixes it with survival horror tropes and elements of Richard Connell's classic 1924 short story "The Most Dangerous Game," as well as borrowing liberally from the 1986 Ozploitation movie *Fair Game*. Matilda Lutz plays the mistress of a wealthy businessman who accompanies him and his two male friends on a hunting trip in the desert. After she is assaulted by the three men and left for dead, she hunts them down and exacts bloody revenge. Less a deconstruction of rape-revenge movie conventions than a full-on re-deployment of them, *Revenge* was marketed as a synthesis of exploitation and feminist film in the wake of the #MeToo movement. However, it might also be considered, like *Raw*, in terms of New French Extremity. "I was aiming for something so excessive that it became almost surreal," Fargeat has said of the film. Like *Baise-Moi*, *Revenge* is an attempt to use the rape-revenge paradigm as way to provoke discussion of, in Fargeat's words, "the violence and inequality that women suffer,"[9] and a number of *Revenge* screenings in the U.K. were followed by special panel discussions on the subjects of rape-revenge cinema, sexual violence and female empowerment.

## The Strange Color of Your Body's Tears

Gender politics suffuses the work of Forzani and Cattet, not only in the films themselves but in the filmmakers' production methods. French-born Forzani and Cattet met in Brussels in 1997; they co-wrote and directed a number of early short films exploring the *giallo*, a subgenre that attracted them as self-taught students of film. The sexual politics of the *giallo* is of particular interest to them as a tool with which to investigate personal themes.

Their first short, *Catharsis* (2001), was, in Forzani's words, "about self-destruction, through *giallo* grammar."[10] Important to note is that their films are not intended as homages to *gialli*, although they readily admit to consciously utilizing elements from specific films. For example, the title *The Strange Color of Your Body's Tears* deliberately evokes the florid titles of several '70s *gialli* including *Lo strano vizio della signora Wardh* (*The Strange Vice of Mrs. Wardh*, 1971) and *Perché quelle strane gocce di sangue sul corpo di Jennifer?* (*The Case of the Bloody Iris*, 1972). Instead, their appropriation of the *giallo* is "because there are strong iconographic elements whose meaning we can subvert."[11] The subversion of meaning, for Forzani and Cattet, partly involves the manipulation of point of view, incorporating both male and female perspectives into their work. As Forzani told *Senses of Cinema* in 2018, "When we made our short films, in one … it was a man who was killed, in the other it was a woman. We wanted to be equal in the violence, and in the male and female aspect."[12] Reference to Sergio Martino's work is especially relevant here, as he was one of the few '70s directors to use women protagonists in his *gialli* as a spin on more traditional male-driven, female-as-victim thrillers. His female-centric *gialli*, such as *Tutti i colori del buio* (*All the Colors of the Dark*, 1972), are, as Michael Mackenzie claims, typically "more languorous [and] psychologically driven."[13] So it is with *Amer*, Forzani and Cattet's debut feature.

*Amer* grew from a desire on the part of its makers to "direct a … male murder, because there's not a lot of male murder in *giallo*, and not a lot of eroticized male murder."[14] *Amer* is essentially the portrait of a young woman's discovery of sexual desire, presented as three stages of her sexual development from child to adult. Forzani and Cattet distill these moments into a series of tableaux that foreground the style and imagery of the *giallo*, largely eschewing the subgenre's usual murder-thriller plot framework.

The story takes place over a period of 30 years in a mansion on the south coast of France. The first section invokes the psycho-sexual primal scene often found in *gialli*. A young child, Ana (Cassandra Forêt), witnesses the death of her grandfather and, later, her parents having sex. It is an enactment of *eros* and *thanatos* typical of the *giallo*, and consciously presented as such by the filmmakers. Tonally, this first section is also akin to the kind of gothic fairy tale favored by Mario Bava, and the filmmakers have in fact referenced, in an interview, the "Drop of Water" segment of Bava's *I tre volti della paura* (*Black Sabbath*, 1963) as a key influence on this first section of their film.

The story resumes a few years later with a now adolescent Ana (Charlotte Eugène Guibbaud) and her mother en route to the hairdresser. Ana finds herself drawn—much to her mother's horror—to a motorcycle gang, and obvious sexual danger. For this second part of the film, Forzani and Cattet consciously drew upon the Japanese *pinku eiga* (erotic film), known for its violent subgenres. The erotic element comes into play in *giallo*, for example, in the dream sequence of Dario Argento's *Tenebrae* (1982), depicting the violent seduction of a transsexual girl by a gang of men. Thus, Forzani and Cattet establish a connection between *giallo* and *pinku eiga* in the second sequence of *Amer*, as they did *giallo* and gothic fairy tale in the first segment.

The third and final section finds Ana as an adult (Marie Bos), returning to the house of her childhood, where her sexual fantasies and reality merge in violent murder. Here the *giallo* tropes come to the fore, in a welter of imagery and sound that emphasizes, above all, the sensorial impact of the *giallo*.

A number of critics have become confused when reading Forzani and Cattet's films as simple homages to *giallo*; few noticed the intersection of genres, deliberately deployed, in *Amer*. What Forzani and Cattet do in *Amer* is explore the crossover points between the three genres, gothic fairy tale, *pinku eiga* and *giallo*. *Amer* exists as a kind of Venn diagram exposing

**Surrealism and the *Giallo*: Manon Beuchot is ravished by the black-gloved killer(s) in *L'étrange couleur des larmes de ton corps/The Strange Color of Your Body's Tears* (2013, Strand Releasing).**

the common elements of these seemingly disparate genres. Key to understanding the film is recognizing the interconnections that the filmmakers find in the genres.

*The Strange Color of Your Body's Tears* takes a similar approach. In terms of the *giallo*, Forzani and Cattet set out to explore the detective trope, often deployed by Argento, this time taking a male point of view. The story involves a man's investigation into the circumstances of his wife's disappearance. Much of the action takes place in a labyrinthine apartment building, into which the man descends in search of clues to his wife's whereabouts. We are introduced to a number of the building's residents, any of whom might hold the key to solving the mystery. As in Argento's films, modernist architecture is of great importance; and *Strange Color* takes its cue from the kaleidoscopic design of the apartment building setting to become in itself a myriad of concealed panels, hidden doors and secret chambers. As in *Amer*, style is foregrounded in order to explore the iconography of *giallo*; indeed, the codes of *giallo* are, as Forzani has claimed, intrinsically "linked to the *mise en scène*."[15]

Forzani and Cattet's method in dealing with *giallo* is to abstract it, or purify it. There are the brief, fleeting shots of the killer dressed in raincoat and black gloves; the loving closeups of the murder weapons (straight razor, knives), and the nightmare and dream sequences that have a psyche-delic effect on the viewer. However, without the traditional narrative conventions in place to give them meaning, the codes of *giallo*, inherent in the *mise en scène*, are unreadable by themselves, "bursting with visual style but suffering from a dearth of discernable narrative."[16]

In this way, *Strange Color*—like *Amer*—can only be understood when the *giallo* elements are considered alongside other things. Whereas *Amer* intersected genres in order to make meaning, *Strange Color* intersects film *types*: thriller, alternative narrative cinema and psychodrama or trance film.

# The Strange Color of Your Body's Tears
## *as Alternative Narrative Cinema*

We can see *The Strange Color of Your Body's Tears* as a throwback to the European art cinema of the 1960s–70s as exemplified by such modernist filmmakers as Michelangelo Antonioni (*L'Avventura*, 1960; *Blow Up*, 1966) and Alain Robbe-Grillet (*Trans-Europ-Express*, 1966). As Penelope Houston wrote of Antonioni: "The comparison would rather be with painting—the plot threads … loosened, the balance between the eye and ear adjusted somewhat towards the eye … increasingly treating the screen as a canvas on which the artist directly registers impressions."[17]

The narrative approach of *Strange Color* places it within the alternative narrative cinema of Antonioni, Resnais and Duras, among others. Instead of the classical Hollywood narrative of set-up, conflict and resolution, Forzani and Cattet divide the narrative into episodes or chapters, like a novel. Throughout, there are numerous digressions in the detective storyline, tangents and fantasy-dream sequences, all of which work against cause and effect in the plot. Although we have the detective protagonist, the filmmakers sometimes shift perspective to other characters; this has a distancing effect on the viewer, undermining the sense of empathy upon which classical Hollywood narrative depends. Unlike classical Hollywood cinema where time and space in the fictional world are clearly delineated, *Strange Color* fails to make its dream sequences and flashbacks obvious to the viewer, leaving us with the impression of more than one fictional world. This brings with it an element of self-reflexivity to the film; where mainstream cinema tries to make the viewer believe in the "reality" of the events on the screen, *Strange Color*, as alternative cinema, disrupts this by drawing attention to the filmmaking process. In this way, style and form in Forzani and Cattet's work are amplified; content becomes secondary.

# The Strange Color of Your Body's Tears
## *as Psychodrama or Trance Film*

A third film type which intersects with the *giallo* and alternative narrative cinema in *Strange Color* is the psychodrama or trance film. Originating in 1940s American avant-garde cinema with such works as *Meshes of the Afternoon* (Alexander Hammid and Maya Deren, 1943) and *Fireworks* (Kenneth Anger, 1947), the psychodrama has been popularized in recent years in the films of David Lynch, with *Lost Highway* (1997) and *Mulholland Drive* (2001) being obvious examples.

According to A.L. Rees, the psychodrama, "modelled on dream, lyric verse and contemporary dance," typically subverts narrative and space-time conventions of mainstream film, to explore themes such as desire, loss, obsession and death.[18] The narrative is shaped by the depiction of dream or a dream state, typically focused on the inner conflicts and states of mind of the central protagonist: "a single guiding consciousness" that may be a stand-in for the filmmakers themselves (certainly in the case of Forzani and Cattet, who create narratives of "personal significance").

In psychodrama, domestic objects take on a metaphorical and symbolic value. An example would be the knives, mirrors and keys that feature in *Meshes of the Afternoon*. There is a clear intersection here with the knives and other symbolic objects of the *giallo*, iconographic elements that are fetishized in Forzani and Cattet's films through the use of extreme closeup. The home itself is seen as oppressive, and it may represent entrapment within the mind of the protagonist. The uncanny use of the home environment in psychodrama creates alienation and disorientation, as familiar territory becomes unsettlingly unfamiliar. Again, this can be seen in *Amer*, but also in the apartment building of *The Strange Color of Your Body's Tears*, which may indeed symbolize the unconscious mind. Finally, psychodrama is characterized by a circular or spiral structure often ending in what P. Adams Sitney calls the "sparagmos": Greek for the literal "tearing of the flesh."[19] A spiraling of events and images is a key element of *Strange Colors*, and the film does in fact conclude with a bloody rending of the flesh.

The psychodrama or trance film derived from the American avant-garde offers obvious appeal to Forzani and Cattet, who consider their work to have a background in Belgian experimentalism. The exploration of the unconscious through surrealism is a major part of their films, and continues in their adaptation of *Let the Corpses Tan*. As the filmmakers told Anton Bitel in 2018:

> Bruno Forzani: We work with the subconscious, when we are writing, because you want to touch the senses through the subconscious, like

in dreams, so that even if you don't understand, you are touched by something sensorial. To find an instance from *Let the Corpses Tan*, in the sequence where you have the machine-gun tearing the girl's dress, it's not in the book. In the book, there is a psychological state explained. You can put a voiceover, and she is saying, "Blah blah blah," okay … and we tried to recreate it….

HÉLÈN CATTET: "visually…"

BRUNO FORZANI: …visually, yes. In an oneiric way. In a surrealistic way. It may be for that [reason] that we tried to work a lot with our subconscious and not to control everything.[20]

# Raw

What is the nature of the pathology of Justine, the young cannibal of *Raw*? This is the underlying question of Julia Ducournau's film, and one that allows the writer-director to explore issues of identity, social conformism and family (dys)function. The film opens on Justine's first day at veterinarian school. Sixteen years old, she is from a family of strict vegetarians. She is following in the family tradition in other ways, too: Both her parents and her older sister Alexia (Ella Rumpf) attended the same vet school in which Justine has been enrolled, Alexia in the year above her.

The school has its own traditions. Among them is hazing, which includes (in a scene reminiscent of Pasolini's *Salò, or the 120 Days of Sodom*, 1975) herding the newbies like cattle through corridors, forcing them into non-consensual sexual activity, and drenching them in blood and paint. Justine, like the other freshers, goes along with this willingly, at least at the start. When she is forced to eat raw lamb's kidney, a violation of her deepest principles, she finds herself becoming voracious for raw meat. She resorts to stealing a beef burger from the college canteen, and raids the fridge late at night for raw chicken. Her body rebels in ways that we might associate with hysterical reaction: She develops a painful rash on her legs and torso, and compulsively eats her own hair, which she then vomits back up. We might read these compulsions, and Justine's inexorable slide into cannibalism, as a form of unconscious protest or hysterical response to the social coercion that has left her feeling deeply compromised.

But the film then shifts focus to Justine's relationship with her older sister Alexia, and this in turn forces us to reconsider our understanding of Justine's developing pathology. In Ducourneau's words, "*Raw* is centered on the construction of identity and moral standards inside a perverted system—that of 'hazing' and that of the family."[21] This shift focuses our attention on the family as the root cause of Justine's problem. It transpires that Alexia, too, is a cannibal, and a more advanced one.

**Veterinary student Justine (Garance Marillier) undergoes a bloody hazing in** *Grave/Raw* **(2016, Focus Word/Universal Pictures International).**

*Raw* opens on an empty road in the French countryside. A car slowly approaches. With startling suddenness, a human figure darts into the road, causing the car to crash into a tree. Later in the film, the significance of this enigmatic opening is revealed as we learn that the figure was Alexia, and that she deliberately caused the crash in order to cannibalize the occupants of the car. But why would Alexia share the same sickness as her younger sister?

Ducournau has described the relationship between the sisters in these terms: "When you're young, you shape your identity as a rebellion against your parents but also against your elders. A sister is also an accomplice with whom you can share an intimacy without any real embarrassment."[22] As a coming-of-age film, *Raw* centers on Justine's attempts to find her own identity in her family's shadow. At first Justine behaves like Alexia, but gradually distances herself from her, morally repelled by her behavior. It becomes clear that Justine is not prepared to follow in Alexia's footsteps. This brings us back to our original question: Why has Justine developed cannibalistic impulses?

The final scene of *Raw* offers answers, while at the same time remaining fascinatingly ambiguous. After Alexia has been imprisoned for murder, Justine's father reveals to Justine:

> It's not your fault…. Or your sister's. When she was born, she was our little princess. We took her everywhere. Our friends loved her. She was full tilt from the start. She should have studied politics or something…. So I guess she got used to being … herself. It's our fault. We didn't find a solution. Your mom was tough at first. Kept saying I was her best friend at school. It drove me nuts. It's not like she had a boyfriend. Just me. And then we had our first kiss. And I understood.

At this point, the father unbuttons his shirt to reveal that his chest is covered in scars, from having been bitten. But who has bitten him during sex?

**Justine (Garance Marillier) battles her cannibalistic urges in *Grave/Raw* (2016, Focus Word/Universal Pictures International).**

His wife (Justine and Alexia's mother) or Alexia? It is unclear which of them he is referring to in his speech. This ambiguity raises two possibilities. The first is that the mother herself is a cannibal and has passed the condition to her two daughters. This would, perhaps, explain her attempts to divert them from eating meat by bringing them up as strict vegetarian. It would also explain the father's guardedness around Justine and her mother throughout the film. He is not "one of them" and understands this in a way that Justine cannot. At the start of the film, the glance that he casts at Justine in the rear view mirror as he and his wife drive her to veterinary school may indicate wariness or, considering the second possibility, may be predatory in nature.

The second possibility is perhaps the more psychologically compelling. If the father has been involved in an incestuous relationship with Alexia, the bite-marks on his torso might be explained as Alexia's fighting back against her father's restraints during sex. Her cannibal pathology has developed as a result of sexual abuse in childhood. We might then understand Justine's own cannibalism, in imitating her sister's abnormal behavior, as a form of sympathetic identification with her abused older sibling on an unconscious level. Either way, *Raw* becomes about Justine's end of innocence and how, by understanding her family's secret, she is able to find her own identity, her own "solution" inside "a perverted system."

*Raw* is, at heart, a Sadean tale of female sexual awakening, and this places it within the New French Extremity alongside the films of Catherine Breillat. As Ducournau states in the film's presskit:

> The name of my character is a reference to *Justine, or the Misfortunes of Virtue by the Marquis de Sade*, the story of the innocent young woman who becomes

an object of sexual pleasure and ends up herself taking pleasure in it.... If sex is significant, atavism is central. My Justine will shape herself around her urges—a family curse. Through contact with her sister, who is afflicted with the same condition, she will become assertive, discover her true self and accept—or reject—her difference."[23]

# 8

# Iran

## *Under the Shadow* (2016)
## and *A Girl Walks Home Alone at Night* (2014)

Set in a Tehran apartment in the 1980s during the Iran-Iraq war, *Under the Shadow* has been compared to *The Babadook* in its story of a mother and child tormented by a malevolent entity, in this case a djinn (Middle Eastern spirit) unleashed by an air raid on their apartment building. Its plot may be similar, but its setting lends *Under the Shadow* a distinctly Iranian flavor. Director Babak Anvari turned not only to Roman Polanski (*Repulsion*, 1965; *Rosemary's Baby*, 1968; *The Tenant*, 1976) but also to Iranian social realist cinema, especially the work of Ashgar Farhadi. *Under the Shadow*'s protagonist is a political activist expelled from medical school due to her past affiliations, and the film addresses the rapid internal, political and cultural transition following the 1979 Iranian Revolution, when decades of progress in women's rights were rolled back (the djinn in the film acts as a metaphor for the oppression of women under the theocratic regime that succeeded the shah in 1979). *Under the Shadow* holds the distinction of being one of only four Farsi-language horror films produced in recent years to have made it to the international scene, the others being *A Girl Walks Home Alone at Night* and the lesser known *Zar* (2017) and *Mahi va gorbeh* (*Fish and Cat*, 2013). The latter is a slasher filmed in one continuous take.

*A Girl Walks Home*, directed by Iranian-American Ana Lily Amirpour, reconfigures the vampire subgenre, regaining control of female sexuality and ethnic identity and, according to some critics, marks reclamation of the monstrous-feminine. The skateboarding, chador-veiled vampire at the heart of the story represents a female monster who is ultimately allowed to *be*, and is accepted by the film's male protagonist (and also the audience) for what she is. Expertly directed in the classical Hollywood style by the 24-year-old Amirpour, the film has also been received by critics as a vindication for women directors coping with glass ceilings in Hollywood.

**Shideh (Narges Rashidi) and her daughter Dorsa (Avin Manshadi) hide from falling bombs in** *Under the Shadow* **(2016, Netflix/Vertical Entertainment).**

## Farsi-Language Horror

Iran has a limited indigenous horror film tradition. Even pre–Iranian Revolution filmmakers shied away from the genre, preferring to focus instead on melodramas and thrillers. *Shab-e bist o nohom* (*The 29th Night*, 1989), directed by Hamid Rakhshani, is generally thought to be the first horror film produced in Iran. Notable for its emphasis on the psychological, it tells the story of Mohtaram (Marjaneh Golchin), a young woman haunted by the spirit of a woman who was once in love with her husband. In an early sequence, Rakhshani uses a subjective camera to take the point of view of the djinn as it moves through the darkened corridors of a Tehran apartment building to terrorize Mohtaram. In other scenes, the djinn is glimpsed only briefly as a chador-clad figure silhouetted against a darkened sky. Although influential on *Under the Shadow* and *A Girl Walks Home Alone at Night* in terms of its theme of female repression (symbolized in the Muslim veil that becomes a dominant image in all three films), *The 29th Night* stands as something of an anomaly in Iranian cinema. Arguably cultural censorship would not allow Iranian filmmakers to follow through in using horror to address issues of women's rights in their own country; it is notable that both *Under the Shadow* and *A Girl Walks Home Alone at Night* were produced outside of Iran, with Jordan and California, respectively, doubling as Tehran.

Shahram Mokri's *Fish and Cat*, by contrast, arises from an experimental tradition of Iranian cinema that informs the work of such directors as Abbas Kiarostami. It takes as its starting point a true story: a restaurant in a remote area of North Iran closed down for serving meat unfit for human consumption, later implicated in the disappearance of several tourists (who had presumably been eaten). From this basic premise, though, it veers away from standard horror narrative in favor of a real-time movie experiment that takes in numerous disparate characters followed by the mobile camera, whose paths intersect in a looping fashion, as time and space appear to fold together in a single overlapping structure.

Mokri is a formalist influenced by theories of cinematic realism, but he is equally inspired by the American horror films that were smuggled into Iran in the 1980s and 1990s. *Fish and Cat* has been described as a postmodern horror film for its self-reflexive use of slasher movie tropes. Furthermore, Mokri recognizes that the horror genre refers "to political and social situations," and *Fish and Cat* is an attempt to convey the anxiety of Iranian life. "[T]he most important characteristic of Iran's society is the suspension in which people are stuck, almost as though they are waiting for an accident every moment of their lives—while driving, in the bank, on an airplane, or waiting for an attack on their home. The Iranian mind is waiting for these incidents and the horror film is the best genre to illustrate their feelings and emotional conditions."[1]

Nima Farahi worked as assistant director to Shahram Mokri before assisting other luminaries of Iranian cinema, including Kiarostami. His debut feature, *Zar*, very much captures the "feelings and emotional conditions" of contemporary Iranians. The setting is a secluded town in north Iran, where newlyweds Amir Hossein Eshgh Abadi and Mohammad Reza Ghaffari spend their honeymoon in a haunted villa. They invite their friends to share the experience, and paranormal activity ensues after a Ouija board séance. Farahi films in a carefully composed, classical style that evokes milestones of the genre such as Robert Wise's *The Haunting* (1963), but the jump-scares and possessed female wraiths are equally reminiscent of J and K horror, with elements of Sam Raimi's *The Evil Dead* (1982) thrown into the mix. *Zar* ends with the couple, and all of their friends, dead except for the Final Girl. The mood is certainly one of impending catastrophe, shared among the young people of the film.

## Under the Shadow

Iranian war cinema began in the early 1980s, almost simultaneously with the Iran-Iraq war itself, and became one of the most popular genres.

Numerous Iranian war films were made in the decades that followed, many of them thinly disguised propaganda pieces. It is interesting that, in addition to social realist cinema and horror film, *Under the Shadow* draws on such Iranian war movies as Mohsen Makhmalbaf's *Arousi-ye Khouban* (*The Marriage of the Blessed*, 1989) in its depiction of ordinary Iranians enduring deliberate attacks on civilian targets, including the bombing of Tehran's civilian population. However, it is important to note that the film's source of horror does not directly arise from its war setting but from the social context of female oppression during the Cultural Revolution. In fact, *Under the Shadow* is arguably as successful as a social realist drama depicting in its early scenes the persecution by the authorities of the main character— an Iranian wife and mother named Shideh (Narges Rashidi)—as it is later on, when it develops into a horror film concerned with a symbolic "return of the repressed."

The film opens with an explanatory title, giving a brief background into the war and how throughout the conflict Iran underwent rapid internal, political and cultural change as a result of the 1979 revolution. The combination of war and regressive social upheaval plunged people's lives "into darkness where fear and anxiety thrived." Documentary footage further sets the scene, depicting Iraq's strategic bombing of Iranian cities. We see civilians fleeing the streets, running into bomb shelters, fortifying their apartment buildings with sandbags and fixing tape to windows. We are taken inside a college building where many of the students are women; in the years following the Iranian Revolution, numerous educated people fled the country and the authorities realized that it was necessary to allow women into universities for the benefit of industry and the economy. However, those who opposed Khomeini during the revolution had their studies suspended, often permanently. This is Shideh's situation. We learn that, as a young medical student, she became involved with a radical left-wing organization, which led to her expulsion from medical school. Now, ten years later, her repeated attempts to convince the university to allow her to continue her training, so that as a doctor she can serve society, fall on deaf ears. The one "mistake" she made during the idealism of her youth has destroyed her career. As she pleads her case, we see through the office window a bomb silently hit an apartment building in the distance. Shideh notices the explosion and momentarily falls silent. A bomb similarly striking her own apartment will bring the djinn into her home. The opening scene thus sets up a connection between the djinn and the political "mistake" of Shideh's past come back to haunt her. The djinn is a return of the repressed; Shideh has been forced to abandon her political beliefs, as well as her goal of becoming a doctor, while living under the shadow of Khomeini. The djinn is an eruption of this repression in nightmare form.

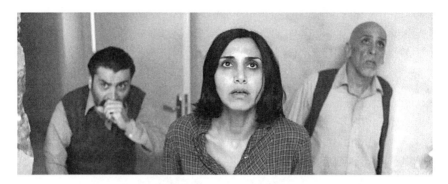

Shideh (Narges Rashidi) and her neighbors Mr. Ebrahimi (Ray Haratian) and Mr. Bijari (Nabil Koni) inspect bomb damage to their apartment block, unaware that an evil djinn has been released, in *Under the Shadow* (2016, Netflix/Vertical Entertainment).

The following scenes establish the oppression Shideh endures in her daily life at the hands of the Khomeini regime (and less overtly, within her marriage), and the effects of this on her personal identity. As she drives home, she is stopped by military guards who scrutinize her and her car. In this short sequence, Anvari conveys the loss of freedom brought by the war and the Cultural Revolution, with striking economy. Women are less likely to walk in the street (and must wear the hijab in public); social interaction is kept to a minimum; men and women no longer mix. Shideh knows the relative freedom that women of her mother's generation enjoyed during the reign of the shah and how, under Khomeini, those liberties have been taken away from her and from her daughter Dorsa (Avin Manshadi). As Shideh collects Dorsa from her neighbor Mrs. Fakur (Soussan Farrokhnia), she is unable to hide her distress. "The climate's not right, now," Mrs. Fakur consoles her. "Don't let it change you."

We see the strain that Shideh is under, as she wearily removes her hijab. *Under the Shadow* is about the sheer weight of political oppression on Iranian women, and how they might buckle beneath it. Shideh tries to cope with her rejection from the university by throwing away her medical textbooks; but she is unable to discard the one given to her by her mother, inscribed with a message of love and pride. This book will reappear later in the film, to remind Shideh of her mother's strength, as Shideh attempts to save herself and Dorsa from the oppressive force of the djinn.

The role of family is further explored in the scene: The camera fixes on a photograph of her mother on the mantelpiece, then pans to the front door of the apartment as Shideh's husband Iraj (Bobby Naderi) returns home from work. Significantly, Shideh hides her mother's textbook in a locked drawer. It represents her refusal to abandon her mother's ambition for her.

But Shideh understands that she must keep her dream of liberation a secret from the male regime, and that includes her husband. "Maybe things will get better after the war," he tells her, trying to be supportive. But Shideh realizes that there is a limit to his sympathy when he remarks, "Maybe it's for the best." Iraj, for all his kindliness and understanding, cannot know Shideh's experience: he himself has been allowed to complete his studies and become a doctor. A sudden cut to darkness indicates a shift in the film's focus.

The opening section of *Under the Shadow* is compelling as social realist drama. Anvari drew on the work of Farhadi in this sequence, particularly *Jodaeiye Nader az Simin* (*A Separation*, 2011) and *Darbareye Elly* (*About Elly*, 2009). Both are set in one house, and concern tangled relationships and marital break-up. Farhadi himself was influenced by Kiarostami's story of a failing marriage, *Gozaresh* (*The Report*, 1977). Iranian social realist drama therefore furnished Anvari with a clear and rich tradition on which to base *Under the Shadow*, and as previously mentioned, this element of the film is wholly successful. As a horror film, *Under the Shadow*, in comparison with *The Babadook*, offers little in the way of genre deconstruction, opting instead to offer fairly straightforward allegory. It is, as one IMDb user put it, a "compelling critique of oppressive Iranian regime subsumed by typical Hollywood-like horror machinations."[2] Like *The Babadook*, however, *Under the Shadow* reminds us of the importance of personal identity, and how socially induced fear of failing (ourselves, our community, our loved ones) will bring horror upon us.

## A Girl Walks Home Alone at Night

Ana Lily Amirpour's debut feature is equally remarkable, not least because it manages to break with Iranian cinematic tradition while simultaneously addressing the issue of emancipation central to female-centric horror, Iranian or otherwise.

The plot is simple: Sheila Vand plays a vampire who pursues her (predominantly male) victims in an Iranian ghost town. The setting is a fictitious place called Bad City, and it is aptly named. Bad City might, in fact, stand in for the Tehran suburbs. Home to prostitutes and drug dealers, it is suffused with an air of despondency and desperation that speaks of economic and moral breakdown. The vampire girl is a vengeful spirit driven to rid Bad City of evil men. Then she meets the sensitive Arash (Arash Marandi), another lost soul. A love story develops, one of mutual acceptance.

Amirpour's own background accounts for the eclectic cultural mix

**The Girl (Sheila Vand) puts on her makeup before seeking a new victim in *A Girl Walks Home Alone at Night* (2014, Kino Lorber).**

that makes up *A Girl Walks Home Alone at Night* (the film has been billed as "an Iranian Vampire Western"[3]). Born in England to Iranian immigrants, she was raised in the U.S. She attended art school in San Francisco and eventually found her way into UCLA's screenwriting program. *A Girl Walks Home* was crowdfunded by Indiegogo on a budget of $55,000, and shot in Southern California with Iranian actors and dialogue in Farsi. Amirpour has cited as specific influences such films as *Once Upon a Time in America* (1984), *Rumble Fish* (1983) and *Blade Runner* (1982). These works are certainly invoked in the visualization of Bad City. However, *A Girl Walks Home* is also reminiscent of early Jim Jarmusch (*Stranger Than Paradise*, 1984, and *Down by Law*, 1986) and early Leos Carax (*Boy Meets Girl*, 1984) in terms of its expressionist black-and-white cinematography revealing a romantic sensibility. It's not too far-out to describe Amirpour's film, as the director herself has, as "like Sergio Leone and David Lynch had an Iranian rock'n'roll baby, and then Nosferatu came and babysat."[4]

The film's theme of female empowerment is reflected in Amirpour's directing style, in her mastery of the classical *mise en scène*. Important to the film's look and feel is the chiaroscuro lighting and the use of the 2.40:1 anamorphic image. Amirpour's visual skill easily rivals that of many Hollywood directors twice her age, with twice the experience. It belies the notion that "professionalism" only comes to those who have worked their way up through the ranks of the Hollywood production system. More to the point, many commentators have questioned how a young female novice might have the technical and craft skills of a Hollywood veteran, as though only middle age, maleness and membership in the Directors Guild of America might confer such mastery on a filmmaker. Jen and Sylvia Soska faced similar criticism following *American Mary* (2012), another film directed in the classical Hollywood style. Credit for that film's cinematic achievements was often given to the cinematographer (a middle-aged male), and the same has happened to Amirpour. However, there is little evidence to suggest that cinematographer Lyle Vincent—rather than Amirpour—"directed" *A Girl Walks Home*. Instead what we have is another example of the horror genre providing a platform for a talented woman filmmaker. In fact, it is remarkable, given the recent explosion of women directors working in the genre, how horror cinema enables directors such as Amirpour to shine.

Given Amirpour's Iranian background, it is not surprising that critics have read a political message into *A Girl Walks Home*, albeit one primarily delivered through the film's imagery. Sheila O'Malley makes the point that the vampire girl targets men who are abusive towards women. O'Malley says that because the vampire girl is dressed in a chador throughout, "one can make all kinds of political and social connections with that storytelling device: She is an avenging angel of dominated and scorned womankind." However, the strength of the film is that the imagery is allowed to carry the film's meaning: "The image of a female vampire skateboarding down a street, her voluminous veil flying out behind her, does the job with more

The chador-clad Girl (Sheila Vand) reveals her fangs in *A Girl Walks Home Alone at Night* (2014, Kino Lorber).

poetic satisfaction and truth than any explicit monologue about the repression of women could ever do."[5]

Like a number of recent horror films in which the female protagonist is the "monster," A Girl Walks Home represents a move towards regaining control of sexuality and ethnic identity, and for women filmmakers a reclamation of the monstrous-feminine. The vampire girl is not destroyed at the end; she reveals her "monstrousness" to Arash (who is presented as a fine upstanding young man) and he accepts the girl on her terms. Amirpour has them drive away together in the final scene, leaving Bad City behind. In so doing, she dramatizes a point made by the scholar Isabel Cristina Pinedo, one that has particular relevance to our discussion of Iranian horror films:

> If a woman cannot be aggressive and still be a woman, then female agency is a pipe dream. But if the surviving female can be aggressive and be really a woman, then she subverts this binary notion of gender that buttresses male dominance.[6]

# 9

# Israel

*Rabies* (2010)
and *Big Bad Wolves* (2013)

Since 2010, Israeli filmmakers have produced a number of films that
can be described as belonging to genre cinema, ranging from zombie movies to psychological thrillers: "Campy takes on the real-life violence fac-
ing Israelis."[1] These include *Tikkun* (2015), *Mesuvag Harig* (*Freak Out*,
2015), *JeruZalem* (2015), *Big Bad Wolves* (2013), *Cannon Fodder* (*Battle of
the Undead*, 2013), *Chatulim Al Sirat Pedalim* (*Cats on a Pedal Boat*, 2011)
and *Kalevet* (*Rabies*, 2010). Israel's film industry has traditionally produced
comedic satires of Israeli society and art house dramas. The turn to horror reflects a shift away from the prestige films that have characterized
recent Israeli cinema—*Vals Im Bashir* (*Waltz with Bashir*, 2008) and *Ajami*
(2009)—toward movies with wider audience appeal. Younger (film school–
educated) directors in the Israeli film industry are looking for an alternative to standard dramas of Israeli family life and war films. Keshales and
Papushado's *Rabies* crossed over to a younger generation of international
filmgoers and was a hit at festivals around the world. Current events have
given Israelis a taste for horror cinema, according to *The Times of Israel*:
"Surrounded by blood and gore in the news and in their lives, Israelis can
find an escape in movies that caricature violence."[2]

This chapter takes *Rabies* as its central focus, along with Keshales
and Papushado's highly acclaimed follow-up *Big Bad Wolves*. Both films
deconstruct the horror genre, or at least play hard and fast with its rules.
In *Rabies*, a brother and sister run away from home to find sanctuary in a
deserted nature reserve. When the sister falls into the trap of a psychopathic
killer, her rescue becomes entwined with a group of young tennis players,
a ranger and his dog, as well as two policemen. All of them commit acts of
violence under duress. The killer makes an early exit from the film while
the ordinary civilians are transformed into "killer machines." The message seems to be that in a country where war and death are commonplace,

violence becomes a language used all too easily by its people. As *Film Slant* commented,

> There are no rabid animals in *Rabies*, only humans who have gone mad (or just gotten really angry) for whatever reason and resort to violence in their agitated states … [T]here's no need for a malevolent force to kill the good guys, because given enough time, the good guys will take care of themselves.[3]

Keshales and Papushado develop this central theme in *Big Bad Wolves*, while debunking the standard torture porn revenge thriller tropes. A pedophile is imprisoned by a cop and a vengeful father who subject him to horrific punishment. The viewer's sympathies switch as Keshales and Papushado subvert the clichés of this scenario: The cop and the father become the psychopaths and the pedophile their victim. In so doing, *Big Bad Wolves* explores ways in which we see violence in our entertainment culture: as a language filmmakers and audiences use too easily.

## The Emergence of Israeli Horror

As journalist Amir Bogen comments, Israeli cinema is no stranger to violence. Notable films emerging from Tel Aviv, Gaza and the West Bank have reflected war-torn regions and atrocities taking place there. As Bogen points out, it is partly this that has brought critical attention—and Oscar nominations—to such films as *Beaufort* (2007), *Waltz with Bashir* and *Ajami*. However, genre cinema has emerged from Israel only recently, with *Rabies* generally cited as the first of a wave of horror-thrillers that expose a different face of violence; in Bogen's words, "the darker, creepier, mysterious, unreal and sometimes supernatural kind favored in the commercial horror films of the United States, Mexico, South Africa, Europe, and East Asia."[4]

There are several reasons why horror cinema has only very recently emerged in Israel. The first is that genre cinema in general has been frowned upon by the Israeli film establishment, as it is in so many countries. Instead, an emphasis has been placed on "quality" drama and comedy that present an authentic, sometimes political or satirical view of Israeli life. In its review of 2014 (Israel's best year at the box office for indigenous Israeli films), *Cineuropa* concluded that Israeli audiences had put their trust in their country's films because "the industry proved that it could produce films of the highest quality, featuring subject matter that managed to create a big enough buzz to shift huge numbers of tickets."[5] The article makes no mention of *Big Bad Wolves*, which had been a sizable hit at home and also played theatrically in Spain, France, Japan and Greece. Lack of support from the Israeli film industry has meant that horror filmmakers had to finance, produce and distribute their films themselves. (The Israel Film Fund is starting to recognize the role of genre cinema.)

Independently financed, *Rabies* managed to attract some of Israel's key film and TV stars, who agreed to appear for minimum fees, an indication perhaps of how the younger generation of film industry players recognize the need to break from tradition in the bid for wider international audiences. Israeli films tended toward art house distribution abroad, but *Rabies* crossed over to genre fans through festival screenings and word-of-mouth in the blogosphere. Its success internationally paved the way for the horror films that followed.

A number of directors of Israeli horror films, including Keshales and Papushado, are graduates of Tel Aviv University Film School. *Battle of the Undead* was developed by students of the Tel Aviv University Film School; while *Cats on a Pedal Boat* originated at the Jerusalem Film School and draws on Troma comedy-horror and Israeli teen sex comedies *à la Lemon Popsicle* (1978) and *The Last American Virgin* (1982). All three horror films display a high level of cine-literacy, as well as a keen sense of popular cinema. At one level, *Big Bad Wolves* is a pastiche of American, English and Asian revenge thrillers and torture-porn slasher movies. "At another level," writes leading Israeli film critic Yair Raveh, "it uses those very movie clichés to explore the ways in which we see violence in our mega-visual culture."[6] Israeli horror films operate on a low-budget aesthetic. *JeruZalem* was filmed in a shaky-cam found-footage style on a budget of $250,000. *Freak Out* cost less than $150,000. And while Israeli star Lior Ashkenazi has acted in Keshales and Papushado's films, many of the other Israeli horror actors have been relative unknowns.

Something more that Israeli horror films have in common is their uniquely Israeli subject matter. In *Big Bad Wolves*, rival Israeli security veterans set out to find the head of a murdered girl. In *Battle of the Undead*, Israeli soldiers fight zombies in Lebanon; while the zombie uprising in *JeruZalem* takes place on Yom Kippur. The films are unmistakably Israeli; however, they are not overtly political. Instead, they are designed as escapist entertainment in a very real sense. As Bogen explains, "It seems fair to suggest that a generation of escapists in Israel have made their way from the devastations of terror in real life to the comforting fictions of films whose lack of realism is at least part of their appeal."[7]

This desire to escape from real-life horror into the fictional world of horror cinema is as much a way for audiences to deal with the violence around them as it is for the filmmakers to do the same. The caricaturing of violence thus becomes a form of catharsis for both filmmaker and audience. As the director of *Freak Out*, Boaz Armoni, explains, "There's something very violent in the day-to-day, in the street. [But] violence in entertainment is liberating. It's not real. It can free up tensions."[8] Yair Raveh describes the emergence of Israeli horror films in the following terms:

> The rise of Israeli horror tells us about one more change in Israeli cinema. While the older film scholars taught us that Israelis cannot make genre movies—the day-to-day life of the ordinary civilian is so ripe with existential tension that genre movies seem fake, they argued—a younger group of directors, who have escaped real life and found solace in American movies, are starting to say the opposite: Real life in Israel is so intense ... that making genre films that are violent, brutal and extreme, where the innocent suffer first, is an authentic aesthetic response.[9]

## Israeli Horror Films

After the success of *Rabies* internationally, Israeli cinema started to become noticed by new audiences abroad, and Israeli filmmakers have responded with an eye to the commercial appeal of horror films. *Cats on a Pedal Boat* describes itself as "a trashy comedy corresponding with American B movies, free of artistic aspirations and willing to only entertain."[10] High school sweethearts Mili (Dana Fridi) and Bill (Nitay Dagan) decide to spend some time on a Tel Aviv lake together. What starts out as a romantic pedal boat ride turns into something unexpected when their cat falls into contaminated water and becomes a bloodthirsty mutant. Added to this is a vicious admiral who pursues the couple. Bill calls on a motley bunch of sea scouts for help, and chaos ensues. Co-directors Yuval Mendelson and Nadav Hollander looked to popular Israeli teen sex comedies of the past, especially those of Boaz Davison, with Bill's frustrated attempts to take Mili's virginity a familiar device in such films as *Lemon Popsicle, Lemon Popsicle 2* (1979) and *Hot Bubblegum* (1981). There is also a strong splatstick element which evokes productions like *The Toxic Avenger* (1984). Many jokes are aimed at an Israeli audience, which helped the film to get a theatrical release at home.

Securing a North American release under the title *Battle of the Undead, Cannon Fodder* was billed as Israel's first zombie movie. It draws primarily on '80s Israeli war movies in its tale of a security task force dispatched to Lebanon, only to be confronted by the living dead. Eitan Gafny's feature debut was financed by an Indiegogo crowdfunding campaign and the Israel Film Fund (which also funded its festival screenings abroad). Despite his government-affiliated funding, Gafny insists that political comment was not his goal. However, the film was criticized in some quarters for its depiction of a heroic Israeli army fighting off mindless zombie hordes in the borderlands. According to the *Miami New Times*,

Many of the zombies—often women in traditional Muslim headscarves—are dispatched with a single bullet to the head after they've already been knocked to the ground. That this is being done by an Israeli military force that has crossed a border into another territory has some uncomfortable resonances.[11]

The *Battle of the Undead* trailer suggests that a more traditional war movie theme lies at the heart of the film. "The fight for borders has lost its meaning," an intertitle tells us. *Battle of the Undead* really explicates the old saying "War is Hell." As the Israeli army struggle to fight off the zombies, *Battle of the Undead* becomes reminiscent of such films as *Apocalypse Now* (1979) and *Saving Private Ryan* (1998), where the madness of conflict makes it easy for us to forget what we are fighting for.

On first glance, *JeruZalem* resembles *Battle of the Undead* in its depiction of an apocalypse that originates in Israel. Despite the obvious nod to *World War Z* (2013), it is more concerned with exploring the mysticism of the ancient city itself, a place where Christianity, Islam and Hebrew religions are considered holy. It is fitting, then, that the End of Days should stem from there, as it does in the film (and in the Bible). Co-directors Yoav Paz and Doron Paz tell the story as a found-footage piece, following three Jewish-American tourists and an Arab hotel owner as they attempt to survive the apocalypse which unleashes demons on the city that possess the living. Shot for $160,000 that the Paz brothers raised themselves, *JeruZalem* was sold to distributors in a number of countries, including in U.S. and the U.K., where it secured release on DVD. In many ways it resembles such generic American demon-possession films as *Constantine* (2005), *The Rite* (2011) and *The Devil Inside* (2012). However, its Jerusalem setting adds some originality. The ending is ambiguous and hints at the regenerative nature of Biblical apocalypse, a resurrection for the city and its people. As the filmmakers told *Starburst*, "The apocalypse starts but what's the next level of the apocalypse? Maybe a new level of something. Maybe a new change in the world."[12] The Paz brothers are currently planning a sequel that explores the need for people to put aside their cultural differences and battle the demons. In the meantime, they remade (in 2018) the silent classic *The Golem*, retaining the folkloric element of the original Jewish legend but with an element of Mary Shelley's *Frankenstein*. It tells the story of a woman who creates a Golem in the image of her dead son, to protect her small 17th century community from neighboring Russian Christians.

A number of Israeli filmmakers have used the horror genre to explore the Israeli experience of national military service. *Freak Out* was one of the first to do so. Set in a military outpost in Palestine, it concerns a young desk clerk sent to join three combat soldiers for a week of guard duty. The soldiers mercilessly bully the clerk. One night they leave him on guard while they go for a jolly time in a nearby town. The clerk soon realizes that he isn't alone on the outpost, and finds himself combatting a killer. A slow-burning film, *Freak Out* is largely devoted to the relationships between the four men, exploring how military service creates fear and aggression in them. The final act turns into a slasher movie, as each man is hunted by the killer. The film is a primarily a dark comedy with a uniquely Israeli feel; again, not too far removed from the coming-of-age comedy of *Lemon Popsicle*, with the barracks replacing the traditional high school locker room as the location of macho humor. Film scholar Ido Rosen says of Israeli army-horror films, "[F]or the young Israeli soldier, army service is a rite of passage, a test of masculinity, a ritual of admission into Israeli society. The makers of these horror films portray this experience as a nightmare."[13]

Eitan Gafny's second feature film, *Yaldey HaStav* (*Children of the Fall*, 2013), set on Yom Kippur in 1973, chronicles the start of the Arab-Israeli war from the point of view of Rachel (Noa Maiman), a Kibbutz volunteer. She has come to Israel to escape from her immigrant background and to convert to Judaism. But the Kibbutz members and soldiers from the nearby Israel Defence Forces are inhospitable to her and other refugee volunteers. When war breaks out on Yom Kippur, a killer stalks the Kibbutz. Like *Freak Out*, *Children of the Fall* uses slasher tropes to explore the incipient violence that exists in a military environment, and how this comes to affect civilians as well as the soldiers themselves.

*Mekulalim* (*The Damned*, 2018) continued this theme. Its director Evgeny Ruman has said, "Horror films are one way of airing and coping with the fears and anxieties that army service stirs up. These are powerful experiences that stay with people who served in the IDF for many years afterwards."[14] In *The Damned*, three soldiers on a desert training exercise find themselves descending into madness and turning against each other, as the desolate landscape plays tricks on their minds. It is reminiscent of *The Blair Witch Project* (1999), both in storyline and in its use of found footage. Are the soldiers acting out a curse placed upon them by a Bedouin woman? Or is isolation bringing on insanity? Either way, *The Damned* concerns young people caught up in a situation that they have no idea how to deal with. That film and the other Israel army-horror movies hinge on the idea of being besieged, the readiness for violent confrontation, and having easy access to weapons. As journalist Nirit Anderman has noted, "The Israeli nightmare is not about monsters and demons, but about the face looking back at us in the mirror."[15]

Avishai Sivan's *Tikkun* has been described as the most disturbing film ever made about Orthodox Judaism. Told in strikingly expressive black and white, the story concerns a Hasidic student, Haim-Aaron (Aharon Traitel), who, after a near-death experience, finds himself deeply alienated from his family and community. The devout life, to which he was once passionately committed, becomes a source of horror to him as, in his "reborn" state, he sees the hermetically sealed world of Judaism in a completely different, oppressive way. The power of Sivan's film lies in the subjectivity of its approach. Religious indoctrination is either desirable or horrible depending on the individual's point of view. Sivan renders this in a series of extraordinary images that take on a dream-like quality as experienced by Haim-Aaron. The effect is very much one of Freudian *Das Unheimliche*: Haim-Aharon's once-familiar world becomes unsettling and strange, to him and to us. It's a device that allows the filmmaker to draw attention to the rites and rituals of a religion in a way that removes us from it. The visual style of *Tikkun* has been compared to that of Darren Aronofsky's *Pi* (1998), and there have also been comparisons to David Lynch's *Eraserhead* (1976) in the way Sivan presents a totally abstracted world. But despite those similarities, *Tikkun* remains a unique—and truly indigenous—horror film.

## Rabies

Keshales and Papushado, the filmmakers behind *Rabies*, wanted to make their debut feature a very Israeli horror film. They were intent on providing something different to American horror movies in order to gain a foothold in the international film market. One of the ways they set out to do this is in the choice of setting. *Rabies* takes place in a nature reserve in Tel Aviv. According to Keshales, "The first gimmick that came into our heads was making the slasher in our film very different to the slasher in other films. Then we asked ourselves, what is more Israeli? Of course, the sun, the Mediterranean climate."[16] The filmmakers made the decision to shoot the entire film out of doors, with the action taking place during the course of a single day. "We thought if we could make people really afraid, if we could achieve proper tension in a film shot in broad daylight, we could really achieve something."[17]

*Rabies* plays adroitly with genre expectation in other ways: The killer is less of a monster than the other characters. His actions merely set off a chain reaction in those around him, and other characters end up killing each other. The filmmakers attribute inspiration for this decision to Pasquale Festa Campanile's 1977 thriller *Autostop rosso sangue* (*Hitch-Hike*), in which escaped bank robber David Hess takes a married couple (Franco Nero and Corinne Cléry) hostage. As the film progresses, the couple proves to be just as morally corrupt as the murderous hitch-hiker, and the film ends with Nero, having used the kidnapping as an opportunity to kill his wife, stealing Hess' money and effectively taking his place on the open

Adi (Ania Bukstein) contemplates the rapid escalation of violence in *Kalevet/ Rabies* (2010, Image Entertainment).

road as the eponymous "hitch-hiker." As Papushado notes, "Marriage is the biggest monster of *Hitch-Hike*."[18] Therefore, with *Rabies*, the filmmakers "wanted to do a film in which the usual monster became the less frightening aspect of the film and all the other characters, whom you expect to behave themselves and be the good guys, are the real monsters."[19]

In *Rabies*, the killer is a catalyst for the inherent aggression of the other characters. The situation they find themselves in (lost in the woods where a killer is on the loose) merely exacerbates existing tensions in the various relationships, and violence becomes the default when those tensions reach a certain point. Friends turn against friends, men against their lovers, women against men, policemen turn against their colleagues; and on it goes, until most of the characters are dead or dying. The film's over-arching theme is how easily violence begets violence in a society predicated on war and aggression. "Does Israel really need a serial killer to do the killing," Keshales and Papushado ask rhetorically, "or do we have enough killing in our country without appointing a trained murderer?"[20] The wilderness setting serves, as it so often does in horror films, to subject the characters to the law of the jungle, where human interaction is reduced to an animalistic level. However, survival alone isn't the cause of violence between the characters. The relationships all hinge on latent social aggression. "It's really a story about families, it's a story about friendships, it's a story about relationships with one thing in common: they're all ruined by intolerance and lack of communication."[21]

In the film, policeman Danny (Lior Ashkenazi) is estranged from his wife. He leaves many phone messages in an attempt at reconciliation. He becomes frustrated when his wife doesn't respond, and the messages become angry. Then, after he does manage to speak to her and patch things up with her, he realizes his error in leaving the abusive phone messages, and tries to be the first one home in order to erase them.

Keshales and Papushado present this latent aggression as symptomatic of a self-defeating behavior that afflicts Israeli society. Such behavior, the film suggests, can only lead to regret afterwards. In another subplot, two friends get into a fight over a woman, and this leads to a completely unnecessary and homicidal retaliation that leaves one of them dead; the tragic killing arises not so much from the heat of the moment, but from a seemingly conscious decision. But, the film asks, why would such an action be seen as an option if not for the state-sanctioned violence afflicting Israeli society?

The film's title is itself a play on genre expectation, as there is no literal rabies infection in the film. Instead, the title is metaphorical: In the film, aggression spreads like a virus, from character to character, infecting them as though they might have rabies, causing them to behave uncontrollably, irrationally and violently, resulting in madness and death. At the heart of this metaphorical "rabies" virus, according to the filmmakers, is social intolerance—and it is spreading on a global scale. As Keshales and Papushado put it, "We thought that the theme of intolerance and lack of communication was a local epidemic, but judging by the reaction abroad, intolerance is a global affair."[22]

## Big Bad Wolves

"What if Dirty Harry wandered by mistake into a Korean revenge film written by the Brothers Grimm?"[23] This is how Keshales and Papushado described their second film, which takes *Rabies'* central theme and focuses it into a "righteous avenger" narrative. In *Big Bad Wolves*, three men capture and torture a suspected pedophile in a story that initially seems like the standard vigilante movie. However, as they did in *Rabies*, the filmmakers challenge genre expectations in terms of tone and plot development. The "Big Bad Wolves" of the title are not so much those who, like the Wolf of "Little Red Riding Hood," prey on innocent children, as the vigilante types who seek vengeance on behalf of their raped and murdered daughters. Like *Rabies*, it ultimately becomes a reflection on the violence inculcated into Israel society. According to Keshales:

Cops Eli (Guy Adler), Arik (Yuval Nadborany) and Micki (Lior Ashkenazi) prepare to beat a confession out of suspected child-killer Dror (Rotem Keinan) in
*Big Bad Wolves* (2013, Magnet Releasing).

With *Big Bad Wolves*, we tried to look at the macho, male-dominated Israeli
society, but not upfront. First of all, it's a revenge comedy thriller, and once
the tone of the movie has been set, you start to think about what you're seeing.
What you're seeing is three guys who were in the army and all their instincts
from that time just come to life when the girl's life is in peril.[24]

*Big Bad Wolves* starts like a dark fairy tale, with lyrical slow-motion
footage of children playing hide-and-seek in the woods. We see one of the
girls hide in a closet inside an abandoned house, whence she is kidnapped
by an unseen assailant. The tone of the opening is unmistakably ironic, the
innocence of childhood as seen through an idealized lens. The filmmakers
have said how they intended the film to be a "revenge on parents" and in
many ways it is a cautionary tale against the lynch mob mentality that can
arise in response to pedophilia. Throughout the film, *Big Bad Wolves* leaves
us guessing whether the suspected murderer, a schoolteacher called Dror
(Rotem Keinan) is guilty or innocent of the crimes of which he is accused.

Following the dream-like opening credits, the film takes us straight
into the harsh reality of torture mentality. To learn the whereabouts of the
missing girl, police officer Micki (Ashkenazi) tortures Dror, an unethical
action captured on a mobile phone by a local teenager and uploaded onto
a website. Micki is suspended. The abducted girl's headless body is later

discovered in a field. Micki sets out to kidnap Dror and exact a confession. But *both* men are kidnapped by the dead girl's father, Gidi (Tzahi Grad), an ex–military man like Micki. Gidi and Micki take turns torturing Dror, who maintains his innocence throughout.

The film's central situation is this extended torture sequence, which takes place in Gidi's cellar. As in a number of torture porn films, the action unfolds in continuous time. However, it is at this point where Keshales and Papushado start to play with our expectations of the torture porn subgenre. The primary text for this scenario is the "ear-slicing" cop-torture scene of *Reservoir Dogs* (1992), elaborated upon in such films as *Saw* (2004) and *Hostel* (2005). It is perhaps no surprise that Quentin Tarantino has praised *Big Bad Wolves*, as it exercises a similarly playful approach to genre as Tarantino's own work. Where *Big Bad Wolves* differs from Tarantino's output is in the way that the generic subversion arises from a desire on the part of the filmmakers to offer a moral commentary. When Gidi's father Yoram (Dov Glickman) arrives unexpectedly, interrupting Dror's torture, we expect the patriarchal figure to intervene, to stop the torture on moral grounds. In other words, we expect the older man to become the film's moral voice. Instead, Papushado and Keshales add a darkly comic twist: Gidi's father is another military veteran, and not only does he *join in*, he reveals himself to be more practiced at torture techniques than the younger men.

With this subversive twist, *Big Bad Wolves* moves firmly towards absurdist black comedy. As the filmmakers explained, "We allowed ourselves to add layers of black comedy to this strange tale of justice because we wanted to show the absurdity in vengeful acts."[25] It becomes clear, as the irony of the scenario comes increasingly to the fore, that the filmmakers are twisting the subgenre towards social commentary. Thematically, *Big Bad*

The distraught Gidi (Tzahi Grad) will go to any lengths to find his daughter's head in *Big Bad Wolves* (2013, Magnet Releasing).

*Wolves* is a continuation of *Rabies*. According to Keshales, "You grow up in an environment where there is war in the air, you absorb it, you develop this survival instinct which is so strong, and sometimes can lead you to do horrific stuff in the name of survival, in the name of our children."[26] However, *Big Bad Wolves* warns against the attempt to legitimize violence. At the end, Micki learns that his own daughter has gone missing, and in the final scene, we discover that she is hidden behind a fake wall in Dror's house, unconscious. Before Micki can ask Dror to reveal the location of his daughter, Gidi kills Dror with a hacksaw. The film thus leaves us with a clear message: If the three Big Bad Wolves had not been intent on exacting violent revenge, the cop's daughter might have survived. As it is, Micki is left with no way of finding or saving his daughter. He has to live with the consequences of his own violent actions.

It is no coincidence that the same actor who plays Micki played the distraught cop in *Rabies*; both characters have to face the fact that violence brings with it consequences and regret. Thus, the events of the films serve as his punishment for his violence. The final word goes to the filmmakers: "We wanted to do a Dirty Harry movie where Dirty Harry gets punished for his deeds—personally, not because someone he knows dies."[27]

# 10

# Mexico

## *Tigers Are Not Afraid* (2017) and *The Untamed* (2016)

Mexican horror cinema has become synonymous with the name of Guillermo del Toro (who made his debut feature with *La invención de Cronos/Cronos* in 1993), but the genre goes much further back in that country's history. As Doyle Greene reports, from approximately 1957 to 1977, horror was one of Mexico's most popular exploitation genres, and featured "an array of vampires, Aztec mummies, mad scientists, ape-men and various other macabre menaces."[1] The best-known "Mexploitation" films are the *lucha libre* (Mexican professional wrestling) movies, often starring wrestling icon El Santo, a *luchador enmascarado* (masked wrestler) who fought assorted monsters, mummies and werewolves between 1958 and 1982. But Mexican horror goes back further still to the 1930s and the *fantástico* films of Juan Bustillo Oro (*Dos Monjes/Two Monks*, 1934; *El misterio del rostro pálido/Mystery of the Ghastly Face*, 1935). In between are the movies of Fernando Méndez, whose gothic works such as *El Vampiro* (*The Vampire*, 1957), *El Ataúd del Vampiro* (*The Vampire's Coffin*, 1958) and *Misterios de ultratumba* (*The Black Pit of Dr. M*, 1958) coincided with Mexican cinema's national decline in the late 1950s.

As Carlos Aguilar notes, in contrast to the nationalized film industry of the 1950s and 1960s, "Mexican horror has always managed to squeeze the genre's tropes into legends that reflect on the culture and struggles of its people at particular points in time."[2] This chapter will focus on two contemporary Mexican horror films that draw on the tradition of the Mexican *fantástico* to explore contemporary societal issues. *Vuelven* (*Tigers Are Not Afraid*, 2017), a social realist-fantasy horror set against the background of Mexico's drug wars, tells the story of Estrella (Paola Lara), a ten-year-old abandoned in a Mexican city after the disappearance of her mother. Estrella suspects that her mom was kidnapped, perhaps even killed by the local cartel. She joins with a gang of street orphans led by the volatile El Shine (Juan

Ramón López), in hopes of escaping both the cartel and the ghosts of those who have died in the drug wars.

*La región salvaje* (*The Untamed*, 2016) delves even deeper into the *fantástico* as a surreal science fiction allegory of domestic violence and repressed sexuality. Simone Bucio plays Verónica, a young woman in a small Mexican town who is drawn into a strange liaison with a couple who host an extraterrestrial creature that seeks interspecies sex with humans. Similarly transgressive to 2016's *Tenemos la carne* (*We Are the Flesh*), *The Untamed* arguably follows in the brutal and visceral tradition of Buñuel's Mexican films of the 1950s to present an explosion of repression and strange monsters from the id.

**Paola Lara as Estrella in *Vuelven/Tigers Are Not Afraid* (2017, Shudder).**

## *Mexican Horror*

Perhaps the most famous Latin American horror film of the 1930s is the George Melford–directed Spanish version of *Dracula* (1931), filmed on the same Universal sets as the Tod Browning version, using international actors and crew as part of Universal's push to supply product to Mexican and Latin American audiences—then as now, a considerable market. Celebrated for its visual flair and its franker portrayal of sexuality than its Bela Lugosi–starring counterpart, Melford's film showcased the formal and thematic experimentation characteristic of Mexican cinema's early talkies.

The influence of Eisenstein and German Expressionism can be keenly felt in horror films made in the 1930s, even as older traditions of magical realism infuse the works. Fernando de Fuentes' *El fantasma del convent* (*Phantom of the Convent*, 1934) is notable for its unusual narrative approach and expressionist style: Three friends get lost in a forest; a monk escorts them to a convent where they experience shifts of personality as their behavior starts to mirror a strange tale told by the monk. Already the filmmaking in this early horror is informed by magic realism in the way that a realistic view of the world is encroached upon increasingly by elements of the *fantástico*.

The screenwriter Juan Bustillo Oro has been described as the father of Mexican horror. A prolific filmmaker (over 60 films as a writer and director), Oro's directorial debut *Two Monks* told the story of two love rivals whose jealousy leads to the death of the woman they both loved. The men enter a monastery, where one suffers horrific hallucinations and tries to kill the other. *Two Monks* was conceived by Oro as a visual experiment: "I wanted to give the film an unreal atmosphere, making it enter an expressionist atmosphere. In this way I felt that I could expand the subject, achieve unusual cinematographic effects and give in to the profound influence that the German masters sealed in my imagination."[3] *Two Monks* was praised by André Breton as "a bold and unusual experiment,"[4] and it is easy to see why its story of *amour fou* struck a chord with surrealist sensibilities. Oro followed it with *Mystery of the Ghastly Face* in 1935, a horror film with science fiction elements: A scientist seeking the cure to a rare disease returns from distant lands accompanied by a mysterious stranger in a pale mask. An enigmatic, dreamlike film, *Mystery of the Ghastly Face* drew on the imagery of *The Cabinet of Dr. Caligari* and Carl Dreyer's *Vampyr*. Oro devoted most of his subsequent career to melodramas but returned to horror with *El hombre sin rostro* (*Man Without a Face*, 1950). A prototype *giallo*, it concerns a faceless killer hunting women, and the shady detective trying to catch him. Like *Two Monks, Man Without a Face* shows that Oro was ahead of his time: The film has been compared to *Psycho* as well as the 1961 Canadian 3D thriller *The Mask*.

As Greene notes, Mexican politics of the 1950s failed to produce "coherent visions of the national past and future,"[5] instead attempting to enculturate an ahistorical Mexican nationalism. The crucial loss of direction in Mexican politics in the 1950s had a damaging effect on cinema, creating a film industry that was unreflective of the problems and conditions of Mexican society. Added to this was a government-controlled film industry that required all films to pass censor boards, precluding any engagement in social or political controversy or criticism of the government. With pressure on producers and studios to fulfill government-stipulated quotas, and stiff competition from Hollywood, the Mexican film industry began concentrating on formula-based, "assembly line" product: "*comedias rancheras*; films based on dance fads; melodramas; horror vehicles *à la* Hollywood; American-style Westerns; and 'superhero' adventures in which masked cowboys or wrestlers took on a variety of evil-doers or monsters."[6]

On television, professional wrestling captured the interest of the nation until a government ban forced it off the small screen; film producers seized the opportunity to combine *lucha libre* with genre cinema. By doing so, not only could they capitalize on the box office appeal of real-life masked wrestling stars like Santo battling criminals and monsters, it allowed extended wrestling matches to be included in films, therefore circumventing the TV ban. The films were hugely popular; around 200 were produced between 1952 and 1983. It is difficult to make any great claims in terms of the quality of these productions (many of which incorporated outlandish and contrived plots), although they did give rise to a few directors of note. One of them, Fernando Méndez, made *Ladrón de cadavers/ The Body Snatcher* (1956) in which a masked grappler fights a mad scientist who replaces athletes' brains with those of gorillas. Méndez also directed a number of influential "straight" horror films in the late 1950s, starting with *The Vampire*. Basically an adaptation of Bram Stoker's novel *Dracula*, *The Vampire* had critical and box office success in Europe and Mexico, reportedly influencing Hammer to produce *Dracula* (*Horror of Dracula*) in 1958. (The plot also resembles that of *The Return of Dracula* [1958].) With rural Mexico as the setting, Germán Robles plays Conde Karol de Lavud, an aristocratic vampire recently arrived from Hungary; he takes a fancy to the throat of a young woman whose aunt has already fallen under his spell. With atmospheric art direction, and moody cinematography by Rosalío Solano, *The Vampire* deserves to be better known. Part of the reason for its neglect may be because in America its release was delayed until 1968, by which time it was taken as a cheap Mexican copy of the Hammer films that it is said to have inspired. However its success at the time helped Mexican producers to mount more gothic horror films outside of the *lucha libre*.

Méndez followed *The Vampire* with a quickly made sequel, *The Vampire's Coffin*, which saw the undead conde still seeking Marta, his lost love from the first film. As Greene notes, both films are typical of Mexploitation's "emphasis on Gothic atmospherics, melodramatics and long stretches of expository dialogue at the expense of taut action and consistent pacing."[7] Both take their cue from the Universal horror films of the 1930s, and appear quite stagebound today.

In *The Black Pit of Dr. M*, Méndez combined gothic horror with science fiction fantasy in a tale of two scientists who make a pact that the first to die will return to tell the other how to glimpse the afterlife; an intriguing premise that would later be used in *Brainstorm* (1983) and *Flatliners* (1990). Méndez continued to explore genre hybrids in *El grito de la muerte* (*The Living Coffin*, 1959), a notable horror-western shot in color. These and other noteworthy Mexican horror films such as *El Barón del terror* (*The Brainiac*, 1961), *El espejo de la bruja* (*The Witch's Mirror*, 1962) and *La maldición de la Llorona* (*The Curse of the Crying Woman*, 1963) were distributed in the U.S. by exploitation producer K. Gordon Murray, who created English-language TV versions and double-bill pairings for the likes of American International Pictures. According to Greene, Murray "single-handedly introduced Mexploitation cinema to America via late night television and drive-ins during the 1960s."[8] Unfortunately, Murray's dubbed versions are also the reason why, in Greene's words, "in the United States, Mexploitation films have been widely ridiculed; at best they are granted a 'so bad they're good' status." More recently, DVD labels such as Casa Negra have released the restored Spanish-language original versions of many of these titles, and modern horror fans are now beginning to appreciate these films, a number of which can be considered classics.

The gothic tradition continued through the 1960s and 1970s in a quartet of films made by Carlos Enrique Taboada, a director who, alongside Oro, Méndez and del Toro, can be considered a master. *Hasta el viento tiene miedo* (*Even the Wind Is Afraid*, 1968) starred Argentinian-Mexican screen idol Marga López as the disciplinarian headmistress of an all-girls boarding school haunted by the vengeful spirit of a student who hanged herself there five years before. Within this simple premise, Taboada weaves a tale of dread and sexual repression worthy of Hitchcock, with imagery reminiscent of Mario Bava's fantasy films. In a particularly striking sequence, Alicia Bonet awakens from a nightmare to see a pair of legs dangling above her bed. A flash of lightning reveals the shadow of the girl on the wall behind her, a noose around her neck. The wraith later appears in her white nightdress in a forest at night, wind blowing the trees violently. It is difficult not to think of Dario Argento's *Suspiria* (1977) in relation to Taboada's film. *Even the Wind Is Afraid* was remade in 2007, but a decent Blu-ray-DVD release of the original has yet to happen.

López returned in Taboada's *El libro de piedra* (*The Book of Stone*, 1969) as the governess of an introverted young girl; the child believes herself to be influenced by the spirit of a boy whose statue stands in the garden. Generally lacking the visuals of *Even the Wind Is Afraid*, *The Book of Stone* instead focuses on the dynamic of the bourgeois family at the center of the haunting. Critics have compared it to *The Innocents*, and the ghost of Henry James certainly looms large. Taboada returned to the horror genre in 1975 with *Más negro que la noche* (*Darker Than Night*). This time Poe is referenced, in the black cat at the heart of the plot. Four young women move into a house that one of them has inherited from her aunt. The will stipulates that the aunt's black cat must be looked after. When the cat turns up dead, the four women find themselves the victims of ghostly goings-on.

*Darker Than Night* is essentially a generation gap horror film: The liberated young are victimized by the vindictive older generation (in the guise of the aunt's ghost). In places it resembles Sergio Martino's *Torso* (1973), although it is far less graphic. (When it was remade in 2014, the reviews were lukewarm.)

Taboada returned in 1984 with what may be his best *fantástico*. *Veneno para las hadas* (*Poison for the Fairies*) again deals with the conflict between tradition and modernity: An aristocratic young girl convinces a new girl at school that she is a witch and enlists her new friend as her accomplice. Together they embark upon a macabre adventure that ends in murder. Taboada tells the story entirely from the perspective of the two children, with adults barely figuring at all. However, traditions of the past as fairy tales and superstition influence the children's behavior despite their modern education that stresses a rational outlook. It is easy to see how Taboada could have an influence on del Toro with this film: It is a very dark fairy tale concerning childhood.

Another strand of Mexican cinema in the 1970s took a much more graphic approach to taboo subject matter. Perhaps most notorious is René Cardona's *La Horripilante bestia humana* (1969). Released in the U.S. as *Night of the Bloody Apes* in 1972, Cardona's low-budget quickie found itself on the "video nasties" list in England during the 1980s for its real-life footage of open-heart surgery (added by the producers for more tolerant foreign markets) and its sexual violence. Cardona had remade his own 1963 *Las luchadoras contra el médico asesino* (*Doctor of Doom*), which like Méndez's earlier *The Body Snatcher* featured masked wrestlers, mad doctors and gorilla-organ transplants, but with extra added gore, medical procedures, nudity, rape and female wrestling footage spliced in for good measure by the producers, who were keen to trade on the increasingly graphic nature of American horror in the early 1970s. This crassly exploitative approach is probably why it met with censorship problems in a number of territories, including Australia. In the U.K., it remained banned until 1999.

Running a close second to *Night of the Bloody Apes* in terms of sheer Mexploitation value is *Sátanico Pandemonium: La Sexorcista* (*Satanico Pandemonium*, 1975), Gilberto Martínez Solares' potent mix of nunsploitation, *The Exorcist*–inspired satanic possession and *The Devils* (1971)–type profanity and forbidden sexual fantasy. Cecilia Pezet is the young nun tempted by Satan to cross over to the dark side. The result: 90 minutes of carnal desire and bloody murder. Like Ken Russell, Solares is not afraid to attack the Roman Catholic Church and its hypocrisies. Not surprisingly, the film was heavily censored by the Mexican government on its first release, but has since become a cult favorite.

A companion piece of sorts is *Alucarda, la hija de las tinieblas*

(*Alucarda*, 1977), another convent-set Satanic horror with many of the same themes as *Satanico Pandemonium*. Based on Sheridan La Fanu's *Carmilla*, it concerns the friendship between two young nuns who fall under the spell of a Pan-like spirit in the woods. Soon they are indulging their sexual desires with each other, performing satanic rituals and leading an orgy of flagellation in the convent. Like Taboada's films, the overarching theme of *Alucarda* is the clash between tradition and modernity, but its director Juan López Moctezuma chooses to dramatize this clash through a series of visibly transgressive actions that exemplify the strand of Mexican horror cinema which celebrates the breaking of screen taboo. We will see this tradition continuing with *The Untamed*.

Although *Cronos* put *fantástico* back on the map in the early 1990s, the current wave of Mexican horror arguably stems from the financial and critical success of Jorge Michel Grau's *Somos lo que hay* (*We Are What We Are*, 2010). Mexican cinema has come into its own in the last 20 years or so with films like *Amores Perros* (2000), which depicts the brutal reality of life in modern Mexico City, a place where (on-screen, at least) life is cheap and survival often calls for desperate measures. At first glance, *We Are What We Are* seems to follow in this school of "poverty cinema" and it shares the same languid pace and formal asceticism of other celebrated Mexican offerings such as Alfonso Cuarón's *Y Tu Mamá También* (*And Your Mother Too*, 2001). But as we get further into the film, it becomes apparent that *We Are What We Are* is also close in theme to classic 1970s English and American horror films like *Frightmare* (1974) and *Death Line* (1972) in its use of the cannibalism motif to explore degenerate families.

In his book *Hearths of Darkness*, Tony Williams wrote of the family as an instrument of repression, as a way of turning out docile members of society.[9] *We Are What We Are* manages to explore this idea pretty neatly within its brief (80-minute) running time. We are firmly in Freudian territory: The Oedipal Trajectory forms the thesis of the film. (That's the process by which male family members are socialized to take on patriarchal roles within the family, and by extension, wider society, thus ensuring the continuance of male power structures.) When the father of a poor Mexican family unexpectedly dies, it falls to his sensitive son, Alfredo (Francisco Barreiro), as the eldest, to take on the role of provider. This family, however, survives by eating human meat and Alfredo seems ill-equipped temperamentally to take on the responsibility of hunting down victims. While his mother Patricia (Carmen Beato) sits in judgment, waiting for Alfredo to prove his mettle, younger brother Julián (Alan Chávez) eyes the father role for himself, while his sister Sabine (Paulina Gaitán) manipulates them *both* like Lady Macbeth, finally goading them into action.

Logically, in the film, cannibalism as the family "ritual" is presented as the social norm, not a deviation from it. Although poverty may be a contributory factor, cannibalism is seen as a monstrous extension of patriarchal family values and a way of holding the family unit together in the face of social change. An image from Buñuel's *Los Olvidados* (*The Young and the Damned*, 1950) springs to mind: In a nightmare, the child sees his mother come towards him holding a dripping hunk of dead flesh. This image, with its evocation of the child's fear of the mother resonates throughout *We Are What We Are*.

The women in the family work towards perpetuating the patriarchal power structure. The Oedipal Trajectory, according to Freud, functions by dissuading the male child from identifying with the mother through the fear of castration—both literally and symbolically through the denial of power within the family structure, a demotion, if you will, within the pecking order—so that the male child should become like his father. The successful completion of the trajectory results in the male child taking on the characteristics of heterosexual masculinity to become the virile, aggressive patriarch. Unfortunately, Alfredo falls short somewhat, harboring homosexual feelings and suffering Oedipal guilt because he is unable to live up to his mother's expectations. During one of his hunts, he picks up a victim in a gay nightclub and brings him home. We have seen Alfredo wrestling with his sexual desires and for a brief moment, we think that he might liberate himself from the repression of his family life by breaking the social norms. But his repression is too great for him to take that step.

Although the women in the film maintain their gender roles within the family structure (the men bring home the meat, the women prepare it), both mother and daughter act out their power envy (or penis envy) in their treatment of Alfredo. Although they devote their frustrated energies to the perpetuation of patriarchy within the family, they are excluded from the wider world of money, power and politics. Their resentment at this exclusion shows itself in their secretly despising Alfredo and his privileged position within the family. Patricia forbids him to bring home a prostitute for them to eat because her husband enjoyed the privilege—as befits the patriarch—of consorting with prostitutes. Patricia later brings home a man for herself, on the pretext of providing a meal for her family, and then is forced to kill him. The film shows that in this patriarchal family, hate masquerades as love. The only priority, Patricia points out, is that in time of crisis, at least one family member survives, so that the ritual can be preserved and continued. This plays itself out in the final scenes as the police close in and a shoot-out ensues. As Patricia flees, leaving her children to their fate, the family finally implodes: Alfredo attacks Sabine and is shot by Julián, who is himself shot and killed by the police.

Interestingly, Grau positions the prostitutes—in their deviation from the social norm—as a potentially positive alternative to the patriarchal family. This is, of course, another reason for Patricia's antagonism towards them: They pose an ideological threat to family values. Grau depicts them as a social collective, a sisterhood with their own moral code (which is more honorable than Patricia's). As Patricia rests after fleeing the police shootout, the whores converge on her and beat her to death.

With the cannibal family wiped out (only Sabine is left alive), is the "family ritual" over? I will not reveal the film's conclusion but suffice it to say that in the patriarchal society of *We Are What We Are* indoctrination runs deep and old ways are hard to change. The clash between tradition and modernity in terms of gender roles remains unresolved.

## Tigers Are Not Afraid

Adopting a social-realist visual aesthetic, Issa López's dark parable of the Mexican drug wars of the last decade and its effect on the children of Mexico City at first glance resembles "child gang" films like Brazil's *Cidade de Deus* (*City of God*, 2003) and South Africa's *Tsotsi* (2005). In these works, we follow the lives of street kids as they attempt to survive the slums of their respective cities; they try to escape the criminal gangs that run their communities but are inevitably drawn into a life of crime, violence and murder. The films comment not only on the huge disparity between rich and poor in their respective countries but on a corrupt political system that gives no protection to those most disadvantaged—the children of poverty. Already mentioned is the *Young and the Damned*, Buñuel's masterpiece about child street gangs in a Mexico City slum; it combined social realism and surrealism. The dream sequence described above is a good example of Buñuel's dictum that neorealist reality is "incomplete, conventional and above all rational," that "the poetry, the mystery, all that completes and enlarges tangible reality is utterly lacking."[10] Instead, Buñuel imbues *The Young and the Damned* (as he does his other films) with dreams, memories and fantasies to express the subjective nature of reality. Similarly, López adopts a child's perspective throughout *Tigers Are Not Afraid*: We experience the world through the eyes of the ten-year-old protagonist, Estrella—and the *fantástico* is incorporated as a part of that.

The film opens with El Shine (Juan Ramón López), leader of a gang of street orphans, stealing the gun and iPhone of drug cartel member Caco (Ianis Guerrero). The cartel, known as the Huascas, is led by local politician El Chino (Tenoch Huerta), who is involved in human trafficking. The Huascas abduct Estrella's mother (and later kill her).

We are then introduced to Estrella at school. Her class is working on an assignment involving a fairy tale prince who wanted to muster the inner strength of a ferocious tiger. (The metaphor will become important to Estrella as a point of identification.) The class is disrupted by a shooting in the street outside. As the pupils crouch on the floor, Estrella's teacher gives the frightened girl three sticks of blackboard chalk, each of which will grant her a wish. Immediately, then, López juxtaposes a social-realist scene (Shine stealing the gun from Caco) with one which signals the *fantástico* to come. In the sequence that follows, surrealism comes to the fore. Estrella walks home and sees the body of

Juan Ramón López plays El Shine, leader of the street gang, in *Vuelven/Tigers Are Not Afraid* (2017, Shudder).

a man shot by the police. A pool of blood develops around his body. A line of his blood appears to follow Estrella home and encroaches into her apartment, as she discovers her mother missing. The line of blood functions as a literalism of the film's central metaphor (as do later scenes of corpses appearing to Estrella): victims of the Mexican drug wars returning from the grave to seek recompense for their deaths. Some critics found this aspect of the film a little obvious. According to the *Los Angeles Times*, "[T]he emotion and the horror might have taken still deeper root if the world of the movie felt less hectic and more coherently realized, if the supernatural touches and occasional jump scares welled up organically from within rather than feeling smeared on with a digital trowel."[11] But there is no disputing that this early scene with the line of blood is genuinely surreal, reminiscent of David Cronenberg's literalization of a philosophical idea as an image of body horror.

Fleeing her apartment into the slums, Estrella is taken under the wing of Shine and his gang. Now she must go through a rite of passage: She is told to shoot Caco, who has kidnapped one of the street kids. Estrella agrees, but uses one of her wishes to ask that she doesn't have to do it. When she arrives at Caco's apartment, she finds him already dead (we later learn that he has been shot by Chino). Realizing that the Huascas are now after them, Shine and the others go into hiding. In a moment of bonding with the boys, Estrella tells them the fairy tale of the prince who must be brave like a tiger. At this point, the film moves into the territory of Stephen King's *It* or even Peter Pan and the Lost Boys. We remember that the protagonists are children battling evils of the adult world, and that their strength lies in their closeness as a group. Throughout the film, the supernatural encroaches ever more keenly on Estrella and we realize that spirits of the dead are seeking vengeance on El Chino (and what he represents). There are shades of del Toro in this aspect of the film, in particular his Mexican-Spanish co-production *El espinazo del diablo* (*The Devil's Backbone*, 2001). Like that film, *Tigers Are Not Afraid* might be described as a humanist ghost story.

However, there is an element of ambiguity in Estrella's ghostly visions that enriches the film: Is Estrella able to see and communicate with the dead? Or is this her fantasy? Are the ghosts a figment of her imagination? The beauty of *Tigers Are Not Afraid* is that both interpretations are valid. Even though her mother is gone, Estrella is able to escape the clutches of the gang, able to escape her fate. The final image shows her climbing out of a burning building and into an open field in which she encounters a tiger that has escaped from the zoo. In the end, through her own inner strength, Estrella, like the tiger, prevails.

## The Untamed

Amat Escalante's *The Untamed* presents a contemporary Mexico where family values are strong, but sex and love fragile, and hypocrisy, homophobia and machismo run rife. Set in a small city in Mexico, the film focuses on the marriage of a young woman called Alejandra (Ruth Ramos). She works at her in-laws' candy factory and raises her two children with husband Ángel (Jesús Meza). Like the brutish husband in Buñuel's *Él* (1953), Ángel sublimates his repressed sexuality in a show of machismo and domestic violence. Alejandra seeks solace from her failing marriage from something that is beyond her control: a tentacled creature, kept by a scientist and his wife in a remote house. The scientist, Signor Vega (Oscar

**Alejandra (Ruth Ramos) prepares to meet a creature of the id in** *La región salvaje/The Untamed* **(2016, Strand Releasing).**

Escalante), explains to Alejandra that the creature is "the primitive part of the self." Like Isabelle Adjani in Andrzej Zulawski's *Possession* (1981), Alejandro finds sexual fulfillment with a creature from the id, the one that lurks behind the rational façade of the everyday.

*The Untamed* opens with Verónica—one in a long line of the creature's victims/human lovers—already in thrall to the pleasure and the pain of sexual congress with it. She emerges from her latest sexual encounter with a deep wound in her side which forces her into hospital. There she meets Fabián, Alejandro's brother, who works as a nurse. The two become friends. (Both are fated to die because of their developing sexual addiction to the creature—which itself can be seen as a reaction to the repression fostered by their environment.)

We then see Alejandra as Ángel makes love to her dispassionately, from behind. Sex with him is unsatisfying for her, and she masturbates in the shower afterwards. Their marriage is failing but they stay together because of the children. There is also the sense that they are keeping up appearances for the sake of Ángel's bourgeois parents, who own the candy factory where Alejandra works on the production line. (Her in-laws will later try to take Alejandra's children away from her.)

Ángel's repressed homosexuality is at the root of the problem with their marriage. Unbeknownst to Alejandra, Ángel is having a love affair with Fabián. However, he will not admit his homosexuality, and instead hides behind a macho homophobia. (He later beats up Alejandra in a display of self-loathing machismo.) Fabián's self-esteem is eroded by his relationship with Ángel, who will not express his true feelings, and he breaks off the affair.

Verónica draws Fabián into her world of sexual pleasure with the creature; the encounter leaves Fabián badly hurt. When he is found naked and unconscious beside a stream, the police believe that he has been the victim of an assault by Ángel. Alejandra discovers text messages between Ángel and Fabián and she informs on her husband, who is arrested. Ángel is forced to move in with his parents and contemplates suicide before attempting a reconciliation with Alejandra. Meanwhile, Verónica introduces Alejandra to the Vegas, and she experiences sexual ecstasy with the creature.

It is interesting that while Verónica (who tries to wean herself off the creature but inevitably returns to it), Fabián and, eventually, Ángel die as a result of their addictions, Alejandra is empowered by her sexual encounters with the creature. Her repression is perhaps less a matter of self-denial than a frustrating but necessary suppression of her sexual needs for the sake of her marriage and children. The final image is of Alejandra with her children. We get the sense that she will not be destroyed like the others; that her affair with the creature is a transition for her, a libidinous one. Her sexuality is "untamed." Escalante's film shows us that Mexican *fantástico* is ultimately a return of the repressed.

# 11

# South Korea

*Train to Busan* (2016)
and *The Wailing* (2016)

In 1999, the success of Hideo Nakata's *Ringu* (*Ring*, 1998) led to a renaissance of Japanese horror (or "J-horror"). Titles that followed include: *Cure* (1997), *Jisatsu sâkuru* (*Suicide Club*, 2002), *Ju-On: The Grudge* (2002), *Honogurai mizu no soko kara* (*Dark Water*, 2002), *Yogen* (*Premonition*, 2004). Distributors in the West were quick to capitalize: The DVD label Tartan Extreme, for example, featured auteurs like Nakata, Kiyoshi Kurosawa (*Akarui mirau/Bright Future*, 2003), Shinya Tsukamoto (*Rokugatsu no hebi/A Snake in June*, 2002) and Takashi Miike (*Ôdishon/Audition*, 1999).

Japan was not the only country to benefit from the Asian Horror "explosion." Thailand contributed with *Gin gwai* (*The Eye*, 2002) and *Shutter* (2004); and while Malaysia also produces many horror films, few of them secure distribution in the West. Perhaps the most significant emergence during this time was South Korean horror, or "K-horror," with key titles that include *Yeogo goedam* (*Whispering Corridors*, 1998), *Pon* (*Phone*, 2002), *Janghwa, Hongryeon* (*A Tale of Two Sisters*, 2003), *Gwoemul* (*The Host*, 2006), *Gosa* (*Death Bell*, 2008), *Ang-ma-reul bo-at-da* (*I Saw the Devil*, 2010), *Gok-seong* (*The Wailing*, 2016) and *Busanhaeng* (*Train to Busan*, 2016). "K-horror" has become so influential that it rivals "J-horror" in terms of its popularity with film fans. As Daniel Martin has pointed out, marketing practices have occasionally resulted in Korean horror films being mistakenly perceived as works of Japanese cinema. There are, of course, crossover points; however, "K-horror" has its own distinct set of culturally specific fears "played out on screen in the form of ghosts and monsters, tales of treachery, revenge and redemption."[1]

The ghost story has a tradition in Japanese horror dating back to *Ugetsu Monogatari* (*Tales of Ugetsu*, 1953), *Kaidan* (*Kwaidan*, 1964) and *Onibaba* (1964). These films drew on the legend of the "hannya," the vengeful female spirit, but also brought in commentary on the effects of modern technology and the relationship between the present and the past. According to James Marriot, Japan's program of rapid modernization after World War II had left many fearing the loss of Japan's traditional culture.[2] Mizoguchi's film, for example, expresses a sense of loss and nostalgia, a harking back to a simpler past. Japanese films continue to explore these themes. But some, like *Ring*, characterize the past as monstrous, repressive and a source of vengefulness.

Many Japanese (and South Korean) films after *Ring* were imitators of "the long-haired, pale-skinned creepy lady,"[3] and the "hannya" cycle eventually exhausted itself in Japan. However, "J-Horror" has diversified to include other subgenres like zombie movies (*Junk*, 2001) and splatstick comedies (*Deddo sushi/Dead Sushi*, 2012).

Beginning in 1999, Korea's new wave was born from the country's economic restructuring of the 1990s. Thanks to hi-tech industrialization, Korea is the world's ninth largest economy, with a large defense budget and a highly urbanized population. The success of action movie *Shiri* (1999) in its own country and abroad sparked interest in Korea's film industry from the West, and Korean distributors started putting out a range of movies that included action, art house and horror.

As Martin observes, *Whispering Corridors* marked a turning point for the Korean horror film industry and proved popular enough to spawn

Lost and alone in the zombie apocalypse: Soo-an (Su-an Kim) in *Busanhaeng/ Train to Busan* (2016, Well Go USA Entertainment).

a new cycle of Korean horror. Within this cycle, two basic types of horror film have emerged: the ghost story that takes its cue from Korean folklore, and the apocalypse-disaster movie that draws heavily on American science fiction–disaster movie tropes. This chapter will focus on two recent "K-horror" movies, *The Wailing* and *Train to Busan*, as recent examples of each school.

## The Importance of Myth and Folklore to K-Horror

As Alison Peirse and Daniel Martin explain in their book *Korean Horror Cinema*, classic Korean horror is a cinema of folklore and ghosts, of "gumiho" and "wonhon," primarily if not exclusively supernatural.[4] Ingrained tales of animal transformation prevalent in Korean culture have permeated into the nation's horror cinema, in the forms of animal spirits that possess characters, as in *Go-hyang-i: Jook-eum-eul bo-neun doo gae-eui noon* (*The Cat*, 2011), and the ubiquitous fox-maiden (gumiho) who has frequented Korean films since *Cheonnyeon ho* (*Thousand Year-Old Fox*, 1969).

Vengeful ghosts (wonhon) have appeared in Korean films since 1924's *Jang-hwa and Hong-ryeon* (*The Story of Jang-hwa and Hong-ryeon*). In the classic Korean horror film, according to Peirse and Martin, when good people die, they return to seek revenge; when bad people commit evil, they are punished by permanent death. Suffering is shared by all parties but justice ultimately prevails. Kim Jee-Woon's break-out hit *A Tale of Two Sisters* is, in fact, based upon the same fable as was *The Story of Jang-hwa and Hong-ryeon* ("The Story of Rose and Lotus"), which tells of two young girls murdered by their stepmother only to return as ghosts seeking retribution. As Martin points out, Korean horror's emergence in the 1960s, and its resurgence in the late 1990s and into the following decades can be seen as a continuation of such myths and folk tales: "a cinema … of killers and avengers both human and monstrous … of secrets and revenge, of justice and tragedy, of suffering both physical and emotional."[5]

In 2009, an article in *Asian Correspondent* posed the question: Why do Korean horror movies have only female ghosts? The article suggests that one reason may be because "in the past, women were systematically repressed and invisible." Through ill treatment, "they entered a freakish state and the result was for them to take care of their grudge through vengeance. The prevalence of women ghosts in so many (Asian) horror movies … can be seen as due to that freakish state brought on by repression."[6] In a number of recent Korean horror films, the focus has been on a person seeking revenge rather than on the victim of a vengeful spirit. This is said to constitute both an attempt by Korean filmmakers to integrate foreign influences into their narratives, in order to appeal to an international market, and an expression of social anger built up in the populace during the country's transition to democracy in the 1990s. *Seuseung-ui eunhye* (*Bloody Reunion*, 2006) concerns a psychologically damaged young woman's revenge on her classmates and the teacher who ruined her life. The film presents the killer as highly sympathetic and her desire for revenge understandable. Andrew Hock Soon Ng has argued that Southeast Asian horror films have proven "refreshingly dissident in their subtle redrawing of gender boundaries" traditionally found in a region "noted for its strict adherence to gender hierarchies that plot women as secondary and inferior to men." According to Ng, in Southeast Asian horror films, women, when transformed into or aligned with monsters, "discover a new and empowered sense of self otherwise denied them."[7] In this way, then, recent South Korean horror movies, while relying on myth and folklore, have become recalibrated in ways that give them modern meanings and often reveal an oppositional stance that questions the logic of the status quo.

## The Impact of Recent Political and Social Change on K-Horror

Martin speaks of an emerging subcycle of Korean cinema designed for the global market, of which films like *I Saw the Devil* and *Bloody Reunion* are notable examples. While these films capitalize on the success of previous Korean hits such as *Oldeuboi* (*Oldboy*, 2003) and/or appropriate Western horror tropes such as the slasher in their narratives (as does *Bloody Reunion*), the films also reflect a great deal of cultural specificity. Korean sci-fi disaster movies, such as *Haeundae* (*Tidal Wave*, 2009), *Ta-weo* (*The Tower*, 2012), *Yeon-ga-si* (*Deranged*, 2012) and *Gamgi* (*Flu*, 2012) are interesting hybrids in this respect. Although heavily influenced by American films like *Outbreak* (1995) and *Deep Impact* (1998), the Korean sci-fi disaster epics speak to contemporary social and political tensions in the region, while also addressing specific cultural concerns, including gender equality.

South Korea is a liberalized society: Asia's most advanced democracy, with high government transparency, universal voting rights, universal healthcare, freedom of religion and women's rights. In contrast to this, though, are its internal stresses. South Korea has high international migration, from China and other countries. The education system is notoriously competitive, with social stigma attached to non-graduates, and a high suicide rate among children and teenagers. The system has been criticized as rigidly conformist, stifling creativity and innovation in industry and commerce. And while the country enjoys international trading partnerships with the E.U., America and Canada, and is one of the G20 summit countries and a part of the United Nations, the influence of the West is also perceived as a potential threat to the Korean identity. Perhaps most pressingly, South Korea has a long history of invasion by nearby countries, and ongoing tensions with North Korea have intensified since Kim Jong-un came to power and stepped up the North's nuclear weapons program. It is perhaps not surprising that a film such as *Flu* should play so heavily on the country's socio-political fears, as well as continuing scientific and medical concerns regarding epidemics of SARS and the H5N1 virus. The COVID-19 world pandemic is an obvious touchstone for future horror films internationally; but past Southeast Asian pandemics have fueled a number of virus-related horror movies in the region.

*Flu* depicts the outbreak of a deadly strain of avian flu in a Seoul suburb. Tellingly, the virus is brought into South Korea by illegal immigrants from Hong Kong. As the epidemic swells, the authorities order a complete lockdown of the city, while politicians, international clinicians and military tacticians try to agree on a containment strategy, aware of the political and humanitarian disaster that is likely to ensue should the virus spread beyond South Korean borders. *Flu* takes its cue from the 2003 SARS outbreak in Hong Kong, which caused international concern about the sudden and seemingly unpreventable nature of modern pandemics. The media coverage of the pandemic and ensuing mass panic becomes another feature of *Flu*'s social commentary. As *Variety* wrote of the film, "It delivers a transfusion of harrowing realism, government duplicity and dripping sentimentality."[8] The country's social infrastructure very quickly collapses, and the government is clearly to blame for its inability to contain the virus. But *Flu* very quickly counterpoints this with recuperation of South Korean authority. When the Americans threaten to take control of the situation, the South Korean president must step up. He orders his soldiers to stop firing on fleeing civilians and forces the Americans to cancel a planned air strike on the city. At the heart of *Flu* is South Korea's fear of losing its autonomy, both as a nation and as a newly formed democracy. The virus outbreak is less of a threat to the country than the resulting political destabilization both internally and in terms of South Korea's international relations. In *Flu*, these threats are assuaged, and trust in the government restored. (Interestingly, South Korea's response to the COVID-19 pandemic of 2020 was thought to be exemplary in the ways the initial outbreak was contained and the economic infrastructure protected, although tensions between civilians and the authorities were also reported.) By contrast, in *Train to Busan*, the reaffirmation of the political status quo is ambiguous at best.

# Train to Busan

In contrast to *Flu*, the point of conflict in Yeon Sang-ho's zombie apocalypse *Train to Busan* is less between the populace and the impositions of authority made upon them in an attempt to contain a deadly virus from becoming a pandemic, and more between the various sectors of South Korean society itself. As in his previous film *Seoulyeok* (*Seoul Station*, 2015), an animated tale of a sex worker's attempt to both free herself from her personal situation and to survive a zombie epidemic, Yeon presents the military as ruthless in their attempts to contain the outbreak, with the government treating fleeing survivors as insurrectionists. In an interview with *Korean Cinema Today*, Yeon said that he wanted to depict society's collective rage in a "simple, powerful way" by making a zombie film "in which zombies are among people protesting for the democratization of Korea."⁹ The government in Yeon's films is the oppressor, and this is presented as a given. Thus negotiation between the individual survivors becomes the main focus instead.

Seok-woo (Yoo Gong) is a fund manager whose workaholism has led to his estrangement from his wife, and his neglect of his young daughter, Soo-an (Su-an Kim). He has spent his adult life helping to enable South Korea's economic growth, but is now beginning to regret the sacrifices he has made in terms of his family. His attempt to get himself and his daughter by train to Busan, where his wife lives, is also an attempt at reconciliation—a desire on his part to atone for his past neglect. The actions of the faceless government in response to the zombie outbreak suggest that Seok-woo's personal sacrifice in the name of his country has been somewhat in vain.

Shortly after boarding the train, father and daughter get caught up in the zombie outbreak along with the other passengers, who form a cross-section of South Korean society. These include a pair of elderly sisters, a man and his pregnant wife, a homeless man and a mercenary businessman. The latter, Coo Yon-suk (Eui-sung Kim), becomes the film's main antagonist; his selfish behavior causes the deaths of several of the survivors and puts him at odds with Seok-woo.

A number of critics have commented on similarities with Bong Joon-Ho's underrated *Snowpiercer* (2013), a dystopian science fiction film set on a futuristic train in which the survivors of an ecological apocalypse have forged a rigidly class-demarcated continuation of society (with the rich enjoying a life of luxury in the front carriages, while the train itself is powered by the workers at the rear). Class conflict is less a factor in *Train to Busan*. Instead, it is the clash between the self-centered Yon-suk and the democratically minded Seok-woo that drives the film. What kind of society

**Seok-woo (Yoo Gong) prepares to battle more zombies in *Busanhaeng/Train to Busan* (2016, Well Go USA Entertainment).**

do South Koreans want to make for themselves, the film asks, suggesting that democracy relies on a willingness to place the welfare of others before our own individual wants and needs.

As in so many zombie narratives, selfish actions lead to zombie infection. Yon-suk's attempts to save himself inevitably lead to the other survivors succumbing to the zombie bite and becoming zombies themselves. A number of characters barricade themselves in the train's carriages, refusing to let others in; as a result, the infection spreads through the train. When they arrive at Daejeon Station, the protagonists find the whole city overrun by zombies and have to *re*-board the train. Gradually the decent, caring citizens such as the homeless man and the two sisters sacrifice themselves to save others.

In the end, Seok-woo, too, has to sacrifice his life to save his daughter. Symbolically, he and the other survivors have boarded a new locomotive—a new start and prospect for their future—but he is bitten as he does battle with Yon-suk (who is in the process of turning into a zombie). As he begins to zombify, Seok-woo throws himself from the train to a certain death, but with the reward of knowing that he has saved the most precious thing in his life.

*Train to Busan* ends ambiguously. Soo-an, the only survivor, arrives at Busan and hurries to safety through a train tunnel where—unbeknownst to her—snipers are stationed to kill the infected. Orders are given for her to be shot. However, when the soldiers hear Soo-an singing a lullaby to herself, they realize that she is not a zombie and spare her. It is the only act of mercy that the authorities perform in the film, and leaves us with the possibility that change may be possible, if only at the level of individuals. At the time of writing, Yeon Sang-ho is completing the sequel *Peninsula* (2020), a title that suggests a wider story scope than the original, and a plot involving a search for a vaccine to halt the zombie virus.

## The Wailing

Like *Train to Busan*, *The Wailing* at first appears to have allegorical meaning. Its director, Na Hong-jin, has stated, "I wanted to make a movie that reflects my feelings on the current climate of our society."[10] That statement is somewhat misleading, as at the heart of *The Wailing* are primarily metaphysical rather than socio-political concerns. *The Wailing* does, however, present a mix of horror tropes—both Western and Korean—that comment intriguingly on the Korean horror genre's conjunction with its Western counterpart. In that sense, *The Wailing* has much to say about contemporary Korea as a country caught between modernity and folklore.

In a mountain village in Gokseong County, police officer Jong-goo (Do-won Kwak) investigates a murder. A local has apparently gone insane and killed his family. Soon similar incidents occur in other parts of the village. The victims seem to be afflicted by some sort of plague. The locals blame a newly arrived Japanese stranger. Jong-goo's young daughter, Hyo-jin (Kim Hwan-hee), begins to behave strangely. A shaman says that she is possessed by an evil spirit and conducts an exorcism. Jong-goo's investigation gradually leads him away from the Japanese stranger as the cause of the village's misfortunes, and toward Moo-myung (Chun Woohee), a mysterious young woman in white who may or may not be a ghost haunting the village.

It is significant that the Korean title of the film is *Gokseong*; the film appears, at first, to be about the community itself and its parochialism. Although existing on the outskirts of what appears to be a modern town with Westernized shops and modern workplaces, the populace lives in mountain huts and observe Korean traditions. Jong-goo is an ambiguous figure; he is a modern lawman, but succumbs quickly to local superstitions. Hong Kyung-pyo's cinematography beautifully captures this schism between the modern world and the majestic, mystical landscape; the film features a great deal of rural imagery. Although the people of the village, like Jong-goo, think of themselves as cosmopolitan, the weight of Korean

**Small town cops Il-gwang (Hwang Jung-min) and Jong-goo (Kwak Do-won) investigate a grisly murder in *Gok-seong/The Wailing* (2016, Fox International/ Well Go USA Entertainment).**

tradition bears down on them. (There is a memorable moment where the shaman changes from his ritual garb to his Nike leisure wear.) This conflict in the psyches of the characters of the traditional and the modern is what gives the film much of its power as it gradually shifts into supernatural territory. As *Variety* noted, the investigation "unleashes a greater terror—that of the paranoid imagination."[11] The provincial mindset of the villagers naturally leads them to point the finger at an outsider, the Japanese stranger. (The telling of "old wives' tales" throughout the story is one of the film's most fascinating aspects.) However, as director Na Hong-jin notes, xenophobia is not his central concern. Instead, as he told *Screen Daily*, he is trying to express the metaphysical: "what it must feel like when evil attacks and invades you." As the setting, Gokseong therefore becomes significant because it is "a place where you can get a feeling of religion and the supernatural" in contrast to the modernity of Seoul (which is, in fact, only 256 kilometers away). Gokseong is a "good place to talk about Korean ghosts and gods."[12]

The co-existence of the two—modernity and superstition—is reflected in *The Wailing*'s blend of genre tropes. *GQ* said that the film "jumbles up ghosts, zombies, body horror, Eastern exorcism, Christian mythology, demonic curses, creepy children and a lot more into one sustained narrative."[13] *The Wailing* mixes these Western and Eastern tropes liberally,

Jong-goo (Kwak Do-won) tries to save his possessed daughter Hyo-jin (Kim Hwan-hee) in *Gok-seong/The Wailing* (2016, Fox International/Well Go USA Entertainment).

but remains curiously ambivalent to both. Moo-myung, for example, is an enigmatic figure. But is she a wonhon? Or a shaman? And what motivates her in the story? These are just a few of the questions that *The Wailing* refuses to answer.

Of course, the movie's ambiguities only served to make it popular as a topic of discussion amongst horror fans on social media. *The Wailing* was financed and distributed by Fox's South Korean arm, and as such it has become one of South Korea's most successful horror film exports to date.

# 12

# Spain

### Painless (2012)
### and The Corpse of Anna Fritz (2015)

Antonio Lázaro-Reboll observes in his 2012 book *Spanish Horror Cinema* that contemporary horror production in Spain gives voice to 21st-century cultural anxieties, such as the role of the media in society and its representation of violence (as in *Tesis* [*Thesis*, 1996] and the [*REC*] franchise); or filmic representations of the Spanish Civil War and its legacy (the works of Mexican director Guillermo del Toro, for example). As Lázaro-Reboll remarks, del Toro's films in particular engage with traumas that are all but erased from the history books, and do so by virtue of their fantasy elements which lend themselves more to political allegory than most mainstream productions.[1] Indeed, since the early 1990s, del Toro has been at the vanguard of a new wave of Spanish-language horror cinema which has also seen works from the likes of Alex de Iglesia and Pedro Almodovar, among others. Many of them have benefited from del Toro's involvement as executive producer.

The high point of Spanish horror production was in the late 1960s-early 1970s, which saw horror films made by Vicente Aranda, Jess Franco, Narciso Ibáñez Serrador and Paul Naschy. After the return to democracy following the 1975 death of General Franco, the Spanish film industry began to focus on how to engage with the historical moment, and horror production halted in favor of political dramas. A decade later, critics like Carlos Aguilar started to reconsider the genre and its place within Spanish cinema history. Sitges and San Sebastian hosted important film festivals and young Spanish filmmakers became influenced by U.S. and European horror cinema. In similar ways to German post-reunification cinema, modern Spanish horror filmmakers have sought to reconnect with the past; none more so than Juan Carlos Medina, whose debut feature, *Insensibles* (*Painless*, 2012), is discussed in this chapter. Medina treats the historical memory of the Spanish Civil War as a theme that "belongs to the unspeakable, that is there, hidden behind a wall of silence and mystery."[2]

During the Civil War, a Catalonian asylum houses a group of children who are completely immune to pain. One of them, Benigno, is prone to violent outbursts. Discovered by Franco's fascists and their German Nazi allies, Benigno is hailed as a new breed of superman, and he is rechristened Berkano after Norse mythology. He is put to work as a torturer for the Franco regime, and remains locked away from view in the asylum until after Franco's fall. *Painless* ends with his rediscovery by the new generation of Spaniards, who are forced to acknowledge their true heritage.

It would be a mistake to attribute anti-authoritarianism as the only theme addressed in contemporary Spanish horror cinema. As Ian Olney has observed, other related themes, patterns and motifs can be found as part of its national identity. Erotic horror is a major theme of Spanish horror, linked, in Olney's words, to Spanish art cinema and, more recently, to anxieties relating to Spain's move from fascism to democracy. Critics have connected the eroticized violence of Spanish horror cinema to a larger leftist critique, to "expose the legacy of brutality and torture that lay hidden beneath the surface beauty of the Fascist and neo–Catholic aesthetics."[3] As Olney comments, one of the most fascinating aspects of Spanish horror is its treatment of gender and sexuality, which "tends to be unconventional and even subversive."[4] This has been found from the very beginnings of the genre, with the recurring figure of the female protagonist, whose role is "to perform a critique of the male power structure by exposing the misogynistic brutality of the monstrous father."[5] In Hèctor Hernández Vicens' controversial *El cadáver de Anna Fritz* (*The Corpse of Anna Fritz*, 2015), a famous actress' corpse is used as a sexual plaything by three young men. The film exposes the misogyny of the male gaze in the fetishized corpse of the actress, but also the brutality of the young men, and how the dominant patriarchal order is still characterized by the fascism of the Franco era. As befits the subversive nature of Spanish horror cinema, it is revealed that Anna Fritz is far from dead, and the male power structure is turned on its head.

## *The Contemporary Spanish Horror Film*

Olney notes that Spanish horror cinema can be divided into three periods:

- a classic era which ran from the early 1960s, from *Gritos en la noche* (*The Awful Dr. Orloff*, 1962), to the early 1980s;

- a "transitional" period from the early '80s to the early 2000s which was relatively fallow in terms of output;
- the contemporary era from the early 2000s to the present, which, in Olney's words, "has witnessed a genre renaissance fuelled by the resurgent popularity of horror cinema among Spanish viewers, the debut of a new generation of horror directors, and the unprecedented success of Spanish horror movies on the international stage."[6]

An early sign of Spanish horror's resurgence was the box office success of *Los otros* (*The Others*, 2001), which helped to revitalize the Spanish horror film industry and paved the way for others. These included Jaume Balagueró, Paco Plaza, Juan Antonio Bayona, Guillem Morales and Jaume Collet-Serra.

Balagueró's debut feature, *Los sin nombre* (*The Nameless*, 1999), was based on a novel by British author Ramsey Campbell. It told the story of a woman's search for her missing daughter, whom she believes has been abducted by a secret sect called The Nameless. Balagueró followed this with the supernatural thrillers *Darkness* (2002) starring Anna Paquin, and *Frágiles* (*Fragile*, 2005) with Calista Flockhart as a nurse in a children's hospital who discovers her patients are imperiled by an evil spirit. Plaza made his debut with *El segundo nombre* (*Second Name*, 2002), also based on a Campbell novel, about a young woman who discovers her family is connected with a group of religious fanatics. His second film, *Romasanta* (*Romasanta: The Werewolf Hunt*, 2004), was based on the true story of Spain's first recorded serial killer who, in 1852, confessed to the murders of 13 people. Together, Balagueró and Plaza made the popular and highly effective found-footage horror movie *[•REC]* (2007), which followed a news crew trapped in an apartment building during a zombie outbreak. *[•REC]*'s success led to a Hollywood remake (*Quarantine*, 2008) directed by John Erick Dowdle, and three sequels: *[•REC²]*, directed by Balagueró and Plaza in 2009, *[•REC³]: Génesis*, directed by Plaza in 2012, and *[•REC⁴]: Apocalypsis* (*[•REC⁴]: Apocalypse*), directed by Balagueró in 2014. Balagueró and Plaza continued to work in the genre, with Balagueró making the apartment building psychological thriller *Mientras duermes* (*Sleep Tight*, 2011) and the dark arts horror *Musa* (*Muse*, 2017). Plaza directed the Ouija board horror *Verónica* in 2017, followed by *La abuela* in 2020.

While Balagueró and Plaza, working together and separately, have been the genre's most prolific directors, a number of important new Spanish horror filmmakers emerged alongside them in the late 2000s. Juan Antonio Bayona's *El orfanato* (*The Orphanage*, 2007) was a traditional ghost story about a family moving into an old house that used to be an orphanage. Soon ghosts from the past, both literal and metaphorical, start to reappear. Bayona's obvious talent in dealing with child actors led him to make the acclaimed British fantasy *A Monster Calls* (2016); while his abiding theme of a family afflicted by horror found a real-life corollary in the true-life story *The Impossible* (2012), about a family holidaying in Thailand caught up in the destruction of the 2004 tsunami.

Guillem Morales directed *Los ojos de Julia* (*Julia's Eyes*, 2010), an intriguing and well-received thriller about a woman who investigates the suspicious death of her twin sister, while at the same time coping with the gradual loss of her sight. Before that, he made *El habitante incierto* (*The Uninvited Guest*, 2004), a psychological thriller in which a man is haunted by an intruder in his house—or is the intruder a figment of his imagination? Morales has a knack for creating an atmosphere of unease. Lately, he has been working in British television on series like *Inside No. 9*.

Another director who moved into television after directing a handful of noteworthy horror films is Miguel Ángel Vivas. *Secuestrados* (2010) was a grueling home invasion horror shot in 12 long takes, a presentation which heightened tension to an almost unbearable degree. This was followed by *Extinction* (2015), a sci-fi–horror set in the aftermath of an epidemic of the living dead. A family of survivors, living alone in a small snowbound town, have to set aside their differences when threatened by a fresh infection. Viva's latest horror film is *Inside* (2016), a Spanish remake of Bustillo and Maury's original (discussed in Chapter 7). Olney has said of these Spanish horror filmmakers that, although they differ in terms of personal style, they share "a commitment not just to horror itself, but to a traditional mode of horror that emphasizes old-fashioned authenticity over postmodern pastiche."[7]

Although Spanish horror cinema has great transnational appeal, with a number of productions taking place outside of Spain, the themes and motifs have, as both Olney and Lázaro-Reboll have noted, remained remarkably consistent. In the classic era, anti-authoritarianism was linked to the underground political opposition to the Franco regime, and appeared in coded form in early horror films. Set in repressive female institutions, Serrador's *La residencia* (*The House That Screamed*, 1969) and Jess Franco's *Der heiße Todd* (*99 Women*, 1969) used the conventions of the women-in-prison movie to make allegorical statements about Spain's totalitarian state. As Olney points out, in these films and others, such as *The Awful Dr. Orloff*, a sadistic or psychotic patriarch or monstrous father is used as a stand-in for Franco himself. Gothic tropes often feature in Spanish horror, such as curses passed down through the generations. Variations on this trope appear in films as varied as *La marca del hombre lobo* (*Frankenstein's Bloody Terror*, 1968) and *The Orphanage*. Spanish horror films in the '60s and '70s often carried an anti-clerical message, stemming from criticism of the Roman Catholic Church's support of the Franco regime. This antipathy in Spanish horror toward representatives of the church has carried forward from movies about the Spanish Inquisition (*Il trono di fuoco/The Bloody Judge*, 1970) to contemporary films like *La monja* (*The Nun*, 2005).

In these films, the sadism of church officials is linked not only to their desire for political power but also to their debased sexual needs. As mentioned, eroticized violence has always played a major part in Spanish horror cinema; examine the films of Jess Franco (*La comtesse noire/Female Vampire*, 1973; *La nuit des étoiles filantes/A Virgin Among the Living Dead*, 1973); José Ramón Larraz (*Vampyres/Daughters of Darkness*, 1974; *Los ritos sexuales del diablo/Black Candles*, 1982) and Paul Naschy (*La orgia de los muertos/The Hanging Woman*, 1973). In a number of these, including *The Awful Dr. Orloff*, the female protagonist(s) struggle against monsters aligned with the dominant patriarchal order. They often turn the tables on these patriarchs, assuming the active gaze in order to usurp or punish their torturers. Olney makes the point that the sadistic patriarchs of classic Spanish horror can also be said to represent the more general threat of regressive forms of Spanish masculinity,[8] and this ties in both with the contemporary horror cinema of *Painless* and *The Corpse of Anna Fritz* and with the debunking of Spanish machismo found in the art house films of Pedro Almodovar (*¡Átame!/Tie Me Up! Tie Me Down!*, 1989), Bigas Luna (*Jamón Jamón*, 1992; *Huevos de oro/Golden Balls*, 1993) and others.

## Painless

Juan Carlos Medina has described *Painless* as metaphorical. The film's title goes "far beyond the children of war who (in the film) do not feel pain."[9] However, it is hard to think of another horror film that confronts the truths of the Franco government as directly—or unflinchingly—as *Painless* does. In some ways, we might see it as the culmination of all the Spanish horror films that have dealt with the civil war and historical memory. Although it resembles some of del Toro's work in these respects (a number of critics have drawn comparisons with *The Devil's Backbone*), it is arguably more explicit in its attempts to expose the brutality and torture of the Fascist regime.

Set in Catalonia, *Painless* interweaves two stories. In the first, which starts during the Spanish Civil War and continues into the 1960s, an asylum's staff attempts to rehabilitate a group of children who feel no pain, by teaching them physical suffering. In the second story, young neurosurgeon

Berkano (Tómas Lemarquis), the torturer insensitive to physical pain, in *Insensibles/Painless* (2012, 101 Films).

David (Àlex Brendemühl) discovers that he needs a bone marrow transplant, and attempts to find his biological parents. Inevitably, the two stories converge, and it is in the convergence of past and present that the meaning of the film becomes clear.

Painless opens in 1931. A group of young children, including Benigno, are brought into the asylum. Because they don't know pain, they are adjudged by Dr. Carcedo (Ramon Fontseré) to be a danger to other people but especially to themselves. His colleague Dr. Holzman (Derek De Lint) believes that the children suffer from an unknown disease, for which there is no cure, but proposes to teach them to understand human pain and to learn compassion. Benigno, whose mother has been taken away from him, is prone to violent outbursts. Attempts to rehabilitate the children are cut short when Franco's troops and German Nazis invade the asylum and kill the staff. Only Benigno survives, and is renamed Berkano ("rebirth") by the Nazis. His growing propensity for sadism (brought about by the abuse he has suffered) and imperviousness to suffering lead the Nazis to train him as a torturer.

Intercut with this is David's story, which takes place in the present day. After a car crash in which his wife is killed, David learns that he has lymphoma and needs a bone marrow transplant. He turns to his estranged parents, only to learn that he was adopted. He attempts to find his biological parents, which eventually leads him to the asylum, where he discovers that Benigno-Berkano—his biological father—is still alive. As David learns the truth about his own identity *and* about his nation's past, the film closes with a short voiceover reminiscent of the Scriptures. Although we are not responsible for the sins of our fathers, we must ensure we are not influenced by them to sin likewise. We must learn from their mistakes.

*Painless* makes clear the links between the Spanish Civil War and rise of Franco, and the need for Spain to learn from the "sins of the fathers," an explicit linking between past and present. The historical memory of Franco's regime, according to Medina, is "hidden behind a wall of silence and mystery. And it deeply affects our present. As a kind of burden that we carry on our backs although we do not know it."[10] As such, *Painless* is a conscious attempt on Medina's part to engage with (to use Lázaro-Reboll's words) "memories and histories that have been erased from official discourses on contemporary Democratic Spain."[11]

But what of its central metaphor of the child who feels no pain? As Olney has stated, the centrality of children is a key pattern of Spanish horror cinema, and this is but one of the tropes that *Painless* uses. Children in Spanish horror, even those that are murderous, are typically victimized by the people closest to them. Although Benigno is treated compassionately by Dr. Holzman, others consider him evil and routinely beat him. Medina presents Benigno in a sympathetic light; casting his tendency for brutality as a product of victimization. In this way, Benigno's violence is directed at the adults around him. In Olney's words, "It is possible to read the antagonism between parents and their children in Spanish horror cinema allegorically as a conflict between the past and the future in which history itself becomes for the young a monster to escape from, vanquish, eliminate and eventually overcome."[12] However, as Olney adds, "It is by no means certain that children represent the promise that history can be remade and rewritten,"[13] and this is certainly the case with Benigno. "Given how often these films' youngsters succumb to the oppressive weight of the past, it is perhaps more accurate to say that they represent Spain's fears that history has already written the present, leaving little hope for the future."[14]

*Painless'* central metaphor suggests that the inability to feel pain, to appreciate the suffering of others, leads to a lack of empathy that, in turn, leads to fascism. Medina based his metaphorical illness on an actual medical condition called Nishida syndrome—the congenital insensitivity to pain. In Medina's words:

> Nishida syndrome is a pretext to treat our relationship with suffering. From the image that was in my head of a tormentor monster, Berkano, I wanted to tell a story about the historical heritage, the relationship between suffering and the truth, and the price we are willing to pay for that truth. Placing the insensitive

children in the context of the recent history of Spain, his tragic life becomes a metaphor for the collective destiny of a country torn by hatred and intolerance.[15]

## The Corpse of Anna Fritz

The excess of *Painless'* torture sequences show us how the eroticized violence of classic era Spanish horror cinema—born out of resistance to fascism—has carried over into contemporary movies. The clinical nature of these types of torture scenes hark back to the beginnings of Spanish horror and *The Awful Dr. Orloff* (which itself borrowed from Franju's *Eyes Without a Face*). The extremity of a film like *The Corpse of Anna Fritz*, and its subject matter of necrophilia, has precedents not only in earlier Spanish horror films of the "transitional" period such as *Aftermath* (1994)—which depicts the mutilation and violation of a woman's body in a morgue—but in *The Awful Dr. Orloff*, too. In Franco's film, we see Dr. Orloff fondle the bare breasts of a victim before surgically removing her face. A similar scene occurs in *The Corpse of Anna Fritz* when the three males take turns fondling Anna's breast as she lies on a gurney in the morgue. These young men have succumbed to the oppressive weight of the past; they are, in many respects, "Franco's children," carrying with them a toxic masculinity that leads them to act immorally.

*The Corpse of Anna Fritz* opens with the media reporting the death of Anna, Spain's most famous and celebrated young actress. We see her corpse being wheeled on a gurney through the morgue corridors. A news broadcast tells us that Anna (played by Alba Ribas) inexplicably died at a private party. News of her death spreads and her fans and followers are desperate to know where her body is being kept. Pau (Albert Carbó), a young morgue attendant on the night shift, leaks photos taken on his phone to his friends Iván (Cristian Valencia) and Javi (Bernat Saumell). Iván and Javi turn up at the morgue on their way to a party and ask to see the corpse; Pau and Iván take turns raping her body, while Javi watches.

Immediately, Vicens establishes a cult of celebrity which has grown around Anna that casts her as a fetish object to her fans. As Ivan coarsely remarks, "Half of Spain would do Anna Fritz. And here we have her naked." The story may well have been inspired by allegations that necrophilia had been committed on Marilyn Monroe's corpse by county morgue employees after she died of an overdose of barbiturates in August 1962. The deputy coroner, Lionel Grandison, described numerous bruises on Monroe's corpse that were not listed on the autopsy report, and claimed that one or more necrophiles had violated it before it was released for burial.[16] Whether these allegations are true or not, the story has passed into urban legend

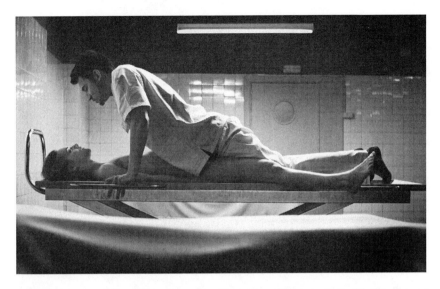

**Pau (Albert Carbó) violates Anna in** *El cadáver de Anna Fritz/The Corpse of Anna Fritz* **(2015, Invincible).**

and speaks to the morbid fascination with celebrity that both iconizes and objectifies the personalities involved.

A number of horror films have used necrophilia as subject matter (and the suggestion of it crops up in many more). The best known of these, perhaps, are the films of Jörg Buttgereit (*Nekromanik*, 1987; *Nekromantik 2*, 1991). *The Corpse of Anna Fritz* uses this subject only tangentially. The film's real focus is regressive masculinity, and in keeping with traditions of Spanish horror cinema, the role of the female protagonist (whom it is revealed is not, in fact, dead, but has been in a coma) is "to perform a critique of the male power structure by exposing the misogynistic brutality of the monstrous father."[17]

Pau and Ivan's acts may be partly explained by their drunkenness and cocaine consumption, but Vicens establishes clearly in earlier scenes how the three men view women as sex objects. As Iván and Javi enter the hospital, they make misogynistic remarks about two young Chinese women who are sitting in the waiting area:

IVÁN: Wouldn't you fuck a Chinese girl?
JAVI: Which one?
IVÁN: Both.
JAVI: Chinese women are flat-chested.
IVÁN: With 3000 euros you get her the tits you want. Chinese girl are docile, you can even put them to work as prostitutes. My colleague did. They are grateful because they are so ugly.

Pau later admits that he has already committed necrophilia on the corpse of another young woman, and has photographs of her naked body on his phone. The men's lack of respect for women, their lack of empathy and the way they see women as sex objects make it possible for them to commit the act of necrophilia. Only Javi shows any semblance of a conscience; indeed, both Pau and Iván are aware that they are committing rape.

As Olney has noted of the horror film in general, "[W]here gender is concerned, horror movies frequently cater to the male, casting women in the roles of fetishized sexual objects or avatars of the monstrous-feminine."[18] Early in *The Corpse of Anna Fritz*, the film appears to take the male gaze, as the men pull back the sheet covering the naked Anna. This is emphasized in the scene where Iván rapes Anna, which is shot from the perspective of Pau and Javi, who watch the depraved act through the morgue door.

The film shifts at the point where Anna awakens; we see her eyes open as Pau is raping her. From there, Anna begins to turn the tables and makes the men the object of her active, inquiring, investigative gaze. At first unable to speak or move, Anna gradually begins to regain her powers. The film continues to intercut her point of view with the perspective of the males, until finally shifting again so that Anna fully assumes the active gaze. Like the female protagonist of *The Awful Dr. Orloff* and numerous other Spanish horror films, she is not punished for "assuming the active male gaze and usurping police and patriarchal authority."[19]

Anna watches as, during a fight between Iván and the penitent Javi, the latter is accidentally killed. At that point, she offers the two remaining

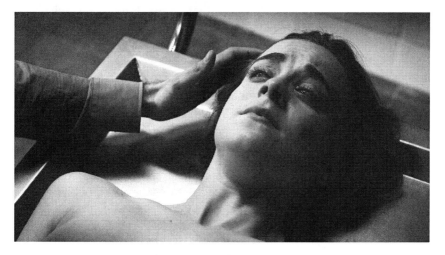

Anna (Alba Ribas) regains consciousness in *El cadáver de Anna Fritz/The Corpse of Anna Fritz* (2015, Invincible).

men the chance to redeem themselves by letting her go. As Olney notes, in many Spanish horror movies, the female protagonist's conflict with the male antagonist(s) serves to illuminate the threat of regressive forms of Spanish masculinity. The pressure Anna attempts to place on Iván and Pau reveals their regressive masculinity fully. Although he feels remorse for Javi's death, Iván's only concern is to avoid prison. If this means killing Anna, so be it. Pau is portrayed as the less dominant of the two men. However, he is easily influenced by Iván, so when Anna attempts to escape, Pau goes along with the attempt to suffocate her.

One of the film's remarkable aspects is the emphasis it places on female agency. Anna is a formidable force, refusing to be suppressed. She literally refuses to die. After Pau has cleaned her body and readied it for the autopsy, he realizes that she is *still* breathing. She awakens again. This time, Pau attempts to hide the fact that Anna is still alive from Iván and pleads with Anna to "play dead." The two men leave the morgue, and at this point the film might have ended—with the remaining characters surviving and Pau keeping Anna's survival a secret. However, Anna's role in the narrative is to change once again, from redeemer to righteous avenger. When Iván returns to retrieve his wallet, he discovers Anna alive. Enraged that Pau has betrayed him, he attempts to strangle Pau. Anna stabs Iván to death. Only she and the penitent Pau remain. But he is not to be spared. The film ends as Anna stabs Pau repeatedly. The final image is of Anna staring off screen, with tears in her eyes and blood spatter on her face.

The conclusion is a curious one. Although Anna prevails, there is little sense of triumph. Instead, the film emphasizes the trauma inflicted on the woman, and the homicidal impulse that this has brought out in her. The film does not show Anna leaving the morgue or her later recovery from her ordeal. The ambiguity of the ending suggests defeat as much as it does triumph. There is the sense that the woman's struggle against patriarchal oppression is far from over. However, as Olney notes of heroines in Spanish horror, even when they do not triumph, "their defeat serves to underscore the repressiveness of the patriarchal rule and the precariousness of women's place within it."[20]

# 13

# Turkey

## Hüddam (2015) and Baskin (2015)

Since 2004, Turkey has seen a significant emergence of horror cinema, compared with previous decades of minimal output. Until the box office successes of Orhan Oğuz's *Büyü* (*Dark Spells*, 2004) and Hasan Karacadağ's *D@bbe* (2006) spearheaded an increase in production of horror films by Turkish producers, the total number of Turkish horror films made since the beginning of Turkish cinema had been less than a dozen. Since 2004, horror film production has steadily increased; and in 2015 there came a mini-boom, with 21 horror films released that year alone. The numbers have continued to rise: At the time of writing, there have been over 90 horror films in total produced in Turkey.

This recent surge of interest has been attributed to the rapid increase of fandom practices, the academic interest in the genre, and the addition of horror to university curriculums. The rise of digital production and the return of audiences to local productions have also contributed to the genre's rise. Horror has in the last few years become a staple of Turkish cinema, and is now the third most popular genre in that country after comedy and romance.

As Kaya Özkaracalar has commented, Turkish horror cinema has been caught "between appropriation and innovation."[1] The few horror films produced up to the current boom were adaptations of European and American horror films, the most famous being *Şeytan* (*Satan*, 1974), a remake of *The Exorcist* (1973). However, the horror films that have emerged since the start of the new millennium categorize the genre (in the words of F. Danaci) as one which "created its own rules by 2014 and made big strides towards becoming an industry on its own."[2] Contemporary Turkish horror films following in the wake of *Dark Spells* and *D@bbe* typically rely on both traditional and Islamic horror motifs. These films "take haunted houses, teen-slashers and other-worldly entities and tailor them to Turkish (and naturally Islamic) culture. Ghosts and zombies become *jinn*, exorcism is

The poster of *Hüddam* featuring Nilgün Baykent as Fatma, the black magician (2015, Hayal Sanat/Bir Film).

done by *hodjas*, and the apocalypse takes its own version from the Quran."[3] The twin themes of black magic and *djinni* have become prevalent in Turkish horror cinema, accounting for more than a third of all Turkish horror films. As Zeynep Koçer remarks, the Turkish horror market has become "flooded with stories of possession by malevolent jinn, as transgressive, volatile figures of abjection."[4]

One such film is Utku Uçar's *Hüddam* (2015), which provides the first focus film of this chapter. The story follows young Can (Çagri Duran), who lives with his mother Derya (Fatma Hun). Their quiet country life is disrupted when Derya is possessed by an evil spirit. With the help of an Imam, Can transports Derya to a town in the Aegean where Asaf (Murat Özen), a mystic, attempts to lift the spell.

According to Sertaç Koyuncu, social attention in Turkey has been given to horror films about *djinni* and black magic because of Islamic belief. Films about *djinni* ("whose names cannot even be pronounced aloud, are thereby referred to as 'three-lettered'"[5]) and films on black magic (which is prohibited in the Quran) have aroused both curiosity and horror. However, the fears of Turkey are not limited to *djinni* and black magic, even as those themes have become *de facto* to that country's mainstream horror films. Social crisis and political turmoil also influence the cultural structure of a society and feed into horror films. *Baskin* (2015) is the first horror film made in Turkey to have won awards at international festivals and to have received international recognition. It concerns black mass rituals taking place in an abandoned Ottoman-era police station and a police investigation that takes the five-man squad through a trap door into Hell itself. In its experimentation with genre and narrative form, *Baskin* can be seen as an alternative Turkish horror film, one which (in the words of Koyuncu) "aims to discover the potentials of horror film production in the country."[6]

## Turkish Horror Cinema 1949–2004

Scholars have cited a number of reasons why horror was a neglected genre in Turkey prior the millennium. It is not that Turkish audiences were averse to horror films: Horror literature became popular in the 1970s, even though its equivalent in Turkish cinema amounted to no more than two or three titles. Turkish producers generally did not have the confidence in the technical aspects of Turkish film production to mount horror success-fully. Inadequacies in special effects, makeup, sound and set design (tech-nical areas which are considered vital in horror production) meant that producers were not willing to take risks on productions that might fail due to technical flaws. Another argument for the shortage of horror films is the absence in Turkish culture of such horror film staples as vampires, were-wolves and serial killers. However, this is offset by the fact that foreign hor-ror films with these elements have always existed in the Turkish horror market, as an important part of the domestic video and DVD market. It was the chance event of *The Spell* in 2004, and its box office popularity, that con-vinced producers that Turkish audiences were interested in "horror motifs from the cultural heritage of Turkey itself."[7]

The first Turkish horror film, *Çiğlik* (*The Cry*, 1949), is thought to be lost. Written and directed by Aydin Arakon, it's an "old dark house" mys-tery about a doctor (Muzzafer Tema) who takes shelter in a mansion on a rainy night where he becomes involved in a plot to drive a young woman (Emine Engin) insane in order to seize her inheritance. All that exists is a poster and an evocative still showing a woman in a nightdress with her hands bound overhead.

The first surviving film is *Drakula Istanbul'da* (*Dracula in Istanbul*, 1953), a loose adaptation of Bram Stoker's novel (by way of a 1928 abridged Turkish version called *Kazikli Voyvoda/The Voivode with the Stakes*). Despite the screen adaptation being based on the "Turkified" novel, it is still a faithful Stoker adaptation. Azimi (Bülent Oran), an Istanbul lawyer, travels to Romania to act for Dracula (Atif Kaptan), who wishes to acquire property in Turkey. A descendent of Vlad the Impaler, Dracula embarks on a vampiric mission on arrival in Istanbul. Produced at a time when Tur-key was undergoing secularization, *Dracula in Istanbul* dispensed with

Christian iconography but did not replace it with Islamic equivalents. For example, Dracula is repelled not with a crucifix or by the Quran, but through garlic alone. *Dracula in Istanbul* lacks a full technical grasp of the vampire film (as evidenced by the poor choice of stock music) and did not lead to more Turkish horror films. The next Turkish horror film did not appear for almost 20 years.

*Ölüler Konusmazki* (*The Dead Don't Talk*, 1970) is the first instance of a Turkish horror film injecting Islamic elements into plots familiar from Western horror films. In this case, a young couple inherits an old house which they find to be haunted by an undead ghoul. They enlist the help of a *hodja* who manages to banish the zombie by reciting from the Quran. While *The Dead Don't Talk* gives an Islamic context to its supernatural tale, it also "appropriates" many visual and audio stylistics from American and European horror, and uses the original musical scores of American films on its soundtrack (including Krzysztof Komeda's score for *Rosemary's Baby*, 1968).

The Turkish film industry's tendency, in the 1970s, to create clones of popular Western films continued with *Aska Susayanlar: Seks Ve Cinayet* (*Thirsty for Love, Sex and Murder*, 1972). A scene-by-scene remake of Sergio Martino's classic *giallo Lo strano vizio della signora Wardh* (*The Strange Vice of Mrs. Wardh*, 1971), it stars Meral Zeren as the ambassador's wife who suspects that either her husband or one of her lovers is a serial killer. Prolific director Mehmet Aslan reproduces a number of Martino's stylish set pieces but also includes some wild flourishes of his own. The producers brazenly lifted the entire Ennio Morricone score from the Italian original for their own version.

Perhaps the most famous "Turkish version" of an American horror film is *Satan*, the Turkish version of William Friedkin's *The Exorcist*. This unauthorized remake was made by producer Hulki Saner to capitalize on the publicity stirred up by the original. If a number of European horror films in the 1970s stole blatantly from *The Exorcist*, then *Satan* simply remade it scene by scene, and at times shot by shot. Directed by Metin Erksan, a once-radical Turkish filmmaker who eventually gave up his social concerns to make market-orientated, popular films, *Satan* comes across as a genuine cultural oddity: In modern-day Istanbul, a secular young girl, Gül (Canan Perver), is possessed by a demon. An Imam performs an exorcism, Gül is cured and embraces Islam.

While the scenes between Gül and her mother (played by glamorous actress Meral Taygun) are almost identical to those of *The Exorcist*, even down to the dialogue, the Catholic scenes with Father Karras posed an obvious problem for Erksan and the producers. Karras (called Tügrul Bilge in the Turkish film and played by Cihan Ünal) is now a psychiatrist who happens to have written a book about witchcraft. His inner conflict no longer has to do with his lack of faith, although he still harbors guilt over the death of his mother. *Satan* does not have the same power as the original partly for that reason; another factor being the primitive filmmaking and poor special effects on display. *Satan* replicates the possession and exorcism scenes of the original but with much less convincing effects. Mike Oldfield's "Tubular Bells" is used throughout, followed by Islamic music in the final scene where Gül finds her belief. The purpose of the original was arguably to reaffirm Catholicism in a secularized world; *Satan* uses the same plot to reaffirm belief in Islam. Kaya Özkaracalar notes that *Satan*'s main theme "is clearly the reconfirmation of Islam's power and validity within the conflict between modernization and tradition in general and between materialism and religion in particular."[8]

## Turkish Horror Cinema After 2004

The success of *Dark Spells*, Turkey's first horror film since the 1970s, is attributable more to the circumstances of its release than to the film's quality. A group of young and good-looking archaeologists, in search of an ancient book, come up against an evil spirit during their excavations. Essentially a teen slasher, and containing rape and gory violence, it was made by a major Turkish producer, Faruk Aksoy, and veteran TV director Orhan Oğuz. A wide release and advertising campaign designed to capitalize on the popularity in the DVD market of American slashers helped secure a large audience, as did national TV news coverage of the premiere, during which a fire broke out threatening the lives of numerous celebrities in the audience. Despite almost universally poor reviews, *Dark Spells* made the box office Top Ten in 2005, paving the way for more Turkish horror films.

One of these was writer-director Hasan Karacadağ's indie *D@bbe*. Koyuncu identifies a secondary theme in a small number of post–2004 Turkish horror films: "a virus epidemic" threatening the world with apocalypse. *D@bbe* presents its apocalypse in the form of *djinni* making connection with people through the Internet and causing their mass suicide. It was a remake of the American horror film *Pulse* (2006), which was itself a remake of the Japanese *Kairo* (*Pulse*, 2001). *D@bbe*'s box office success led to no fewer than five sequels (with *D@bbe 7* currently in production), all directed by Karacadağ.

*D@bbe* may well be Turkey's first and most successful horror film franchise; a number of others have followed. The most recent include the six-film black magic franchise *Siccîn* (2014–2019); from the same director

(Alper Mestçi), *Musallat* (*Haunted*, 2007) and *Musallat 2: Lanet* (2011); *Sir-Ayet* (2019) and *Sir-Ayet 2* (2019), and three films in the *Araf* (*Limbo*) franchise (2012–2019). As Koçer notes, the titles of many Turkish horror films are names of particular *djinni* (*Dabbe, Marid, Azazil, Ammar*) or references to the Quran (*Semum, Siccin, Ceberrut, Bezm-I Ezel*).

In 2008, Karacadağ directed *Semum*, based on *The Exorcist*, highlighting a third theme of many Turkish horrors: spirit possession causing illness or miscarriage; according to Koçer, these stories rely on "Islamic cosmology and the character of the jinn as their choice of monster."[9] As tales of abjection which play on the trope of the "monstrous-feminine," many of these films are about the hellish punishments visited on their female protagonists as a result of extra-marital affairs, abortions or being impregnated by djinni. Pregnancy holds a significant place within the Turkish horror genre, according to Koçer, with an example being *Haunted*, whose female protagonist "begins to be depicted as monstrous in relation to her maternal capacity and as a woman has also become abject." Horror in Turkish cinema is culturally gendered and thus, in Koçer's words, "provides many opportunities to investigate the internal mechanisms of power dynamics and patriarchal ideology through its depictions of gender."

That is not to say that all Turkish horror films are essentially conservative. *Limbo*, the story of a woman haunted by the ghost of her aborted child, was supported by the Islamist fundamentalist media but actually avoids taking a clear-cut anti-abortion stance (although, as Özkaracalar notes, is more problematic when it comes to the woman's extra-marital relationship, the cause of her pregnancy).[10] Other Turkish horror films, such as *Gen* (*Gene*, 2006), have sought to avoid local motifs, instead looking to American films for their role models. Still other Turkish horror films take their inspiration from real-life domestic social issues rather than from cultural motifs that traditionally inform Turkish horror cinema. *Küçük Kiyamet* (*The Little Apocalypse*, 2006) speculates on the possibility of Istanbul being destroyed by earthquake following tremors which killed 20,000 people in 1999.

## Hüddam

Directed by Utku Uçar, *Hüddam* is a good example of the kind of low-budget independent horror films that have emerged in the wake of the horror boom, distributed by small-scale Turkish distributors looking to take a share of the market through horror cinema. In this case, Utku Uçar, as well as writing, producing, directing and composing the music, distributed the film through his own company Hayal Sanat. The film's modest success has allowed him to make and distribute the film's two sequels, as well as act as distributor for a number of other horror films including the second, third and fourth in the *Araf* series.

Although produced with limited resources, *Hüddam* skillfully incorporates a number of tropes that have become synonymous with modern Turkish horror cinema: *Djinni*, possession, black magic and female abjection feature prominently in its narrative. It opens in 1968 with a black magic spell being cast by a woman called Fatma (Nilgün Baykent). We cut to present-day Istanbul. Can is throwing a birthday party for his mother, Derya. Can's best friend, Melih (Eray Logo), is present, as are their respective girlfriends. They are apparently modern (Westernized) and secular in their views. The conversation revolves around jobs and house-buying. The occasion is filmed on Can's handycam. In part, *Hüddam* utilizes elements of the found-footage horror movie, which adds a low-budget verisimilitude. The influence of the *Paranormal Activity* franchise is in evidence, not only in the theme of possession but also in the presentation of a domestic setting captured on consumer video camera. For the rest of the film, Utku Uçar shoots on digital video, with atmospheric lighting and careful color grading. There is a basic competence in the filmmaking that ensures commercial viability as a horror film, but also many scenes that resemble a television soap opera in terms of the bland décor of the locations.

After the party, Derya begins to exhibit her first signs of possession. *The Exorcist* provides an obvious touchstone for *Hüddam,* as it continues to do for many Turkish horror films. Briefly taken over by the evil spirit within her, she writes on the wall in Aramaic (a language she doesn't know) with her own blood. Can and Melih are able to watch the footage on their camcorder (which was accidentally left on after the party). This immediately leads to a dilemma for Can: Should he take his mother to the hospital or call in the *hodja*? Thus the conflict caused by the opposition of tradition/ religion vs. Westernization/modernization—which, according to Koçer, "remains not only at the forefront of the Turkish political scene but deeply embedded within the Turkish socio-cultural psyche"[11]—is immediately introduced, and follows into the next sequence.

Before calling in the *hodja*, Can asks for help from his friend Begüm (Hande Oktan), a trainee psychiatrist. Her diagnosis is "a possession form of schizophrenia." Like in *The Exorcist*, rationalism is attacked by the demon and Begüm's medical worldview is shattered by the evil spirit within Derya. Interestingly, Utku Uçar does not attempt to use makeup or special effects to portray Derya's possessed state. This is, no doubt, because of the film's tiny budget. (*Huddam* 2 [2019] was considerably more expensive in terms of its production values, locations and special effects, which includes a levitation sequence that has become standard in possession films.) Instead, he relies on the effective performance by Fatma Hun as Derya, as well as a spooky score and occasionally dubbed voices.

After Begüm's hasty exit from the narrative, Can brings in the *hodja*, who informs him that they are dealing with a very powerful djinn. Can believes that his grandfather, himself a mystic, has placed a spell on Derya. Together with Melih and Derya, he sets out on a journey to the town in the Aegean to find a cure for the spell placed on his mother. There he enlists the help of another mystic, Asaf, who uncovers the truth.

One of *Hüddam*'s flaws is an often confusing script: As the film goes on, increasingly lengthy dialogue exchanges attempt to explain the story. What does transpire, though, is that the real target of the djinn's attack (and therefore the focus of the film) is not Derya (who is portrayed as the abject woman of the story), but Can. In 1968, a spell was placed on Derya by Fatma, who wanted a male child. That child turns out to be Can; and *Hüddam*'s conclusion sees Can discover that his real mother is Fatma. His whole identity is thus called into question.

As Koçer notes, in Turkish horror films, male characters tend to fall into two main categories: "With slight variations, they are either depicted as the devout elderly male *hoca* who saves victims of possession or constructed as the rational bystander who yields to Islamic belief and reaffirms his faith."[12] Can clearly belongs to the latter category: He is the young Westernized male who, by the end of the narrative, is forced to reject his rational outlook and embrace belief in Islam as the antidote to the black magic spell cast on him. Essentially *Hüddam* is a cautionary tale, not against black magic, but against leading an excessively Westernized way of life. In Koçer's words:

> Modernization/Westernization has always been encouraged as long as it does not threaten the patriarchal ideology and remains within the lines drawn by the dominant political structure … [T]his mainly male crisis of reconstructing and sustaining patriarchal ideology still manifests itself in the politics, culture and collective consciousness of Turkish society.[13]

## Baskin

Unlike *Hüddam*, *Baskin* offers very little in the way of a frame of reference, especially with regards to Turkish horror; it is a film that demands to be taken on its own terms. In some respects, it is perhaps more akin to surrealism in that it defies meaning: We have to look to the film itself to tell us how it should be understood. A remarkable technical achievement on the part of director Can Evrenol, *Baskin* affects the viewer in a profound and powerful manner through sound and image, and in its use of nightmare syntax. It is a film about horror and about the aesthetics of horror cinema. Evrenol's masterful use of camera, production design, lighting and sound present a vision of Hell of some description, although the film avoids a definitive interpretation of this.

*Baskin* (Turkish for "Raid") splits into two parts. The first is arguably the more accomplished as it presents a normal, rational situation—a recognizable reality. But through the accretion of detail seemingly extraneous to the main action on screen, it creates an atmosphere of deep unease for the viewer. Its first 45 or so minutes is a case of fear being most acute when we are not exactly sure of what we are meant to be afraid of; when our fear takes no tangible form. The film's second half presents a more recognizable horror scenario, but one that is still rich with ambiguity. Like the policemen in the film, who, summoned to an abandoned building, find themselves confronted by a terrifying cult, we feel compelled to watch the inexplicable horrors taking place when we should look away, because the need to try to comprehend what it is we are seeing and experiencing is so great.

As *Baskin* unfolds, a number of questions are raised in the viewer's mind. Are we in a literal "Hell"? Is there a rational explanation for what we are seeing (are the inhabitants of the building, in fact, a cult of cannibals)? Are we seeing the individual private hells of each of the policemen being enacted for them? Are we locked inside the recurring childhood nightmare of protagonist Arda (Gorkem Kasal)? That the film might encompass all of these interpretations is a key to its power. It is a film that asks to be fully "felt" rather than understood in rational terms.

Mehmet Cerrahoglu plays Baba, leader of the cult, in *Baskin* (2015, IFC Midnight).

There *is* some guidance along the way. The main antagonist Baba (Mehmet Cerrahoglu) tells us, "Hell is not a place you go to, but something that you carry around inside of you." There is also the fact that Evrenol based *Baskin* on his earlier short film of the same name. That short, according to the IMDb, was shot "during the height of the police brutality and Gezi resistance that hit the headlines worldwide."[14] One can conclude that the short contained some element of allegory that may have carried over into the feature-length version. (In fact, the feature film version is very much like a short film narrative in that it revolves around a single event).

A film of socio-political relevance, *Baskin* addresses the construction of masculinity, the nature of repressive institutions such as the military and the police, and the repression of the self in conforming to gender roles. And yet these do not seem to constitute its deeper meaning. Its aim may well be simply to present "Hell" (in a similar way to how Gasper Noé's films present a kind of living hell), and it does so vividly, and with remarkable immediacy.

*Baskin* opens with a boy waking from a bad dream and hearing the sound of his parents having sex in their bedroom. The camera pans across a shelf in the boy's room. We see a picture of Kemal Atatürk and a toy police car, an indication perhaps of the boy's desire to someday serve his country. As he goes into the hallway to investigate the noise, a hand appears out of the darkness (this same image is featured on the film's poster)—an unnerving intrusion of horror into domestic normality.

From this pre-titles sequence, we move into the film's main action of the first half: an extended dialogue scene in a restaurant featuring the five policemen. The dialogue, concerning sexual deviance, is like the chit-chat we get in Tarantino's films—genre characters making everyday conversation. It is ostensibly a scene about male camaraderie. However, the scene's real "meaning" seems to be contained in the action taking place in the restaurant kitchen. Intercut with the policemen are a series of details and interactions involving the chef and a mysterious visitor. The sequence opens with an extended Steadicam shot that follows a hooded figure delivering meat to the chef. We then see the meat being cut up and cooked over coals. The emphasis placed on the meat creates a sense of unease. It also foreshadows the rending of human flesh and eating of human meat that we fleetingly glimpse later in the sequence that takes place in Inceagac.

This unease builds when one of the men, Seyfi (Sabahattin Yakut), goes to the rest room to vomit (we wonder if he has been poisoned by the meat) and screams in terror in the mirror. The moment is never fully explained but clearly Seyfi is repressing fear, perhaps in precognition of what is to come in Inceagac. (In the rest room he sees a frog in the soap dish, which also perhaps foreshadows Inceagac where they come across a bucketful of frogs.)

The men travel by police van to Inceagac. (Koyuncu's socio-political reading of *Baskin* hinges on the 2013 social movement for and against the government which saw political activists attacked by the police; the police violence was featured in Turkish news. It is possible to see the police "raid" on the cultists in *Baskin* in these terms.)[15] The van appears to hit a naked person in the road and crashes into a river. At this point, Evrenol introduces the non-linear looping structural motif that becomes an important part of *Baskin*'s narrative design. We are suddenly back in the restaurant. A newbie policeman, Arda describes his childhood dream to his mentor, Remzi (Ergun Kuyucu); this is when we learn that Arda is the child at the start of the film. Remzi and Arda are both able to see the hooded figure in the restaurant. Remzi claims this figure has haunted him his whole life. At this point, we are unsure whether structurally the film has taken us into a flashback of a part of the restaurant sequence that we did not see, or whether this is, indeed, a dream that Arda is experiencing (and whether the childhood sequence was a dream-within-a-dream). Surrealism encroaches as blood appears to seep through the policemen's table cloth. It is a dream-like moment. Arda pitches backward in his chair and submerges in water. A giant hand (like the one we saw in the hallway at the start of the film) reaches to him in the water. We then return to what we assume is present reality as the other policemen pull Arda from the river. We can now begin to understand the film as being subjective from Arda's (conscious and unconscious) experience. This bookending of Arda's dream-nightmare also brings the first part of the film to a close.

*Baskin*'s second section involves the police officers' hellish descent; it's depicted as a kind of subterranean dwelling place of the cult members, who indulge in sexual depravity, torture, cannibalism and totem-building. The policemen die one by one, strikingly in ways that seem to follow their own repressed fears. For example, Yavuz (Muharrem Bayrak) is made to have sex with a woman wearing a goat's head. Again we can begin to understand that the second section is a mirror image of the first. Earlier, Yavuz divulged to his colleagues that he once had sex with a man whom he thought was a woman—a shapeshifter. The main action of the second section is the protracted torture of the surviving officers, Apo (Mehmet Fatih Dokgoz), Yavuz and Remzi, and Arda's eventual escape from Inceagac. It is notable that some of the ways in which Evrenol portrays "Hell" or purgatory are reminiscent of Western horror films such as *Jacob's Ladder* (1990) and *Event Horizon* (1997)—fleetingly glimpsed atrocities that resemble the paintings and literature of late medievalists, like the hellscapes of Hieronymus Bosch. The Quran's description of *Jahannam* may figure as an

**One of the many visions of Hell in *Baskin* (2015, IFC Midnight).**

influence but more recognizable is the kind of S&M imagery that features in Clive Barker works such as *Hellraiser* (1987), a kind of sado-sexual hell, combined with the torture and cannibalism sequences of *Bone Tomahawk* (2015). Like Pinhead in the *Hellraiser* films, Baba in *Baskin* provides us with a tangible monster, a master of ceremonies–cult leader who instigates the torture of the cops.

But before *Baskin* can provide us with some markers by which we can orient ourselves and gain some understanding of the horror we are experiencing, it confounds us with a final narrative loop. Arda may manage to escape Baba, and in the process throw off the repression of his childhood which has resulted in his becoming a policeman, but this is undercut by the film's conclusion. As Arda runs naked down the road away from Inceagac, he is hit by an approaching police van. We assume at first that this is yet another convoy on its way to battle the cult. However, we quickly realize that it is the same five policemen as before. Arda was the naked man that they originally hit. The narrative loop presents a hell that is seemingly inescapable: for Arda, the other policemen, and for us. It is just one of the many conundrums that confront *Baskin*'s viewers and which remain with them after the film ends, making *Baskin* all the more disturbing.

# 14

# U.S. and Canada

*Most Beautiful Island* (2017)
and *The Transfiguration* (2016)

International instability post–9/11 created a context for the re-emergence of horror cinema in North America and other countries in the last 20 years; a flourishing which, if anything, has intensified since we entered the second decade of the millennium. As James Aston and John Wallis remark in the introduction to their book *To See the Saw Movies*: "Horror has never been more vibrant in American cinema than in the past decade and has circulated through mainstream, independent, exploitation, underground and alternative indices and connected with audiences worldwide."[1]

Since 2008, there has been a corresponding increase in the number of women involved in American independent horror film as writers and directors, as well as women taking more active roles as primary characters in horror film narratives. This goes against the traditional "glass ceiling" in the film industry generally. Feminist film theories on horror and gender have been disseminated via academic film courses into filmmaking practice, influencing a new generation of university-educated filmmakers (both men and women); and digital production tools, online networking and promotional platforms have helped to democratize the filmmaking process by lowering costs and broadening access, particularly within independent film. Beyond that, break-out hits such as *It Follows* and *American Mary* have proven that there is a market for female-centered, female-centric horror; and that there exists a large and growing community of female horror fans. This chapter will focus firstly on the growth of feminist horror in America and Canada.

*It Follows* serves as a primary example of what Donato Totaro has described as "female-centric" horror.[2] It shows a move toward surrealism or even hyper-realism in its depiction of American suburban life; a corresponding sense of dislocation or alienation from the middle-class

171

American ideal of gender. To an extent, *It Follows* debunks the tropes of the 1980s slasher, presenting an ambiguous view of teenage sexual identity, and expresses cultural anxieties surrounding marriage and family. Director David Robert Mitchell draws on the photographic tradition of Gregory Crewdson to present a suburbia that is not unlike the dream-like vision of David Lynch.

The film I have chosen to examine in detail is *Most Beautiful Island*, a remarkable debut feature written and directed by and starring Ana Asensio as an undocumented immigrant from Barcelona struggling to survive in New York, working menial jobs. A tip-off from a friend sees her become involved in an underground betting game run by the wealthy who wager on the outcome of extreme scenarios. It's essentially a recessionary narrative, but from the perspective of a female immigrant. Asensio brings a unique, female-centric viewpoint to the genre.

As well as seeing more women filmmakers going into the horror genre, and the genre addressing feminist concerns, we are, in North America, seeing more Black horror films made by Black filmmakers, bringing new vision and a new radicalism. In the way that *Get Out* allegorizes (and satirizes) white liberal America's co-optation of Black identity, it pushed Black horror into new areas. Jordan Peele's follow-up, *Us*, and Nia DaCosta's reimagining of *Candyman* further mark a reclamation of Black identity in horror, an attempt to seize the reins of Black representation from white Hollywood. Less publicized than Peele's box office hit, but arguably with a similar agenda, is *The Transfiguration* (2016), Michael O'Shea's meditation on race, class and gender in the guise of a modern vampire movie—or a movie about a modern vampire. Drawing on previous films about vampirism and identity like George A. Romero's *Martin* (1977), *The Transfiguration* tells the story of Milo (Eric Ruffin), a lonely young boy obsessed with horror movies, who starts to believe that he might be a vampire. Like Peele's work, *The Transfiguration* re-examines classic horror tropes through a Black lens, and is driven by its political ideas, if more implicitly than *Get Out*.

## *Recent Feminist Developments in North American Horror Cinema*

In his 2014 essay "Women Who Kill," Donato Totaro notes the changing landscape of North American horror since the mid–2000s in terms of the increasingly active roles women have taken in the genre, both in the narratives of horror films, and as creatives behind the camera. In this way, North American horror has moved ahead of 1960s Euro-horror films, which often showcased powerful female agency, such as in the female-centered *gialli* of directors like Martino. As Totaro writes:

> "the intricacies of the female experience" have evolved into slightly uncharted territory for North American horror films since the mid–2000s. Female killers as monsters (zombies, vampires, werewolves, etc.) have remained a fairly constant presence in horror films over decades, but the difference now is that women are killers in a more realist context as well, as serial killers and psychopaths.[3]

Totaro offers a number of social, cultural and industrial reasons for the increase of women-who-kill in recent American horror films. The first is the influence of 1970s Euro horror on emerging North American filmmakers, helped by the importance of international film festivals as a showcase and a meeting place for like-minded filmmakers. Also to thank are DVD and Blu Ray labels such as Arrow, Shameless, Blue Underground, Kino Lorber, Severin, Scream Factory and others who have made these Euro horror films available in North America, often for the first time.

A second reason is the impact of feminist scholarship on horror and gender, which has spread beyond academia into practical filmmaking, film programming and Internet-based film criticism. There are, as Totaro notes, more women writing about horror films and more female horror viewers, "knowing there are more women watching horror translates to better female roles."[4]

Another important reason, says Totaro, is the impact of digital technology on the filmmaking process. It has tended to "demystify the technology of the film apparatus"[5] and made it cheaper to make and promote films, particularly in the independent sector. Finally, there has been a huge increase in the number of women working behind the camera in production capacities since 2000. To name but a few: Mary Harron (*American Psycho*, 2000; *The Moth Diaries*, 2011), Elza Kephart (*Graveyard Alive*, 2003); Izabel Grondin (Montreal-based horror short filmmaker), Kimberly Peirce (*Carrie*, 2013), Axelle Carolyn (*Soulmate*, 2013; *Tales of Halloween,* 2015), Karyn Kusama (*Jennifer's Body*, 2007; *The Invitation*, 2015; *XX*, 2017), Jennifer and Sylvia Soska (*Dead Hooker in a Trunk*, 2008; *American Mary,* 2012; *See No Evil 2,* 2014; *Rabid*, 2019), Jennifer Lynch (*Hisss*, 2010; *Chained*, 2012), Ana Lily Amirpour (*A Girl Walks Home Alone at Night,* 2014; *The Bad Batch*, 2016), Annette Ashlie Slomka (co-director of *The Secret Life of Sarah Sheldon*, 2006), Jovanka Vuckovic (*XX*, 2017), Karen Lam (*Evangeline*, 2013; *7 from Etheria,* 2017; *The Curse of Willow Song*, 2020), Maude Michaud (*Dys-*, 2014; *At the Door,* 2018), Kate Robbins (*Candy Stripers,* 2006), Natalia Leite (*M.F.A.*, 2017), Marianna Palka (*Bitch*, 2017), Audrey Cummings (*She Never Died*, 2019) and Amy Seimetz (*She Dies Tomorrow,* 2020).

According to Totaro, the increased presence of women in North American horror films has been so marked that critics have labeled this growth as a subgenre, "the female-centered horror film." However, Totaro also notes, it is possible to distinguish between female-centered horror (where the lead character is female) and female-centric (where themes are part of the female experience and address issues such as pregnancy, rape, date rape, abortion, sexism, chauvinism, sexual and work harassment and lesbianism). "A good many are directed (or at least written by) women; some are directed by men but feature a strong female character as the central point of identification; or in some cases feature a predominantly female cast."[6]

Totaro does, however, contend that recent female-centered and female-centric North American horror has departed from the Freudian or post–Freudian patriarchal model where the woman is either the victim or, if she manages to turn the tables on the antagonist-monster-killer, loses her femininity in the process by becoming a masculinized killer. In recent North American horror films where women feature as killers (such as *American Mary*), they do so while retaining their sexuality-femininity, something they have in common with Euro-horror films of the 1970s. That there are now so many more North American female-centric, female-centered horror films comes down to the increase in female spectators and the gains that women have made socially and in the film industry that enable men to identify with the female protagonist-antagonist in horror cinema. As Totaro puts it, the contemporary North American horror film is not just about the Final Girl, it is about the *Primary* Girl: The woman is primary within the narrative, either as a killer or as a woman who fights back (or both). Many of these films deal with issues to do with the female experience, which the male spectator can sympathize with but never fully experience: the woman's "acts of murder being justified within the narrative as a situation, if perhaps exaggerated, of real world experience: physical or mental abuse in the workforce, rape, and sexual harassment being the most common triggers for violence. The audience is meant to understand, if not condone or empathize with, the social, political, cultural or psychological pressures that have led the female character in question to commit these violent crimes."[7]

Since Totaro's essay in 2014, a number of North American horror films have centered on women-who-kill. *Starry Eyes* (2014) was a potent combination of Satanic thriller, body horror and Hollywood make-over story: Sarah (Alexandra Essoe), a young waitress in Hollywood, gets the chance to star in a movie being made by a company called Astraeus Pictures. At first, she is suspicious of the producers, but spurred on by her self-centered friends, she goes the "casting couch" route in her bid for stardom. She begins to undergo a frightening physical transformation as her body starts to deteriorate: She suffers hair loss, develops sores on her face and body, her teeth start to fall out. The producer tells her that she must accept this transformation or die. She decides to embrace the changes—and murders her friends one by one. Finally she takes part in a rebirth ritual held by the people at Astraeus Pictures, who are revealed to be devil worshippers. Sarah emerges from the ritual as a physically flawless Hollywood starlet who is, in fact, a demon incarnate.

As the synopsis suggests, *Starry Eyes* is a horror film version of the Hollywood rags-to-riches narrative. However, its makers' (Kevin Kölsch and Dennis Widmyer) attitude toward Sarah's rise to fame becomes clear from the film's diabolical central metaphor: Her fame comes at a terrible price. Sarah literally has to sell her soul to the Devil to become a star. The metaphor may be obvious, but the film's combination of body horror and women-who-kill tropes makes for a disturbing watch. Like Sarah, her friends are narcissistic millennials with little loyalty to one another. Sarah, however, shows that she is willing to go far beyond the usual jealousy and betrayal in her bid for stardom. As her decaying body becomes increasingly repulsive to her, her desperation forces her to murder her friends in horrible ways (through suffocation and stabbing). These brutal killings, which bring to mind the Manson murders, complete Sarah's rite of passage, her proof to the sect that she is willing to act entirely without conscience in pursuit of her dream. Her reward is rebirth as a glamorous but soulless movie star. The final scene presents her complete physical transformation from a cadaverous wreck into a perfect, blemish-free Hollywood beauty. The message of *Starry Eyes* seems clear. Behind the glamor of stardom lies the demon of self-compromise; the Hollywood dream is a Faustian pact. In this sense, Sarah and her friends are victims of a culture that promotes selfish ambition. And that is the film's true source of horror: We never once think that success will bring Sarah the happiness she craves, but we understand the pressure on her as an actor to be beautiful and successful, and her reluctant willingness to go along with the "casting couch" to advance her acting career.

The #MeToo movement, which exposed the sexual harassment systemic in the music and film industries, and saw the investigation of Jeffrey Epstein and trial of Harvey Weinstein, provides an undercurrent to *Starry Eyes* (and a number of other female-centric movies, both in and out of the horror genre) as it does to another controversial North American horror film, *M.F.A.* (2017). Although it uses the established tropes of the rape-revenge thriller, *M.F.A.* broadens the narrative to focus on the systemic sexual abuse of female students that has become prevalent on North American university campuses. The avenging angel character no longer

seeks vengeance for her own rape alone, but for that of her fellow classmates, each of whom has experienced sexual assault in the past.

Francesca Eastwood's Noelle is an introverted, socially awkward
young artist pursuing a Masters in Fine Art degree at a California university. In an early scene, she is told by her (male) professor, and her fellow students, that her work lacks inspiration. She has a crush on a good-looking
boy in her class—a boy who then rapes Noelle at a party. She confronts
him the following day, and accidentally causes his death. Suddenly empowered, both in her artistic expression and in her sexuality, she takes vigilante
action against other male students who have sexually assaulted her friends.

*M.F.A.* neither condones nor condemns Noelle's vigilante killings;
instead, it presents her violent actions as a response to the silence that sur-
rounds sexual assault. As is revealed in the course of the narrative, a number of the women around Noelle have suffered sexual assault, like she has,
but have been pressured to keep quiet. Director Natalie Leite based the
film on her own experience as an art student, and aimed to create in the
Noelle character the kind of anti-hero that is often portrayed as male but
rarely as female. As Leite comments: "While there are countless examples
of likable men doing bad things in film and television—Don Draper, Walter White, Lester Burnham, Tony Montana—we rarely see a likable female
anti-hero."[8] The purpose of *M.F.A.* is to open a discussion about a rape culture that has, in the past, been shrouded by "amnesia." As Leite told *Explore
Entertainment*:

> I wanted to tell this story because we live in a world that doesn't fully acknowl-
> edge the severity of sexual assault or its effect on the victims. Women are con-
> stantly bullied into being silent and feeling responsible for someone else's crime.
> That silence manifests itself in psychological effects that can be seen even years
> after the assault takes place. While violence is never a solution for any matter, in
> creating a female Dexter-type character, I aimed to give these women a cathartic
> experience—the sense of relief that comes from vengeance through the safety of
> fiction.[9]

*M.F.A.* is as much a conscious political statement as it is a piece of genre
filmmaking. At the end, Noelle receives her Masters in Fine Art and gives
an acceptance speech. The film ties in so closely her art with her killing that
the award is clearly intended as being for both. At the same time, *M.F.A.*
shows that the voices of the #MeToo movement are influencing art and
culture.

Much more tongue-in-cheek, but with a underlying seriousness in its
presentation of female empowerment, is *Tragedy Girls*, a 2017 black comedy about two high school friends, Sadie and McKayla (played by Alexandra Shipp and Brianna Hildebrand), who go on a killing spree in an attempt
to gain a mass following for their true-crime blog. They try to enlist the

help of a local serial killer, Lowell Orson Lehmann (Kevin Durand); when he refuses, they hold him captive and commit the murders in his name. Eventually the whole town becomes embroiled in an increasingly convoluted plot in which the loyalties of the two girls are tested as factions begin to develop between the police, the major, the kidnapped killer and the girls' friends and boyfriends. As Totaro notes, in many female-centric horror films, the female characters go unpunished, and this is the case in *Tragedy Girls*. Despite attempts by the male characters to turn Sadie and McKayla against each other, the conclusion sees them reconciled, and together they set fire to their high school during the prom, killing all of the prom-goers. The murders are pinned on Lehmann, while Sadie and McKayla get off scot-free. Like *M.F.A.*, *Tragedy Girls* revels in its female anti-heroes, and in the solidarity between the two friends, which the film holds up as being of primary importance. It is because they refuse to break that solidarity that they go unpunished. The final scene sees Sadie and McKayla head off to college together, no doubt to wreak havoc there too.

## Most Beautiful Island

Totaro defines the female-centric/female-centered horror film as one in which the woman is the primary figure of the narrative, either as the killer or as a survivor who fights back. Asensio's *Most Beautiful Island* takes survival as its theme, although the film actually pushes the definition of a horror film in that, rare for the genre, there are no killings or deaths in the story. There are, however, human monsters who, in Asensio's words, "are capable of paying in brutality."[10] There are also survivors, like Luciana (played by Asensio), who represents the experience of poor immigrants in Manhattan, the "most beautiful island" of the film's title.

Asensio begins the film with a sequence of almost random consequence. The camera follows a number of immigrant women on the New York streets as they go about their daily business. Eventually the camera finds Luciana and stays with her for what will be the next 24 hours of her life, as events lead her into an increasingly bizarre and desperate situation. This slice-of-life sense of *verité* is a key feature of the film. Among her influences, Asensio lists the Dardenne brothers, whose naturalistic films (*Rosetta*, 1999), *La Fille inconnue* (*The Unknown Girl*, 2016) as previously noted show young people on the fringes of society (often immigrants or displaced people themselves) struggling to survive physically and spiritually; and the Romanian drama-thriller *4 luni, 3 săptămâni și 2 zile* (*4 Months, 3 Weeks and 2 Days*, 2007) which follows a young student's harrowing attempts to get an illegal abortion. Although Asensio has not included

**Luciana (Ana Asensio) prepares to play a dangerous game in *Most Beautiful Island* (2017, Samuel Goldwyn Films/Orion Pictures).**

it as an influence, Hitchcock's *Psycho* also bears comparison, especially in the opening sequence. Like *Most Beautiful Island*, *Psycho* opens in a city and selects a character to follow seemingly at random, the implication being that what happens to that person might equally happen to another person living in that same environment. In Luciana's case, we get the sense that what happens to her might have happened, or will happen to others in her situation. (In fact, Asensio based the story on her own experiences as an immigrant in New York.) This is later confirmed when Luciana finds others like herself at the underground betting game.

Also, like *Psycho*, we follow the female protagonist through a mundane reality, marked by financial desperation that leads, almost inexplicably, into the horrific. To survive without the support of friends or family, Luciana routinely takes menial "gigs": babysitting brattish children, handing out leaflets on the street. She does this not only to eat, but to buy phone cards so that she can keep in touch with her mother in Barcelona. (It is ultimately revealed that Luciana fled Spain after the death of her child, in an attempt to leave behind trauma that she cannot overcome.) An early scene speaks to Luciana's desperate situation and her anxious state of mind. As she sits in the bath in her squalid apartment, cockroaches stream from a hole in the wall into the water with her. She makes no attempt to kill them; to her, they have as much right to live as she does. She is on the same level as they. This scene of insects on her bare skin prefigures what is yet to come, and perhaps provides a clue as to why Luciana, and others like her, are survivors. They are able to endure what others cannot—not by choice but by necessity. Asensio is not afraid to make Luciana unsympathetic at times—such as when she abandons the brattish children—the reality being that people in Luciana's situation can only afford to think of themselves and not others.

Luciana has chosen to settle in a city where she can be anonymous, where she can start from scratch and escape her past. In this sense, the film's title takes another meaning. Luciana is, herself, an "island": cut off, adrift. In the course of the narrative, she learns the importance of protecting the sanctity of one's body and of one's self. The "most beautiful island" is that of the self. It is this subjectivity that gives the film its power. Again, it resembles *Psycho* in the way it uses subjectivity to restrict our experience to that of the protagonist. Like Luciana, we are never sure where events are taking us, and we are forced to follow helplessly as she finds herself drawn into the inexplicable.

The film shifts its style in its second act. It moves away from social realism into a more expressionist mode, particularly in terms of its heightened use of sound to suggest Luciana's anxious state of mind. Here we can detect the conscious influence of *4 Months, 3 Weeks and 2 Days*, which shifts from naturalism into a claustrophobic depiction of impending danger. *Most Beautiful Island* moves us from the exteriors of Manhattan to the interior of a building's basement, where Luciana has to confront her own internal fears.

This sense of subjectivity is really the film's cleverest trick: The narration is restricted to what Luciana knows and nothing more; and this invites the viewer to predict the nature of the danger that she faces. Is she being lured into prostitution? Human trafficking? Organ harvesting? Asensio uses the techniques of misdirection masterfully in these sequences, so that when the reveal comes, it is completely unexpected and impossible to guess (although subtly foreshadowed in the earlier "cockroach" sequence). Here the recessionary narrative comes to the fore, which, I suggest, is the film's underlying project.

Like in *4 Months, 3 Weeks and 2 Days*, the real horror of the female protagonist's situation lies in a political system that creates stark polarities between wealth and poverty, between the educated elite and the working class. The class conflict in *Most Beautiful Island* is between Luciana (and the other immigrants in her situation) and Manhattan's wealthy one-percent, depicted in the film as the partygoers who seek to exploit Luciana's desperate situation for their own pleasure in the form of the betting game.

In relation to this, it is worth briefly considering the character of Olga (Natasha Romanova), the "finder" who lures Luciana into the betting game. Like Luciana, she is an undocumented immigrant, but appears to enjoy a more lavish lifestyle and has more expensive clothes. Of course, her money comes from aiding and abetting the super-rich. She is, in fact, a traitor to her kind. But she becomes more sympathetic as we realize that she acts under duress. When Olga is forced to take part in the betting game alongside Luciana, she is clearly frightened. This, in turn, brings out the survival instinct in Luciana, but also her compassion. She saves Olga during the game, and reveals great inner strength and personal integrity. Here, again, it becomes apparent that Asensio speaks from personal experience:

> I wanted to talk about a type of immigration that isn't often touched upon—and yet I've met so many girls hoping to get visas as models or actresses. We walk past them on the streets and don't think they have any problems, when really sometimes they don't even have enough to eat. The contrast interested me: this false cruel and bittersweet glamour that consists of only being able to eat when invited to parties. It's degrading. I also wanted to show how the property-owning classes, who can buy anything, are capable of paying in brutality.[11]

Finally, then, we might see that Asensio's intention with *Most Beautiful Island* was to make a cautionary tale for others who are—or *will* be—in that situation. The conclusion sees Luciana offered Olga's job as the wealthy partygoers' recruiter. But Luciana's newfound strength and self-awareness is such that she is able to turn down the offer, rather than help perpetuate the exploitation of others like herself. Instead, she takes the money she has earned and flees into the night.

## Race Horror and Emerging Black Horror Filmmakers

Peele's *Get Out* was similarly unequivocal in the way it vindicated Chris (Daniel Kaluuya), the film's Black protagonist, even to the point of his leaving his duplicitous white girlfriend Rose (Allison Williams) to die at the end of the film. This can be read as a statement on class inequality underlying racism in America: As a white, middle-class liberal, Rose is part of the problem, not part of the solution. She and her family are following an agenda that serves their interests alone, not those of the African-American people. Peele's film is unambiguous in the way it presents no sympathetic white characters or allies, thereby positioning Chris as its true hero. Not only that, Chris is allowed to live at the end of the film and is not apprehended by the police. He does not become a sacrificial victim of racism. His unquestionable triumph, and the film's willingness to go against conventional race horror tropes, reinvigorated the genre, and *Get Out*'s phenomenal box office success showed that Black and white audiences alike were ready to empathize with a radical Black horror film hero. In short, *Get*

*Out* marked the reclamation of race horror for Black audiences and Black filmmakers.

In the 1990s and 2000s, there had been attempts to do this by Black filmmakers working in the genre: Rusty Cundieff (*Tales from the Hood*, 1995) and Ernest Dickerson (*Bones*, 2001). These filmmakers and others sought to reverse the African-American stereotypes that had become set in the genre over the decades and were prevalent in the teen horror films of the late 1980s and 1990s.

The Blaxploitation horror films *Blacula* (1972), *Blackenstein* (1973) and *Dr. Black, Mr. Hyde* (1976) serve as interesting precursors to modern Black horror films. Although these now tend to be dismissed as camp, they did at least allow African-American audiences to see themselves represented on screen, even if commentators are divided over whether those representations are racist. Harry Benshoff has argued that many Blaxploitation horror films "reappropriated the mainstream cinema's monstrous figures for black goals, turning vampires, Frankenstein monsters and transformation monsters into agents of Black pride and Black power."[12] Others feel that the films simply offer variations on traditional genre norms, with Black actors taking the roles usually occupied by whites, but without any fundamental subversion or reworking of generic formula. Critics of Blaxploitation claim that the representation of race in these films is inauthentic. Certainly, Blaxploitation was the product of the predominantly white film industry. They were intended for an African-American urban audience but designed also to cross over to white audiences.

At the heart of *Get Out* is the taboo issue of miscegenation, a key concern of race horror that predates even Blaxploitation. As Peter Hutchings points out, in the early history of the horror genre, Blackness tended to be shown in terms of "primitivism and exoticism."[13] The emphasis, particularly in the horror films of the 1930s and '40s, was on non–American Blacks, while African-American characters were seen only occasionally on-screen, often as comic relief. In *White Zombie* (1932) and *I Walked with a Zombie* (1943), the Black characters encountered by whites in exotic locales have been said to represent white colonialist fears of subservient peoples rising up against their masters. Black and white interbreeding, meanwhile, played out in coded form, often in the pairing of gorilla and white girl—a genre staple in the 1920s and 1930s in such movies as *The Gorilla* (1927), *Ingagi* (1930) and *Murders in the Rue Morgue* (1932). *King Kong* (1933) is, of course, a prime example, and serves as a precursor for a number of race horror films, including *Candyman* (1992).

The late 1980s and early '90s saw a resurgence of race horror films, including two notable efforts by Wes Craven, *The Serpent and the Rainbow* (1988) and *The People Under the Stairs* (1991). The latter is significant as it featured a Black child as its protagonist. However, Black characters remained marginalized in most horror films of those decades, even ones that purported to address the issue of racism (such as *The Craft*, 1996). Reclamation of race horror for Black audiences could only come about with the increase of Black filmmakers making horror films. Director James Bond III's *Def by Temptation* (1990) marked the first in a series of Black horror films by African-American filmmakers, paving the way for the works of Cundieff and Dickerson, as well as a number of lesser-known titles such as *Ax 'Em* (1992) and *Eve's Bayou* (1997). As Robin R. Means Coleman has noted, "Rather than simply including black characters, many of these films are created by blacks, star blacks or focus on black life and culture."[14]

## The Transfiguration

Michael O'Shea's *The Transfiguration* coincides with an effort by white filmmakers (especially those working in TV) to acknowledge racism in American society. TV dramas such as *Little Fires Everywhere* (2020), based on the book by Celeste Ng, confronted white middle-class entitlement in the face of Black experience, and underlying racism through the issue of gentrification. In the NBC series *This Is Us* (2016– ), a white father who has a Black adopted son comes to understand the need to acknowledge his son's Black identity. He has to move on from the mindset of "I don't think of you as Black, I think of you as my son" in order to recognize that his son will encounter social prejudice in his everyday life. *The Transfiguration* marks an interesting attempt by a white filmmaker to present Black experience through the generic lens of the horror film. As such, it is at times problematic, in much the same way that films like *Candyman* and *Night of the Living Dead* (1968) can be criticized for not entirely managing to escape racist tropes.

The film introduces Milo as an outsider in his community. He is orphaned and lives with his brother in a low-income housing complex in the Rockaway Peninsula of Queens, New York. He spends his time reading books, watching films about vampires and dodging the local gang who regard him as a "freak." He is in psychiatric counseling after killing animals. Nobody knows that he has already murdered at least one person in order to drink their blood. He meets Sophia, a self-harmer who lives with her abusive grandfather, and the two develop a close and—for Milo—potentially redemptive bond.

O'Shea reveals Milo's backstory obliquely. We learn that his vampire obsession stems from the death of his mother. In a flashback we see that she has apparently committed suicide by cutting her own wrists and throat.

Eric Ruffin (Milo) and Sophie (Chloe Levine) become friends in *The Transfiguration* (2016, Strand Releasing).

Milo discovers her body on the bed. Morbid curiosity leads him to taste her blood. Just as his mother sought an "escape" through suicide, we can see Milo's resulting fascination with vampires as an escape into fantasy; an attempt to redefine his identity through the cultural mythology of the vampire.

O'Shea has admitted that Romero's *Martin* was a conscious influence on *The Transfiguration*. Both films comment on their relationship to vampire culture self-reflexively. In *The Transfiguration*, this takes place largely in the dialogue scenes in which Milo and Sophia discuss vampire films like *Let the Right One In* (2008), *Twilight* (2008) and *Nosferatu* (1922). Early scenes showing the poor neighborhood where Milo lives also resemble that of *Martin* in the way that setting is used to establish the identity of the protagonist. Also, like *Martin*'s titular vampire, Milo travels outside of his own working class neighborhood to stalk his victims.

In this way, it is significant that Milo's victims of choice are white middle-class males. As O'Shea has commented, "I wanted to explore two New Yorks—the sad, lonely, barren, rundown New York, and the gentrified New York that's slowly overtaking it. That's where Milo goes hunting; where all the bikes and baby strollers are."[15] That Milo's victims are without exception white, and that he considers himself a "hunter," speaks to his viewing white people with suspicion, and of subconsciously placing the blame for his problems on his being poor and Black. Later in the film, when a white middle-class student asks Milo where he can buy drugs, Milo lures him into the basement of a building where the gang shoots him. Sophia and Milo become close friends, and she offers him sex. He declines and withdraws his friendship from her for a time. There is the sense that this is not just because he is afraid of intimacy, but because he is wary of her color.

Sophia also offers the possibility of Milo escaping his hopeless situation: She plans to hop on a bus and leave her problems behind. In O'Shea's words, "Sophie is more of a Faulkner character. To me, Faulkner has this funny idea that the only way for salvation is to get out. There is that barn-burning story where the kid is in the background and he is just running. For Sophie, salvation comes through leaving a very bad situation and finding hope on the other end."[16] Sophia asks Milo to leave with her, so that they start again together somewhere else. This is where *The Transfiguration* arguably becomes problematic.

Instead of offering Milo salvation in the same way that Sophia is given hope of a better life somewhere else, O'Shea seeks redemption for the character. In a later sequence, Milo inadvertently kills a small white child while on a "hunt." He is filled with remorse and contemplates suicide, but believes that, as a vampire, he is unable to kill himself. His view of himself as a "monster" is reinforced when he imagines killing Sophia and sucking her blood. This influences his decision not to leave with her: He fears that he will eventually kill her because of his bloodlust. Instead, he arranges a situation where the gang shoots him dead in revenge for turning them over to the police for killing the student.

In terms of its conclusion, *The Transfiguration* comes close to perpetuating the Black horror stereotype of (in the words of Robin R. Means Coleman) the "Sacrificial Negro,"[17] the Black character who gives up his or her life so that the white character(s) can survive. O'Shea might have had Milo escape with Sophia, but instead, Milo gives up his life so that she can live. We might, of course, equally interpret Milo's self-sacrifice as an act of love. However, by virtue of Milo's color, *The Transfiguration* cannot fully escape this ambiguity.

# Afterword

The world has entered a new period of economic, social and political instability, and horror cinema will inevitably respond. In the U.K. and America, populist anti-establishment movements led to Brexit and the election of Donald Trump; there is growing distrust of globalization as inequality becomes ever more widespread; middle-class incomes in Western economies have suffered from the effects of automation in burgeoning markets, such as China; nationalism is rising in a number of European countries. Horror cinema by its nature is sure to reflect such social and political upheaval in its themes and concerns, even if the potential collapse of the European Union threatens the co-productions that have given the genre—in Europe, at least—its life blood.

This afterword offers a brief summary of some of the notable horror films released during the late stages of this book; and discusses some of the future directions of international horror cinema that critics predict in light of the COVID-19 pandemic that is taking place as I write this in 2020.

It is likely that we will continue to see the rise of Indigenous horror in a number of countries including America, Canada and Australia. More female-centric horror films will emerge, including from countries like Turkey. There are signs that this is already taking place. Indigenous filmmakers promise to offer new angles on established horror tropes as they take different perspectives on the cultural concerns of genre production.

*Blood Quantum* (2019) presents the familiar scenario of zombie apocalypse, but from a unique viewpoint: On a Native reserve in Canada, the Indigenous population is immune to a virus that turns non–Natives into zombies. Their reserve becomes a refuge for survivors, including white people seeking shelter. But the white refugees bring with them the virus and the threat of destruction, and the Natives are putting themselves at risk by letting them onto their land. The film offers a reconfiguration of classic zombie tropes of the 1930s and 1940s where the zombies were often the Black natives menacing the white colonialists. More to the point, it presents a metaphor for the colonialization of Native North American lands, the genocide of the Indian wars and the trauma that took place afterwards for Natives on the reserves.

The film's early sequences depict everyday life on the reserve: The men are trying to stay sober and out of trouble, the women are just trying to cope. Writer-director Jeff Barnaby drew on his own experience in presenting life on the reservation: "The sole inspiration for everything I do is the community I grew up in. Rez life and rez representation is what I do well. I kind of grew up red trash. And that's what I bring to the screen. Those characters are not refined. A lot of them are hard-partying drunks. They like to fight and fuck."[1] *Blood Quantum* deals with the anger of the rez Indian in having to deal with white people, and the idea that the people best equipped to survive in a post-apocalyptic world are those who have already survived an apocalypse. As Barnaby told *NOW Magazine*, "Everybody said the zombie movie is a played-out genre. So I was like, we got to take a different approach. What if the Natives were immune? It turned into the retelling of the colonization story. It wrote itself. The mechanics of the zombie genre just lends itself to Native history."[2]

Another example of an Indigenous filmmaker turning to horror and science fiction is Inuit director Nyla Innuksuk, whose *Slash/Back* (2020) is a coming-of-age story set in the Canadian Arctic Archipelago. It tells the tale of a group of teenage girls fighting off an alien invasion. Again it concerns an outside force trying to invade an Indigenous community. Innuksak wrote the script but another director was originally slated for the film. Eventually the producers agreed to Innuksak as a first-time director. *Slash/Back* is a film of many firsts. The cast is made up of first-time actors and *Slash/Back* is, in fact, the first film ever to be shot in the Baffin Island hamlet of Pangnirtung.

According to Barnaby, an Indigenous perspective of the genre is the concern with environmental catastrophe, the natural world being polluted and corrupted. The land is the basis of these stories; and both *Blood Quantum* and *Slash/Back* can be described as environmental apocalypse films. Another Indigenous horror film produced in 2019 is *Dark Place*, an Australian anthology featuring five Indigenous stories from different directors and with a largely Indigenous cast. The stories tackle a range of issues and themes through a genre lens: female oppression and revenge; sanity and insomnia; the haunting of a housing commission estate; horror in the woods of an outback town; and outback zombies. The stories are united by the overarching theme of post-colonial Aboriginal history, and historical parallels drawn through genre.

*AV: The Hunt* (2020) is another breakthrough in Turkish horror cinema: possibly the first horror film of that country with a female-centric theme, and a premise that we would associate more with films like *Revenge* and *Cold Hell*. Billur Melis Koç plays Ayse, a young Turkish woman who is caught in the arms of her lover by a corrupt cop. She manages to escape but her lover is murdered. She is forced to go on the run from her own family, who set out to kill her to protect their honor. Taking honor killing as its theme, *AV: The Hunt* is a hard-hitting thriller about Ayse's journey from hunted to hunter: To survive, she has no choice but to become as ruthless as the men chasing her. In the process, director Emre Akay tackles the woman's fight for survival in a patriarchal society.

Both *Dark Place* and *AV: The Hunt* played at London's Frightfest horror film festival in 2020. Like a number of film festivals happening during COVID-19, screenings took place entirely online, as a digital festival, and it remains to be seen how the global coronavirus pandemic will affect cinema production and distribution long-term. Horror cinema is arguably at its most powerful when viewed with an audience, and the prospect of it being restricted to viewing on personal devices has implications for the genre; not to mention the issue of social distancing placing restrictions on film production and the likely impact on the form and presentation of films themselves. We have already seen a number of horror films made entirely on computer screens, concerning stories of the Internet and found-footage horror. (In *Host*, 2020, a group of friends accidentally invite the attention of a demonic presence during an online séance.) These questions now preoccupy filmmakers and other industry people. At Frightfest 2020, a panel of industry figures considered the issue of "Horror in Lockdown" and the questions it raises. How has the horror genre been affected by the pandemic? What do filmmakers do when productions have to be shut down? How are horror writers coping with lockdown? How are the stories we want to hear affected by our changed world? And what might the genre look like on the other side?

Assuming that physical group film production will ultimately resume, this final question remains relevant. In a recent article for the popular U.K. genre magazine *Starburst*, Laura Potier discussed horror movies in times of crisis; how the genre reflects contemporary concerns and engages with the processing of trauma. Her comments on the likely impact of the pandemic on future horror cinema are intriguing, and serve as a fitting conclusion here.

According to Potier, coronavirus has laid bare many of modern society's most fundamental failings, "from an increased awareness of socio-economic inequalities and the failures of capitalism, to the incompetence of right-wing governments and their money-first approach to the value of human life."[3] We might expect, then, a wave of cross-genre films in which corporations and governments are cast as villains, favoring wealth and economic growth over human life. There is likely to be an increase in pandemic-related horror and science fiction films, zombie movies and medical dramas like *Contagion* (2011). Other movies are likely to be inspired by our experience of the pandemic and its links to global climate anxieties such as cross-species transmission of viruses like Ebola, SARS, bird flu and coronavirus. Hand in hand with this is growing anxiety about the loss of biodiversity and the depletion of natural resources: an inextricable link between the increased risk of pandemics, in an interconnected world, to the climate emergency. As Potier writes:

> In the face of these "invisible enemies," the anticipated cinematic reaction will likely most resemble what we saw in the 1950s. The invisible enemy will be manifested into something more tangible, an enemy with a face. As a result, expect stories of dystopian societies with one of two types of villain: the insatiable capitalist elite, à la *The Handmaid's Tale* (1990), *Snowpiercer* (2013), *Gattaca* (1997) or *The Hunger Games* (2012), or an enemy that's recognizably monstrous like zombies in *Train to Busan* and *World War Z* (2013) or alien creatures in *A Quiet Place* (2018) and *Invasion of the Body Snatchers* (1978).[4]

# Chapter Notes

## Introduction

1. Brenda S. Gardenour Walter, "Ghastly Transmissions: The Horror of Connectivity and The Transnational Flow of Fear," in *Transnational Horror Across Visual Media: Fragmented Bodies* Dana Och and Kirsten Strayer, eds., p. 17 (London: Routledge, 2014).

2. Philippa Hawker, "Killing Ground Gives Aaron Pedersen the Chance to Be a Villain," *The Australian*, August 26, 2017. Accessed February 14, 2018, https://www.theaustralian.com.au/arts/review/killing-ground-gives-aaron-pedersen-the-chance-to-be-a-villain/news-story/a105ac304d0e1 4f54a7473c3e73d0aa0.

3. Andrew Hock Soon Ng, "Sisterhood of Terror: The Monstrous Feminine of Southeast Asian Horror Cinema," in *A Companion to the Horror Film*, Harry H. Benshoff, ed., p. 444 (Oxford: John Wiley and Sons, 2014).

4. Quoted in Sertaç Koyuncu, "'Baskin': The Horror of the Scapegoats," in *The New Wave in Turkey's Cinema*, Tage T. E. Luxembourgeus and Mumin Baris, eds., p. 126 (N.p.: Proverbial Elephant, 2018).

5. George A. Romero, "Foreword," in *Night of the Living Dead*, John A. Russo (New York: Pocket Books, 1974).

6. Anton Bitel, "Francesca," *Projected Figures*, August 26, 2016. Accessed August 24, 2020, https://projectedfigures.com/2016/08/26/francesca-2016/.

## Chapter 1

1. Charles Newbery, "Argentina Horror Films Going Low Budget," *Variety*, February 8, 2008. Accessed October 11, 2017, http://variety.com/2008/scene/markets-festivals/argentina-horror-films-going-low-budg-1117980500/.

2. Zebbie Watson, "5 Great Horror Films from Latin America You've Probably Never Heard Of," *Inverse Entertainment*, May 11, 2016. Accessed October 11, 2017, https://www.inverse.com/article/15505–5-great-horror-movies-from-latin-america-you-ve-probably-never-heard-of.

3. John Hopewell, "Adrian Garcia Bogliano Sets First Swedish Movie 'Black Circle,'" *Variety*, May 13, 2016. Accessed October 11, 2017, http://variety.com/2016/film/festivals/adrian-garcia-bogliano-first-swedish-movie-black-circle-1201773794/.

4. "Hypersomnia," *Netflix*. Accessed October 11, 2017, https://www.netflix.com/gb/title/80159025.

5. Philippa J. Page, *Politics and Performance in Post-dictatorship Argentine Film and Theatre* (Rochester, NY: Boydell and Brewer, 2011), p. 98.

6. Emiliano De Pablos and John Hopewell, "Argentina's De la Vega Re-launches Supernatural Horror Pic 'White Coffin,'" *Variety*, December 7, 2013. Accessed November 23, 2017, http://variety.com/2013/film/global/argentinas-de-la-vega-re-launches-supernatural-horror-pic-white-coffin-1200929639/.

7. Kat Hughes, "Frightfest 2016: 'White Coffin' Review," *The Hollywood News*, August 27, 2016. Accessed November 23, 2017, http://www.thehollywoodnews.com/2016/08/27/frightfest-2016-white-coffin-review/.

8. Chris Banks, "White Coffin," *Flickfeast*, February 7, 2017. Accessed November 23, 2017, https://www.flickfeast.co.uk/reviews/white-coffin-2016/.

9. Bitel, "Francesca."
10. "Oh the Horror! Interview with Luciano & Nicolás Onetti," *Popcorn Frights Film Festival*, July 31, 2016. Accessed November 27, 2017, http://www.popcornfrights.com/oh-the-horror-interview-with-luciano-and-nico-onetti/.
11. Bitel, "Francesca."
12. "Oh the Horror! Interview with Luciano & Nicolás Onetti."

## Chapter 2

1. Jonathan Hatfull, "Australian Genre Cinema: Living in the Past or a Brave New World?" *SciFi Now*, August 19, 2016. Accessed February 14, 2018, https://www.scifinow.co.uk/blog/australian-genre-cinema-living-in-the-past-or-a-brave-new-world/.
2. Paul MacInnes, "The Babadook: 'I wanted to talk about the need to face darkness in ourselves,'" *The Guardian*, October 18, 2014. Accessed February 14, 2018, https://www.theguardian.com/film/2014/oct/18/the-babadook-jennifer-kent.
3. Luke Buckmaster, "'Hounds of Love' Review—Savagely Intense Australian Horror Is the Scariest Film of the Year," *The Guardian*, May 23, 2017. Accessed February 14, 2018, https://www.theguardian.com/film/2017/may/23/hounds-of-love-review-savagely-intense-australian-horror-is-the-scariest-film-of-the-year.
4. Hatfull, "Australian Genre Cinema: Living in the Past or a Brave New World?"
5. Robert Hood, "Australian Horror Films," *Tabula Rasa*, [undated]. Accessed February 14, 2018, www.tabula-rasa.info/AusHorror/OzHorrorFilms1.html.
6. Lindsay Coleman, "Wake in Fright by Tina Kaufman," *Senses of Cinema*, March 2011. Accessed February 14, 2018, http://sensesofcinema.com/2011/book-reviews/wake-in-fright-by-tina-kaufman/.
7. Hatfull, "Australian Genre Cinema: Living in the Past or a Brave New World?"
8. Hawker, "'Killing Ground' Gives Aaron Pedersen the Chance to Be a Villain."
9. Anton Bitel, "Fantasia First Look: 'Killing Ground,'" *SciFi Now*, July 17, 2017, https://www.scifinow.co.uk/cinema/killing-ground-fantasia-first-look/.
10. Hatfull, "Australian Genre Cinema: Living in the Past or a Brave New World?"

11. *Ibid.*
12. Christina Newland, "Cate Shortland on Her One-night-stand Abduction Drama, 'Berlin Syndrome,'" *The Guardian*, June 8, 2017. Accessed February 14, 2018, https://www.theguardian.com/film/2017/jun/08/cate-shortland-on-her-one-night-stand-abduction-drama-berlin-syndrome.
13. Hatfull, "Australian Genre Cinema: Living in the Past or a Brave New World?"
14. "beDevil" (1993) Press Kit, p. 8.
15. MacInnes, "The Babadook: 'I wanted to talk about the need to face darkness in ourselves.'"
16. *Ibid.*
17. Heather Wixson, "Interview: Writer/Director Ben Young Talks 'Hounds of Love,'" *Daily Dead*, October 5, 2017. Accessed February 20, 2018, https://dailydead.com/interview-writerdirector-ben-young-talks-hounds-of-love/.

## Chapter 3

1. Catherine Chapman, "'Goodnight Mommy' Is the Rebirth of Austrian Horror," *Creators.Vice.Com*, September 20, 2015. Accessed March 8, 2018, https://creators.vice.com/en_us/article/vvyyqm/goodnight-mommy-is-the-rebirth-of-austrian-horror.
2. Emma Myers, "Interview: Veronika Franz and Severin Fiala," *Film Comment*, September 9, 2015. Accessed March 8, 2018, https://www.filmcomment.com/blog/goodnight-mommy-interview-veronika-franz-severin-fiala/.
3. Ryan Gilbey, "'Goodnight Mommy' Is a Chilling Austrian Horror Film with National Guilt at Its Heart," *New Statesman*, March 3, 2016. Accessed March 8, 2018, https://www.newstatesman.com/culture/film/2016/03/goodnight-mommy-chilling-austrian-horror-film-national-guilt-its-heart.
4. Myers, "Interview: Veronika Franz and Severin Fiala."
5. *Ibid.*
6. A. A. Dowd, "Guessing the Twist Won't Save You from the Horrors of 'Goodnight Mommy,'" *AV Club*, September 10, 2015. Accessed March 8, 2018, https://film.avclub.com/guessing-the-twist-won-t-save-you-from-the-horrors-of-g-1798184821.

## Chapter 4

1. Ana Maria Bahiana, "The Blair Witches of Brazil," *BBC*, July 6, 2007. Accessed August 6, 2018, http://www.bbc.com/culture/story/20170701-the-blair-witches-of-brazil.

2. Márcio Ferrari, "Horror, Brazilian Style," *Pesquisa*, June 2017. Accessed August 6, 2018, https://revistapesquisa.fapesp.br/en/2017/12/14/horror-brazilian-style/#prettyPhoto.

3. Larry Rohter, "A Cult Figure Conjures the Macabre," *New York Times*, October 19, 2001. Accessed August 6, 2018, https://www.nytimes.com/2011/10/23/movies/jose-mojica-marins-brazilian-filmmaker-conjures-macabre.html.

4. Stephanie Dennison and Lisa Shaw, *Popular Cinema in Brazil* (Manchester: Manchester University Press, 2004), p. 141.

5. Robert Stam, João Luis Vieira and Ismail Xavier, "The Shape of Brazilian Cinema in the Postmodern Age," in *Brazilian Cinema*, Randal Johnson and Robert Stam, eds., (New York: Columbia University Press, 1995), p. 405.

6. Roberto Pinheiro Machado, *Brazilian History: Culture, Society, Politics 1500–2010* (Newcastle-Upon-Tyne: Cambridge Scholars Publishing, 2018), p. 356.

7. Bahiana, "The Blair Witches of Brazil."

8. Jack Ahnold, "Horror Film Festival 'Hell do Janeiro' Arrives in Rio Tonight," *The Rio Times*, September 12, 2018. Accessed November 13, 2018, https://riotimesonline.com/brazil-news/rio-entertainment/horror-film-festival-hell-do-janeiro-arrives-in-rio-this-wednesday/.

9. Jenny Barchfield, "'Hard Labor' Serves Up Brazil Sans Bikinis," *The Washington Times*, May 13, 2011. Accessed November 13, 2018, https://m.washingtontimes.com/news/2011/may/13/hard-labor-serves-up-brazil-sans-bikinis/.

10. Gustavo Beck, "Dark Aspects: Juliana Rojas and Marco Dutra Discuss 'Good Manners,'" *MUBI*, August 6, 2017. Accessed November 13, 2018, https://mubi.com/notebook/posts/dark-aspects-juliana-rojas-marco-dutra-discuss-good-manners.

11. Walter Lima Jr., "Director's Statement." Accessed November 15, 2018, http://www.throughtheshadowmovie.com/about.

12. *Ibid.*

13. Jennie Kermode, "Through the Shadow," *Eye for Film*, August 27, 2016. Accessed November 15, 2018, https://www.eyeforfilm.co.uk/review/through-the-shadow-2016-film-review-by-jennie-kermode.

14. Anton Bitel, "'Our Evil' Film Review: Hitman Horror with a Supernatural Twist," *Sci-Fi Now*, December 12, 2017. Accessed November 17, 2018, https://www.scifinow.co.uk/reviews/our-evil-film-review-hitman-horror-with-a-supernatural-twist/.

15. Benedict Seal, "Frightfest Review: 'Our Evil' Is Emotionally Charged and Violent," *Bloody Disgusting*, August 30, 2017. Accessed November 17, 2018, https://bloody-disgusting.com/reviews/3456019/frightfest-review-evil-emotionally-charges-violent/.

## Chapter 5

1. See "Classification Guidelines," *British Board of Film Classification*. Accessed August 4, 2020, https://www.bbfc.co.uk/about-classification/classification-guidelines.

2. Shellie McMurdo, "'We Are Never Going in the Woods Again': The Horror of The Underclass White Monster in American and British Horror," *Cine Excess*, volume 4 (2020). Accessed August 4, 2020, https://www.cine-excess.co.uk/lsquoweare-never-going-in-the-woods-againrsquo-the-horror-of-the-underclass-white-monster-in-american-and-british-horror.html.

3. Kat Ellinger, "The Gorgon," *Scream*, July/August 2018, p. 32.

4. Adam Scovell, *Folk Horror: Hours Dreadful and Things Strange* (Liverpool: Liverpool University Press, 2017), p. 17.

5. *Ibid.*

6. *Ibid.*, p. 18.

7. Dawn Keetley, "'Eden Lake' (2008): Folk Horror for a Disenchanted World," *Horror Homeroom*, December 16, 2015. Accessed August 4, 2010, http://www.horrorhomeroom.com/eden-lake-2008-folk-horror-for-a-disenchanted-world/.

8. Kim Newman, "The Ghoul," *Empire*, August 1, 2017. Accessed August 4, 2020, https://www.empireonline.com/movies/reviews/ghoul-2-review/.

9. Kim Newman, "Sightseers," *Empire*, November 25, 2012. Accessed August

4, 2020, https://www.empireonline.com/sightseers-2-review/.

10. Ian Cooper, *Frightmares: A History of British Horror Cinema* (Leighton Buzzard: Auteur, 2016), p. 10.

11. Peter Bradshaw, "'Prevenge' Review—A Mother of a Serial-killer Film," *The Guardian*, September 1, 2026. Accessed August 4, 2020, https://www.theguardian.com/film/2016/sep/01/prevenge-review-alice-lowe-mother-of-a-serial-killer-film.

12. Jonathan Rigby, *English Gothic: A Century of Horror Cinema* (London: Reynolds and Hearn, 2004), p. 292.

13. Dawn Keetley, "'Doomwatch': Hybrid Folk Horror," *Horror Homeroom*, September 13, 2019. Accessed August 5, 2020, http://www.horrorhomeroom.com/doomwatch-hybrid-folk-horror/.

14. John Wyndham, *The Day of the Triffids* (London: Michael Joseph, 1951), p. 27.

## Chapter 6

1. Josh Millican, "12 Amazing Scandinavian Horror Movies Guaranteed to Chill Your Bones," *Dread Central*, February 2, 2018. Accessed November 17, 2018, https://www.dreadcentral.com/news/265526/12-amazing-scandinavian-horror-movies-guaranteed-chill-bones/.

2. "Nordic Noir," *Wikipedia*. Accessed November 17, 2018, https://en.wikipedia.org/wiki/Nordic_noir.

3. Ditte Fiil Ravn, "'Sorgenfri' Instructor Bo Mikkelsen: 'I spent a fair amount of my research on looking at bodies,'" *Soundvenue*, April 1, 2016. Accessed November 17, 2018, http://soundvenue.com/film/2016/04/sorgenfri-instruktoer-bo-mikkelsen-jeg-brugte-rimelig-meget-af-min-research-paa-at-se-paa-lig-192307.

4. *Ibid.*

## Chapter 7

1. Gerardelson, "Interview: Hélène Cattet & Bruno Forzani, Makers of *Amer*," *Desktop*, June 28, 2010. Accessed September 1, 2019, https://desktopmag.com.au/blogs/interview-helene-cattet-bruno-forzani-makers-of-amer/.

2. Jordan Hageman, "The History of the Horror Renaissance of the 1970s," Odyssey, September 27, 2016. Accessed September

1, 2019, https://www.theodysseyonline.com/1970s-horror-history.

3. Quoted in Steven Higgins, *Still Moving: The Film and Media Collections of The Museum of Modern Art* (New York: The Museum of Modern Art, 2006), p. 130.

4. Frank Lafond, "A Hand Full of Horrors," *Kinoeye*, February 18, 2002. Accessed September 1, 2019, https://www.kinoeye.org/02/04/lafond04.php.

5. David Hinds, *Fascination: The Celluloid Dreams of Jean Rollin* (Truro, UK: Headpress, 2016), p. 4.

6. Quoted in James Walker, "The New French Extremity: An Endeavour into Excessive Violence," *The Artifice*, May 25, 2013. Accessed September 1, 2019, https://the-artifice.com/new-french-extremity/.

7. Alexandra West, *New French Extremity: Visceral Horror and National Identity* (Jefferson, NC: McFarland, 2016), p. 5.

8. Darren Amner, "Horror's New Frontier(s)," *Eye for Film*, October 24, 2007. Accessed September 1, 2019, https://www.eyeforfilm.co.uk/feature/2007-10-24-xavier-gens-interview-about-front ieresfrontiers-feature-story-by-darren-amner.

9. Quoted in "*Revenge* Screening Information Pack."

10. Anton Bitel, "Fragments of Hélène Cattet and Bruno Forzani," *Senses of Cinema*, June 2018. Accessed September 1, 2019, http://sensesofcinema.com/2018/split-screen-cattet-forzani-helene-cattet-and-bruno-forzani-interview/.

11. Virginie Sélavy, "Interview with Hélène Cattet and Bruno Forzani," *Electric Sheep Magazine*, April 10, 2014. Accessed September 1, 2019, http://www.electric sheepmagazine.co.uk/tag/all-the-colours-of-the-dark/.

12. Bitel, "Fragments of Hélène Cattet and Bruno Forzani."

13. Michael Mackenzie, "Blood and Black Gloves," *Cult Cinema: An Arrow Video Companion* (Shenley, UK: Arrow Films, 2016), p. 169.

14. Bitel, "Fragments of Hélène Cattet and Bruno Forzani."

15. *Ibid.*

16. "The Strange Color of Your Body's Tears," *Rotten Tomatoes*. Accessed September 1, 2019, https://www.rottentomatoes.com/m/the_strange_color_of_your_bodys_tears.

17. Penelope Houston, "Michelangelo Antonioni," in *Cinema: A Critical Dictionary*, Richard Roud, ed. (London: Secker & Warburg, 1980). p. 87.

18. A.L. Rees, *A History of Experimental Film and Video: From the Canonical Avant-garde to Contemporary British Practice* (London: BFI, 1999) p. 58.

19. P. Adams Sitney, "American Avant-Garde Cinema," in *Cinema: A Critical Dictionary*, Richard Roud, ed. (London: Secker & Warburg, 1980). p. 29.

20. Bitel, "Fragments of Hélène Cattet and Bruno Forzani."

21. Quoted in "*Raw* Press Kit," www.wildbunch.biz/movie/raw/.

22. *Ibid.*

23. *Ibid.*

## Chapter 8

1. Amir Ganjavie and Leila Passandideh, "Interview with Shahram Mokri About Fish & Cat (2013)," *Offscreen*, March 2015. Accessed September 18, 2019, https://offscreen.com/view/shahram-mokri.

2. Turfseer, "Review of 'Under the Shadow,'" *Internet Movie Database*, February 19, 2007. Accessed September 18, 2019, https://www.imdb.com/review/rw3642382/?ref_=tt_urv.

3. Charlie Lyne, "A Girl Walks Home Alone at Night: 'The first Iranian vampire western.'" *The Guardian*, July 24, 2015. Accessed September 18, 2019, https://www.theguardian.com/film/2015/jul/24/a-girl-walks-home-alone-at-night-dvd-blu-ray.

4. Ana Lily Amirpour, "Director's Statement," *A Girl Walks Home Alone at Night* Press kit, p. 3, https://4f399d350e4882ff73b9-0f00c87f9e216dcd5acfbe5f7dfb64d7.ssl.cf2.rackcdn.com/production/documents/AGIRLWALKHOMEALONEATNIGHT_Presskit.pdf.

5. Sheila O'Malley, "A Girl Walks Home Alone at Night," *Roger Ebert.com*, November 21, 2019. Accessed September 18, 2019, https://www.rogerebert.com/reviews/a-girl-walks-home-alone-at-night-2014.

6. Isabel Cristina Pinedo, *Recreational Terror: Women and the Pleasures of Horror Film Viewing* (Albany: State University of New York Press, 1997) p. 83.

## Chapter 9

1. Ben Sales, "Israeli Audiences Warm to Home-grown Horror Movies," *Jewish Telegraphic Agency*, April 27, 2016. Accessed September 20, 2019, https://www.jta.org/2016/04/27/culture/israeli-audiences-warm-to-home-grown-horror-movies.

2. *Ibid.*

3. Robert Tumas, "Rabies," *Film Slant*, April 19, 2011. Accessed September 20, 2019, https://www.slantmagazine.com/film/rabies/.

4. Amir Bogen, "Israeli Zombies, Killers, Torturers, and Human Parasites Invade World Cinema," *Tablet*, January 14, 2014. Accessed September 20, 2010, https://www.tabletmag.com/jewish-arts-and-culture/158659/israeli-horror-movies.

5. Daniel Litani, "A Glowing 2014 for the Israeli Film Industry," *Cineuropa*, January 21, 2015. Accessed September 20, 2019, https://cineuropa.org/en/newsdetail/283492/.

6. Yair Raveh, "Letting the Right One in: The Rise of the Israeli Horror Film," *Fathom*, Autumn 2013. Accessed September 20, 2019, https://fathomjournal.org/letting-the-right-one-in-the-rise-of-the-israeli-horror-film/.

7. *Ibid.*

8. Quoted in Sales, "Israeli Audiences Warm to Home-grown Horror Movies."

9. Raveh, "Letting the Right One In: The Rise of the Israeli Horror Film."

10. "Cats on a Pedal Boat," *Israeli Films Catalogue*. Accessed September 20, 2019, http://www.israelifilms.co.il/Cats-on-a-Pedal-Boat.html.

11. B. Caplan, "Israel's First Zombie Movie, Cannon Fodder: 'We Tried to Piss Everyone Off,'" *Miami New Times*, October 22, 2013. Accessed September 20, 2019, https://www.miaminewtimes.com/arts/israels-first-zombie-movie-cannon-fodder-we-tried-to-piss-everyone-off-6488693.

12. Doc Charlie Oughton, "The Paz Brothers—JeruZalem," *Starburst Magazine*, September 14, 2015. Accessed September 20, 2019, https://www.starburstmagazine.com/features/paz-brothers-interview.

13. Quoted in Nirit Anderman, "Why So Many Israeli Horror Films Take Place in the Army," *Haaretz*, January 4, 2019. Accessed September 20, 2019, https://www.

haaretz.com/israel-news/culture/movies/.
premium.MAGAZINE-why-so-many-
israeli-horror-films-take-place-in-the-
army-1.6808066.
14. Quoted in Anderman, "Why So
Many Israeli Horror Films Take Place in the
Army."
15. Anderman, "Why So Many Israeli
Horror Films Take Place in the Army."
16. "Rabies—Aharon Keshales and
Navot Papushado in Conversation with
Phil Newton," *Fright Fest* (YouTube),
September 26, 2011. Accessed September 20, 2019, https://www.youtube.com/
watch?v=oxQiCBJZeWg.
17. *Ibid.*
18. *Ibid.*
19. *Ibid.*
20. *Ibid.*
21. *Ibid.*
22. *Ibid.*
23. Ollie Charles, "Aharon Keshales
Interview—Big Bad Wolves—UK Jewish Film Festival," *Front Row Reviews*,
November 11, 2013. Accessed September 20, 2019, http://www.frontrowreviews.
co.uk/features/aharon-keshales-interview-
%E2%80%93-big-bad-wolves-%E2%80%-
93-uk-jewish-film-festival/26177.
24. Pam Jahn, "Big Bad Wolves: Interview with Aharon Keshales and Navot Papushado," *Electric Sheep*, December 5, 2013.
Accessed September 20, 2019, http://www.
electricsheepmagazine.co.uk/2013/12/05/
big-bad-wolves-interview-with-aharon-
keshales-and-navot-papushado/.
25. *Ibid.*
26. *Ibid.*
27. *Ibid.*

## Chapter 10

1. Doyle Greene, *Mexploitation Cinema: A Critical History of Mexican Vampire, Wrestler, Ape-Man, and Similar Films,
1957–1977* (Jefferson, NC: McFarland,
2005), p. 1.
2. Carlos Aguilar, "15 Movies to Get
You Started with Mexican Horror," *Vulture*, August 28, 2019. Accessed August 12,
2020, https://www.vulture.com/2019/08/
mexican-horror-movies-15-films-to-watch.
html.
3. Quoted in "Dos Monjes," *Películas Del Cine Mexicano*. Accessed August
12, 2020, https://web.archive.org/

web/20110518101600/http://cinemexicano.
mty.itesm.mx/peliculas/monjes.html.
4. *Ibid.*
5. Greene, *Mexploitation Cinema*, p. 5.
6. *Ibid.*, p. 6.
7. *Ibid.*, p. 8.
8. *Ibid.*, p. 1.
9. Tony Williams, *Hearths of Darkness:
The Family in the American Horror Film*
(Madison, NJ: Fairleigh Dickinson University Press, 1996), pp. 134–135.
10. Quoted in Robert Sklar, *Film: An
International History of the Medium* (London: Thames and Hudson, 1990), p. 324.
11. Justin Chang, "Review: A Grim Fairy
Tale, 'Tigers Are Not Afraid' Peers at War
Through a Child's Eyes," *Los Angeles Times*,
August 21, 2019. Accessed August 12, 2020,
https://www.latimes.com/entertainment-
arts/movies/story/2019–08–21/tigers-are-
not-afraid-horror-mexico-review.

## Chapter 11

1. Daniel Martin, "South Korean Horror Cinema," in *A Companion to the Horror
Film* Harry H. Benshoff, ed. (Oxford: John
Wiley and Sons, 2014), p. 24.
2. James Marriott, *Horror Films* (London: Virgin Books, 2004), p. 297.
3. *Ibid.*
4. Alison Peirse and Daniel Martin,
"Introduction," in *Korean Horror Cinema*, Alison Peirse and Daniel Martin, eds.
(Edinburgh: Edinburgh University Press,
2013), p. 6.
5. Martin, "South Korean Horror Cinema," p.427.
6. Nathan Schwartzman, "Why Do
Korean Horror Movies Have Only Female
Ghosts?" *Asian Correspondent*, June
21, 2009. Accessed June 3, 2020, http://
asiancorrespondent.com.
7. Ng, "Sisterhood of Terror: The Monstrous Feminine of Southeast Asian Horror
Cinema," p.444.
8. Maggie Lee, "Film Review: Flu," *Variety*, September 24, 2013. Accessed June
7, 2020, https://variety.com/2013/film/
reviews/film-review-flu-1200665907/.
9. Kim Su-yeon, "Seoul Station Director Yeon Sang-ho," *Korean Cinema Today*,
September 17, 2014. Accessed June 3,
2020, http://koreanfilm.or.kr/webzine/sub/
interview.jsp?mode=A_VIEW&wbSeq=120.

10. Na Hong-jin, "The Making of 'The Wailing,'" DVD extra.

11. Maggie Lee, "Cannes Film Review: 'The Wailing,'" *Variety*, May 19, 2016. Accessed June 3, 2020, https://variety.com/2016/film/reviews/the-wailing-review-goksung-cannes-1201776287/.

12. Jean Noh, "Cannes Q&A: Na Hong Jin, 'The Wailing,'" May 19, 2016. Accessed June 3, 2020, https://www.screendaily.com/cannes/cannes-qanda-na-hong-jin-the-wailing/5104060.article.

13. Lincoln Michel, "'The Wailing' Is the Spookiest Movie on Netflix," October 6, 2018. Accessed June 3, 2020, https://www.gq.com/story/the-wailing-is-the-spookiest-movie-on-netflix.

## Chapter 12

1. Antonio Lázaro-Reboll, *Spanish Horror Film* (Edinburgh: Edinburgh University Press, 2012).

2. Julián Garciá, "Juan Carlos Medina: The Historical Memory Is There, Behind a Wall," *elPeriódico*, October 6, 2012. Accessed July 9, 2020, https://www.elperiodico.com/es/sitges/20121006/juan-carlos-medina-la-memoria-historica-esta-ahi-tras-un-muro-2220025.

3. Ian Olney, "Spanish Horror Cinema," in *A Companion to the Horror Film*, Harry H. Benshoff, ed. (Oxford: John Wiley and Sons, 2014), p. 379.

4. *Ibid.*, p. 380.

5. *Ibid.*, p. 381.

6. *Ibid.*, pp. 365–366

7. *Ibid.*, p. 375.

8. *Ibid.*, p. 381.

9. Garciá, "Juan Carlos Medina: The Historical Memory Is There, Behind a Wall."

10. *Ibid.*

11. Lázaro-Reboll, *Spanish Horror Film.*

12. Olney, "Spanish Horror Cinema," p. 379.

13. *Ibid.*

14. *Ibid.*

15. Garciá, "Juan Carlos Medina: The Historical Memory Is There, Behind a Wall."

16. Anil Aggrawal, *Necrophilia: Forensic and Medico-legal Aspects* (Boca Raton, FL: CRC Press, 2011), p. 16.

17. Olney, "Spanish Horror Cinema," p. 381.

18. *Ibid.*, p. 380.

19. *Ibid.*, p. 381.

20. *Ibid.*

## Chapter 13

1. Kaya Özkaracalar, "Between Appropriation and Innovation: Turkish Horror Cinema," in *Fear Without Frontiers: Horror Cinema Across the Globe*, Steven Jay Schneider, ed. (Guildford, UK: Fab Press, 2003), p. 205.

2. Quoted in Zeynep Koçer, "The Monstrous-feminine and Masculinity as Abjection in Turkish Horror Cinema," in *Gender and Contemporary Horror in Film*, Samantha Holland, Robert Shail and Steven Gerrard, eds. (Bingley: Emerald Publishing, 2019), ebook.

3. Emrah Güler, "Turkish Horror Cinema Continues to Haunt Audience," *Hürriet Daily News*, March 24, 2014. Accessed August 18, 2020, https://www.hurriyetdailynews.com/turkish-horror-cinema-continues-to-haunt-audience-63971.

4. Koçer, "The Monstrous-feminine and Masculinity as Abjection in Turkish Horror Cinema."

5. Koyuncu, "'Baskin': The Horror of the Scapegoats," p. 108.

6. *Ibid.*, p. 110.

7. Kaya Özkaracalar, "Horror Films in Turkish Cinema: To Use or Not to Use Local Cultural Motifs, That Is Not the Question," in *European Nightmares: Horror Cinema in Europe Since 1945*, Patricia Allmer, Emily Brick and David Huxley, eds. (London: Wallflower Press, 2012), p. 250.

8. *Ibid.*, p. 252.

9. Koçer, "The Monstrous-feminine and Masculinity as Abjection in Turkish Horror Cinema."

10. Özkaracalar, "Horror Films in Turkish Cinema: To Use or Not to Use Local Cultural Motifs, That Is Not the Question," p. 251.

11. Koçer, "The Monstrous-feminine and Masculinity as Abjection in Turkish Horror Cinema."

12. *Ibid.*

13. *Ibid.*

14. "Baskin (short)," *Internet Movie Database.* https://www.imdb.com/title/tt3188880/?ref_=tt_sims_tt.

15. Koyuncu, "'Baskin': The Horror of the Scapegoats," p. 112.

## Chapter 14

1. James Aston and John Walliss, "Introduction," in *To See the Saw Movies: Essays on Torture Porn and Post-9/11 Horror*, James Aston and John Walliss, eds. (Jefferson, NC: McFarland, 2013), p. 3.

2. Donato Totaro, "When Women Kill: Recent North American Horror Films," *Offscreen* 18, issue 8 (August 2014). Accessed July 27, 2020, https://offscreen.com/view/when-women-kill.

3. *Ibid.*

4. *Ibid.*

5. *Ibid.*

6. *Ibid.*

7. *Ibid.*

8. Clark Collis, "Francesca Eastwood Is Warned Against Talking About Her Sexual Assault in M.F.A. clip," *Explore Entertainment*, October 13, 2017. Accessed July 27, 2020, https://ew.com/movies/2017/10/13/francesca-eastwood-sexual-assault-mfa-clip/.

9. *Ibid.*

10. Alfonso Rivera, "Private Producers Believed in My Passion," *Cineuropa*, October 11, 2017. Accessed July 27, 2017, https://cineuropa.org/en/interview/338794/.

11. *Ibid.*

12. Harry M. Benshoff, "Blaxploitation Horror Films: Generic Reappropriation or Reinscription?" *Cinema Journal* 39, no. 2 (Winter 2000), p. 37.

13. Peter Hutchings, *The Horror Film* (Harlow, Essex: Pearson Educational, 2004), p. 110.

14. Robin R. Means Coleman, "We're in a Golden Age of Black Horror Films," *The Conversation*, May 29, 2019. Accessed July 27, 2020, https://theconversation.com/were-in-a-golden-age-of-black-horror-films-116648.

15. Jacob Knight, "Writer/Director Michael O'Shea Talks 'The Transfiguration' and Writing Vampire Rules," *Birth. Movies. Death.*, April 7, 2017. Accessed July 27, 2020, https://birthmoviesdeath.com/2017/04/07/writer-director-michael-oshea-talks-the-transfiguration-and-writing-vampire.

16. Joseph Owen, "'The Transfiguration': An Interview with Director Michael O'Shea," *The Up Coming*, May 17, 2016. Accessed July 27, 2020, https://www.theupcoming.co.uk/2016/05/17/the-transfiguration-an-interview-with-director-michael-oshea/.

17. Robin R. Means Coleman, *Horror Noire: Blacks in American Horror Films from the 1890s to the Present* (New York: Routledge, 2011), pp. 145–168.

## Afterword

1. Quoted in Radheyan Simonpillai, "TIFF 2019: Indigenous Artists Are Using Horror to Unpack Colonial Trauma," *NOW Magazine*, September 4, 2019. Accessed August 25, 2020, https://nowtoronto.com/movies/news-features/indigenous-horror-blood-quantum-tiff-2019.

2. *Ibid.*

3. Laura Potier, "Movies in Times of Crisis," *Starburst*, June 2020, p. 61.

4. *Ibid.*

# Bibliography

Aggrawal, Anil. *Necrophilia: Forensic and Medico-legal Aspects*. Boca Raton, FL: CRC Press, 2011.

Aguilar, Carlos. "15 Movies to Get You Started with Mexican Horror." *Vulture*, August 28, 2019. Accessed August 12, 2020, https://www.vulture.com/2019/08/mexican-horror-movies-15-films-to-watch.html.

Ahnold, Jack. "Horror Film Festival 'Hell do Janeiro' Arrives in Rio Tonight." *The Rio Times*, September 12, 2018. Accessed November 13, 2018, https://riotimesonline.com/brazil-news/rio-entertainment/horror-film-festival-hell-do-janeiro-arrives-in-rio-this-wednesday/.

Amirpour, Ana Lily. "Director's Statement." *A Girl Walks Home Alone at Night* Press kit. https://4f399d350e4882ff73b9–0f00c87f9e216dcd5acfbe5f7dfb64d7.ssl.cf2.rackcdn.com/production/documents/AGIRLWALKHOMEALONEATNIGHT_Presskit.pdf.

Amner, Darren. "Horror's new *Frontier(s)*." *Eye for Film*, October 24, 2007. Accessed September 1, 2019, https://www.eyeforfilm.co.uk/feature/2007–10–24-xavier-gens-interview-about-frontieresfrontiers-feature-story-by-darren-amner.

Anderman, Nirit. "Why So Many Israeli Horror Films Take Place in the Army." *Haaretz*, January 4, 2019. Accessed September 20, 2019, https://www.haaretz.com/israel-news/culture/movies/.premium.MAGAZINE-why-so-many-israeli-horror-films-take-place-in-the-army-1.6808066.

Aston, James, and John Walliss. "Introduction." In *To See the Saw Movies: Essays on Torture Porn and Post-9/11 Horror*, James Aston and John Walliss, eds., 1–11. Jefferson, NC: McFarland, 2013.

Bahiana, Ana Maria. "The Blair Witches of Brazil." *BBC*, July 6, 2007. Accessed August 6, 2018, http://www.bbc.com/culture/story/20170701-the-blair-witches-of-brazil.

Banks, Chris. "White Coffin." *Flickfeast*, February 7, 2017. Accessed November 23, 2017, https://www.flickfeast.co.uk/reviews/white-coffin-2016/.

Barchfield, Jenny. "'Hard Labor' Serves up Brazil Sans Bikinis." *The Washington Times*, May 13, 2011. Accessed November 13, 2018, https://m.washingtontimes.com/news/2011/may/13/hard-labor-serves-up-brazil-sans-bikinis/.

Beck, Gustavo. "Dark Aspects: Juliana Rojas and Marco Dutra Discuss 'Good Manners.'" *MUBI*, August 6, 2017. Accessed November 13, 2018, https://mubi.com/notebook/posts/dark-aspects-juliana-rojas-marco-dutra-discuss-good-manners.

Benshoff, Harry M. "Blaxploitation Horror Films: Generic Reappropriation or Reinscription?" *Cinema Journal* 39, no. 2 (Winter 2000): 31–50.

Bitel, Anton. "Fantasia First Look: Killing Ground." *SciFi Now*, July 17, 2017, https://www.scifinow.co.uk/cinema/killing-ground-fantasia-first-look/.

Bitel, Anton. "Fragments of Hélène Cattet and Bruno Forzani." *Senses of Cinema*, June 2018. Accessed September 1, 2019, http://sensesofcinema.com/2018/split-screen-cattet-forzani/helene-cattet-and-bruno-forzani-interview/.

Bitel, Anton. "Francesca." *Projected Figures*, August 26, 2016. Accessed November 27, 2017, http://projectedfigures.com/2016/08/26/francesca-2016/.

Bitel, Anton. "'Our Evil' Film Review: Hitman Horror with a Supernatural Twist." *Sci-Fi*

*Now*, December 12, 2017. Accessed November 17, 2018, https://www.scifinow.co.uk/reviews/our-evil-film-review-hitman-horror-with-a-supernatural-twist/.

Bogen, Amir. "Israeli Zombies, Killers, Torturers, and Human Parasites Invade World Cinema." *Tablet*, January 14, 2014. Accessed September 20, 2010, https://www.tabletmag.com/jewish-arts-and-culture/158659/israeli-horror-movies.

Bradshaw, Peter. "'Prevenge' Review—A Mother of a Serial-killer Film." *The Guardian*, September 1, 2026. Accessed August 4, 2020, https://www.theguardian.com/film/2016/sep/01/prevenge-review-alice-lowe-mother-of-a-serial-killer-film.

Buckmaster, Luke. "'Hounds of Love' Review—Savagely Intense Australian Horror Is the Scariest Film of the Year." *The Guardian*, May 23, 2017. Accessed February 14, 2018, https://www.theguardian.com/film/2017/may/23/hounds-of-love-review-savagely-intense-australian-horror-is-the-scariest-film-of-the-year.

Caplan, B. "Israel's First Zombie Movie, Cannon Fodder: 'We Tried to Piss Everyone Off.'" *Miami New Times*, October 22, 2013. Accessed September 20, 2019, https://www.miaminewtimes.com/arts/israels-first-zombie-movie-cannon-fodder-we-tried-to-piss-everyone-off-6488693.

"Cats on a Pedal Boat." *Israeli Films Catalogue*. Accessed September 20, 2019, http://www.israelifilms.co.il/Cats-on-a-Pedal-Boat.html.

Chang, Justin. "Review: A Grim Fairy Tale, 'Tigers Are Not Afraid' Peers at War Through a Child's Eyes." *Los Angeles Times*, August 21, 2019. Accessed August 12, 2020, https://www.latimes.com/entertainment-arts/movies/story/2019-08-21/tigers-are-not-afraid-horror-mexico-review.

Chapman, Catherine. "'Goodnight Mommy' Is the Rebirth of Austrian Horror." *Creators. Vice.Com*, September 20, 2015. Accessed March 8, 2018, https://creators.vice.com/en_us/article/vvyyqm/goodnight-mommy-is-the-rebirth-of-austrian-horror.

Charles, Ollie. "Aharon Keshales Interview—Big Bad Wolves—UK Jewish Film Festival." *Front Row Reviews*, November 11, 2013. Accessed September 20, 2019, http://www.frontrowreviews.co.uk/features/aharon-keshales-interview-%E2%80%93-big-bad-wolves-%E2%80%93-uk-jewish-film-festival/26177.

Coleman, Lindsay. "Wake in Fright by Tina Kaufman." *Senses of Cinema*, March, 2011. Accessed February 14, 2018, http://sensesofcinema.com/2011/book-reviews/wake-in-fright-by-tina-kaufman/.

Collis, Clark. "Francesca Eastwood Is Warned Against Talking About Her Sexual Assault in M.F.A. Clip." *Explore Entertainment*, October 13, 2017. Accessed July 27, 2020, https://ew.com/movies/2017/10/13/francesca-eastwood-sexual-assault-mfa-clip/.

Cooper, Ian. *Frightmares: A History of British Horror Cinema.* Leighton Buzzard: Auteur, 2016.

Dennison, Stephanie, and Lisa Shaw. *Popular Cinema in Brazil.* Manchester: Manchester University Press, 2004.

De Pablos, Emiliano, and John Hopewell. "Argentina's De la Vega Re-launches Supernatural Horror Pic 'White Coffin.'" *Variety*, December 7, 2013. Accessed November 23, 2017, http://variety.com/2013/film/global/argentinas-de-la-vega-re-launches-supernatural-horror-pic-white-coffin-1200929639/.

"Dos Monjes." *Películas Del Cine Mexicano*. Accessed August 12, 2020, https://web.archive.org/web/20110518101600/http://cinemexicano.mty.itesm.mx/peliculas/monjes.html.

Dowd, A. A. "Guessing the Twist Won't Save You from the Horrors of 'Goodnight Mommy.'" *AV Club*, September 10, 2015. Accessed March 8, 2018, https://film.avclub.com/guessing-the-twist-won-t-save-you-from-the-horrors-of-g-1798184821.

Ellinger, Kat. "The Gorgon." *Scream* 49 (July/August 2018).

Ferrari, Márcio. "Horror, Brazilian Style." *Pesquisa* 256 (June 2017).. Accessed August 6, 2018, https://revistapesquisa.fapesp.br/en/2017/12/14/horror-brazilian-style/#prettyPhoto.

Ganjavie, Amir, and Leila Passandideh. "Interview with Shahram Mokri about Fish & Cat (2013)." *Offscreen*, March 2015. Accessed September 18, 2019, https://offscreen.com/view/shahram-mokri.

Garciá, Julián. "Juan Carlos Medina: The Historical Memory Is There, Behind a Wall." *elPeriódico*, October 6, 2012. Accessed July 9, 2020, https://www.elperiodico.com/

es/sitges/20121006/juan-carlos-medina-la-memoria-historica-esta-ahi-tras-un-muro-2220025.

Gardenour Walter, Brenda S. "Ghastly Transmissions: The Horror of Connectivity and the Transnational Flow of Fear." In *Transnational Horror Across Visual Media: Fragmented Bodies*, Dana Och and Kristen Strayer, eds., 17–29. London: Routledge, 2014.

Gerardelson. "Interview: Hélène Cattet and Bruno Forzani, Makers of *Amer*." *Desktop*, June 28, 2010. Accessed September 1, 2019, https://desktopmag.com.au/blogs/interview-helene-cattet-bruno-forzani-makers-of-amer/.

Gilbey, Ryan. "'Goodnight Mommy' Is a Chilling Austrian Horror Film with National Guilt at Its Heart." *New Statesman*, March 3, 2016. Accessed March 8, 2018, https://www.newstatesman.com/culture/film/2016/03/goodnight-mommy-chilling-austrian-horror-film-national-guilt-its-heart.

Greene, Doyle. *Mexploitation Cinema: A Critical History of Mexican Vampire, Wrestler, Ape-Man, and Similar Films, 1957–1977.* Jefferson, NC: McFarland, 2005.

Güler, Emrah. "Turkish Horror Cinema Continues to Haunt Audience." *Hürriet Daily News*, March 24, 2014. Accessed August 18, 2020, https://www.hurriyetdailynews.com/turkish-horror-cinema-continues-to-haunt-audience-63971.

Hageman, Jordan. "The History of the Horror Renaissance of the 1970s." *Odyssey*, September 27, 2016. Accessed September 1, 2019, https://www.theodysseyonline.com/1970s-horror-history.

Hatfull, Jonathan. "Australian Genre Cinema: Living in the Past or a Brave New World?" *SciFi Now*, August 19, 2016. Accessed February 14, 2018, https://www.scifinow.co.uk/blog/australian-genre-cinema-living-in-the-past-or-a-brave-new-world/.

Hawker, Philippa. "'Killing Ground' Gives Aaron Pedersen the Chance to Be a Villain." *The Australian*, August 26, 2017. Accessed February 14, 2018, https://www.theaustralian.com.au/arts/review/killing-ground-gives-aaron-pedersen-the-chance-to-be-a-villain/news-story/a105ac304d0e14f54a7473c3e73d0aa0.

Higgins, Steven. *Still Moving: The Film and Media Collections of The Museum of Modern Art.* New York: The Museum of Modern Art, 2006.

Hinds, David. *Fascination: The Celluloid Dreams of Jean Rollin.* Truro, UK: Headpress, 2016.

Hood, Robert. "Australian Horror Films." *Tabula Rasa* [undated]. Accessed February 14, 2018, www.tabula-rasa.info/AusHorror/OzHorrorFilms1.html.

Hopewell, John. "Adrian Garcia Bogliano Sets First Swedish Movie 'Black Circle.'" *Variety*, May 13, 2016. Accessed October 11, 2017, http://variety.com/2016/film/festivals/adrian-garcia-bogliano-first-swedish-movie-black-circle-1201773794/.

Houston, Penelope. "Michelangelo Antonioni." In Richard Roud, ed., *Cinema: A Critical Dictionary*, Richard Roud, ed., 83–95. London: Secker & Warburg, 1980.

Hughes, Kat. "Frightfest 2016: 'White Coffin' review." *The Hollywood News*, August 27, 2016. Accessed November 23, 2017, http://www.thehollywoodnews.com/2016/08/27/frightfest-2016-white-coffin-review/.

Hutchings, Peter. *The Horror Film.* Harlow, Essex: Pearson Educational, 2004.

"Hypersomnia." *Netflix.* Accessed October 11, 2017, https://www.netflix.com/gb/title/80159025.

Keetley, Dawn. "'Doomwatch': Hybrid Folk Horror." *Horror Homeroom*, September 13, 2019. Accessed August 5, 2020, http://www.horrorhomeroom.com/doomwatch-hybrid-folk-horror/.

Keetley, Dawn. "'Eden Lake' (2008): Folk Horror for a Disenchanted World." *Horror Homeroom*, December 16, 2015. Accessed August 4, 2010, http://www.horrorhomeroom.com/eden-lake-2008-folk-horror-for-a-disenchanted-world/.

Kermode, Jennie. "Through the Shadow." *Eye for Film*, August 27, 2016. Accessed November 15, 2018, https://www.eyeforfilm.co.uk/review/through-the-shadow-2016-film-review-by-jennie-kermode.

Knight, Jacob. "Writer/Director Michael O'Shea Talks 'The Transfiguration' and Writing Vampire Rules." *Birth. Movies. Death.*, April 7, 2017. Accessed July 27, 2020, https://birthmoviesdeath.com/2017/04/07/writer-director-michael-oshea-talks-the-transfiguration-and-writing-vampire.

Koçer, Zeynep. "The Monstrous-feminine and Masculinity as Abjection in Turkish Horror Cinema." In *Gender and Contemporary Horror in Film*, Samantha Holland, Robert Shail, and Steven Gerrard, eds., ebook. Bingley: Emerald Publishing, 2019.

Koyuncu, Sertaç "'Baskin': The Horror of the Scapegoats." In *The New Wave in Turkey's Cinema*, Tage T. E. Luxembourgeus and Mumin Baris, eds., 107–126. Proverbial Elephant, 2018.

Lafond, Frank. "A Hand Full of Horrors." *Kinoeye* 2, issue 4, February 18, 2002. Accessed September 1, 2019, https://www.kinoeye.org/02/04/lafond04.php.

Lázaro-Reboll, Antonio. *Spanish Horror Film*. Edinburgh: Edinburgh University Press, 2012.

Lee, Maggie. "Cannes Film Review: 'The Wailing.'" *Variety*, May 19, 2016. Accessed June 3, 2020, https://variety.com/2016/film/reviews/the-wailing-review-goksung-cannes-1201776287/.

Lee, Maggie. "Film Review: Flu." *Variety*, September 24, 2013. Accessed June 7, 2020, https://variety.com/2013/film/reviews/film-review-flu-1200665907/.

Lima, Walter, Jr. "Director's Statement." *Through the Shadow*. Accessed November 15, 2018, http://www.throughtheshadowmovie.com/about.

Litani, Daniel. "A Glowing 2014 for the Israeli Film Industry." *Cineuropa*, January 21, 2015. Accessed September 20, 2019, https://cineuropa.org/en/newsdetail/283492/.

Lyne, Charlie. "A Girl Walks Home Alone at Night: 'The first Iranian vampire western.'" *The Guardian*, July 24, 2015. Accessed September 18, 2019, https://www.theguardian.com/film/2015/jul/24/a-girl-walks-home-alone-at-night-dvd-blu-ray.

Machado, Roberto Pinheiro. *Brazilian History: Culture, Society, Politics 1500–2010*. Newcastle-Upon-Tyne: Cambridge Scholars Publishing, 2018.

MacInnes, Paul. "The Babadook: 'I wanted to talk about the need to face darkness in ourselves.'" *The Guardian*, October 18, 2014. Accessed February 14, 2018, https://www.theguardian.com/film/2014/oct/18/the-babadook-jennifer-kent.

Mackenzie, Michael. "Blood and Black Gloves." In *Cult Cinema: An Arrow Video Companion*, 164–171. Shenley: Arrow Films, 2016.

Marriott, James. *Horror Films*. London: Virgin Books, 2004.

Martin, Daniel. "South Korean Horror Cinema." In *A Companion to the Horror Film*, Harry H. Benshoff, ed., 423–441. Oxford: John Wiley and Sons, 2014.

McMurdo, Shellie. "'We Are Never Going in the Woods Again': The Horror of the Underclass White Monster in American and British Horror." *Cine Excess* Volume 4, 2020. Accessed August 4, 2020, https://www.cine-excess.co.uk/lsquowe-are-never-going-in-the-woods-againrsquo-the-horror-of-the-underclass-white-monster-in-american-and-british-horror.html.

Means Coleman, Robin R. *Horror Noire: Blacks in American Horror Films from the 1890s to the Present*. New York: Routledge, 2011.

Means Coleman, Robin R. "We're in a Golden Age of Black Horror Films." *The Conversation*, May 29, 2019. Accessed July 27, 2020, https://theconversation.com/were-in-a-golden-age-of-black-horror-films-116648.

Michel, Lincoln. "'The Wailing' Is the Spookiest Movie on Netflix." *GQ*, October 6, 2018. Accessed June 3, 2020, https://www.gq.com/story/the-wailing-is-the-spookiest-movie-on-netflix.

Millican, Josh. "12 Amazing Scandinavian Horror Movies Guaranteed to Chill Your Bones." *Dread Central*, February 2, 2018.

Myers, Emma. "Interview: Veronika Franz and Severin Fiala." *Film Comment*, September 9, 2015. Accessed March 8, 2018, https://www.filmcomment.com/blog/goodnight-mommy-interview-veronika-franz-severin-fiala/.

Newbery, Charles. "Argentina Horror Films Going Low Budget." *Variety*, February 8, 2008. Accessed October 11, 2017, http://variety.com/2008/scene/markets-festivals/argentina-horror-films-going-low-budg-1117980500/.

Newland, Christina. "Cate Shortland on Her One-night-stand Abduction Drama, 'Berlin Syndrome.'" *The Guardian*, June 8, 2017. Accessed February 14, 2018, https://www.theguardian.com/film/2017/jun/08/cate-shortland-on-her-one-night-stand-abduction-drama-berlin-syndrome.

Newman, Kim. "The Ghoul." *Empire*, August 1, 2017. Accessed August 4, 2020, https://www.empireonline.com/movies/reviews/ghoul-2-review/.

Newman, Kim. "Sightseers." *Empire*. November 25, 2012. Accessed August 4, 2020, https://www.empireonline.com/sightseers-2-review/.

Ng, Andrew Hock Soon. "Sisterhood of Terror: The Monstrous Feminine of Southeast Asian Horror Cinema." In *A Companion to the Horror Film*, Harry H. Benshoff, ed., 442–459. Oxford: John Wiley and Sons, 2014.

Noh, Jean. "Cannes Q&A: Na Hong Jin. 'The Wailing.'" *Screen Daily*, May 19, 2016. Accessed June 3, 2020, https://www.screendaily.com/cannes/cannes-qanda-na-hong-jin-the-wailing/5104060.article.

"Nordic Noir." *Wikipedia*. Accessed November 17, 2018, https://en.wikipedia.org/wiki/Nordic_noir.

"Oh the Horror! Interview with Luciano and Nicolás Onetti." *Popcorn Frights Film Festival*, July 31, 2016. Accessed November 27, 2017, http://www.popcornfrights.com/oh-the-horror-interview-with-luciano-and-nico-onetti.

Olney, Ian. "Spanish Horror Cinema." In *A Companion to the Horror Film*, Harry H. Benshoff, ed., 365–389. Oxford: John Wiley and Sons, 2014.

O'Malley, Sheila. "A Girl Walks Home Alone at Night." *Roger Ebert.com*, November 21, 2019. Accessed September 18, 2019, https://www.rogerebert.com/reviews/a-girl-walks-home-alone-at-night-2014.

Oughton, Doc Charlie. "The Paz Brothers—JeruZalem." *Starburst*, September 14, 2015. Accessed September 20, 2019, https://www.starburstmagazine.com/features/paz-brothers-interview.

Owen, Joseph. "The Transfiguration: An interview with Director Michael O'Shea." *The Up Coming*, May 17, 2016. Accessed July 27, 2020, https://www.theupcoming.co.uk/2016/05/17/the-transfiguration-an-interview-with-director-michael-oshea/.

Özkaracalar, Kaya. "Between Appropriation and Innovation: Turkish Horror Cinema." In *Fear Without Frontiers: Horror Cinema Across the Globe*, Steven Jay Schneider, ed., 205–216. Guildford: Fab Press, 2003.

Özkaracalar, Kaya. "Horror Films in Turkish Cinema: To Use or Not to Use Local Cultural Motifs, That Is Not the Question." In *European Nightmares: Horror Cinema in Europe Since 1945*, Patricia Allmer, Emily Brick and David Huxley, eds., 249–260. London: Wallflower Press, 2012.

Page, Philippa J. *Politics and Performance in Post-dictatorship Argentine Film and Theatre*. Rochester, NY: Boydell and Brewer, 2011.

Pam, Jahn. "Big Bad Wolves: Interview with Aharon Keshales and Navot Papushado." *Electric Sheep*, December 5, 2013. Accessed September 20, 2019, http://www.electricsheepmagazine.co.uk/2013/12/05/big-bad-wolves-interview-with-aharon-keshales-and-navot-papushado/.

Peirse, Alison, and Daniel Martin. "Introduction." In *Korean Horror Cinema*, Alison Peirse and Daniel Martin, eds., 1–20. Edinburgh: Edinburgh University Press, 2013.

Pinedo, Isabel Cristina. *Recreational Terror: Women and the Pleasures of Horror Film Viewing*. Albany: State University of New York Press, 1997.

Potier, Laura. "Movies in Times of Crisis." *Starburst*, June 2020, 58–61.

"Rabies—Aharon Keshales and Navot Papushado in Conversation with Phil Newton." *Fright Fest* (You Tube), September 26, 2011. Accessed September 20, 2019, https://www.youtube.com/watch?v=oxQiCBJZeWg.

Raveh, Yair. "Letting the Right One in: The Rise of the Israeli Horror Film." *Fathom*, Autumn 2013. Accessed September 20, 2019, https://fathomjournal.org/letting-the-right-one-in-the-rise-of-the-israeli-horror-film/.

Ravn, Ditte Fiil. "'Sorgenfri' instructor Bo Mikkelsen: 'I spent a fair amount of my research on looking at bodies.'" *Soundvenue* April 1, 2016. Accessed November 17, 2018, http://soundvenue.com/film/2016/04/sorgenfri-instruktoer-bo-mikkelsen-jeg-brugte-rimelig-meget-af-min-research-paa-at-se-paa-lig-192307.

Rees, A. L. *A History of Experimental Film and Video: From the Canonical Avant-garde to Contemporary British Practice*. London: BFI, 1999.

Rigby, Jonathan. *English Gothic: A Century of Horror Cinema*. London: Reynolds and Hearn, 2004.

Rivera, Alfonso. "Private Producers Believed in My Passion." *Cineuropa*, October 11, 2017. Accessed July 27, 2017, https://cineuropa.org/en/interview/338794/.

Rohter, Larry. "A Cult Figure Conjures the Macabre." *New York Times*, October 19, 2001. Accessed August 6, 2018, https://www.nytimes.com/2011/10/23/movies/jose-mojica-marins-brazilian-filmmaker-conjures-macabre.html.

Romero, George A. "Foreword." In *Night of the Living Dead*, John A. Russo. New York: Pocket Books, 1974.

Sales, Ben. "Israeli Audiences Warm to Home-grown Horror Movies." *Jewish Telegraphic Agency*, April 27, 2016. Accessed September 20, 2019, https://www.jta.org/2016/04/27/culture/israeli-audiences-warm-to-home-grown-horror-movies.

Schwartzman, Nathan. "Why Do Korean Horror Movies Have Only Female Ghosts?" *Asian Correspondent*, June 21, 2009. Accessed June 3, 2020, http://asiancorrespondent.com.

Scovell, Adam. *Folk Horror: Hours Dreadful and Things Strange*. Liverpool, UK: Liverpool University Press, 2017.

Seal, Benedict. "Frightfest Review: 'Our Evil' Is Emotionally Charged and Violent." *Bloody Disgusting*, August 30, 2017. Accessed November 17, 2018, https://bloody-disgusting.com/reviews/3456019/frightfest-review-evil-emotionally-charges-violent/.

Sélavy, Virginie. "Interview with Hélène Cattet and Bruno Forzani." *Electric Sheep Magazine*, April 10, 2014. Accessed September 1, 2019, http://www.electricsheepmagazine.co.uk/tag/all-the-colours-of-the-dark/.

Simonpillai, Radheyan. "TIFF 2019: Indigenous Artists Are Using Horror to Unpack Colonial Trauma." *NOW Magazine*, September 4, 2019. Accessed August 25, 2020, https://nowtoronto.com/movies/news-features/indigenous-horror-blood-quantum-tiff-2019.

Sitney, P. Adams. "American Avant-Garde Cinema." In *Cinema: A Critical Dictionary*, Richard Roud, ed., 28–47. London: Secker & Warburg, 1980.

Sklar, Robert. *Film: An International History of the Medium,* London: Thames and Hudson, 1990.

Stam, Robert, João Luis Vieira, and Ismail Xavier. "The Shape of Brazilian Cinema in the Postmodern Age." In *Brazilian Cinema*, Randal Johnson and Robert Stam, eds., 387–472. New York: Columbia University Press, 1995.

"The Strange Color of Your Body's Tears." *Rotten Tomatoes*. Accessed September 1, 2019, https://www.rottentomatoes.com/m/the_strange_color_of_your_bodys_tears.

Su-yeon, Kim. "Seoul Station Director Yeon Sang-ho." *Korean Cinema Today*, September 17, 2014. Accessed June 3, 2020, http://koreanfilm.or.kr/webzine/sub/interview.jsp?mode=A_VIEW&wbSeq=120.

Totaro, Donato. "When Women Kill: Recent North American Horror Films." *Offscreen* 18, issue 8 (August 2014). Accessed July 27, 2020, https://offscreen.com/view/when-women-kill.

Tumas, Robert. "Rabies." *Film Slant*, April 19, 2011. Accessed September 20, 2019, https://www.slantmagazine.com/film/rabies/.

Turfseer. "Review of 'Under the Shadow.'" *Internet Movie Database*, February 19, 2007. Accessed September 18, 2019, https://www.imdb.com/review/rw3642382/?ref_=tt_urv.

Walker, James. "The New French Extremity: An Endeavour into Excessive Violence." *The Artifice*, May 25, 2013. Accessed September 1, 2019, https://the-artifice.com/new-french-extremity/.

Watson, Zebbie. "5 Great Horror Films from Latin America You've Probably Never Heard Of." *Inverse Entertainment*, May 11, 2016. Accessed October 11, 2017, https://www.inverse.com/article/15505-5-great-horror-movies-from-latin-america-you-ve-probably-never-heard-of,

West, Alexandra. *New French Extremity: Visceral Horror and National Identity*. Jefferson, NC: McFarland, 2016.

Williams, Tony. *Hearths of Darkness: The Family in the American Horror Film*. Madison, NJ: Fairleigh Dickinson University Press, 1996.

Wixson, Heather. "Interview: Writer/Director Ben Young Talks 'Hounds of Love.'" *Daily Dead*, October 5, 2017. Accessed February 20, 2018, https://dailydead.com/interview-writer director-ben-young-talks-hounds-of-love/.

Wyndham, John. *The Day of the Triffids*. London: Michael Joseph, 1951.

# Index

Numbers in **bold italics** indicate pages with illustrations